A Chanticleer Press Edition

Taylor's Guide to Annuals

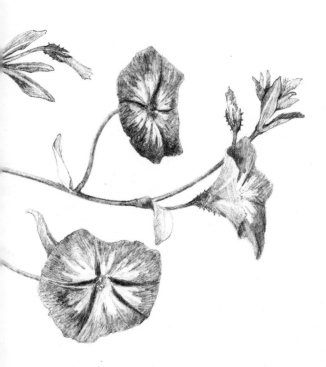

Houghton Mifflin Company Boston 1986

Contributors

Gordon P. DeWolf, Jr., Ph.D.

Coordinator of the Horticulture Program at Massachusetts Bay Community College in Wellesley Hills, Massachusetts, Gordon DeWolf revised and edited the fifth edition of *Taylor's Encyclopedia of Gardening,* upon which this guide is based. DeWolf previously served as Horticulturist at the Arnold Arboretum at Harvard University.

Pamela Harper

General consultant for this book and its principal photographer, Pamela Harper is the coauthor of *Perennials: How to Select, Grow, and Enjoy* published by HPBooks. A well-known horticultural writer, lecturer, and photographer, her articles have appeared in such magazines as *Flower and Garden, Horticulture,* and *Pacific Horticulture.* Harper has also taken more than 80,000 photographs of plants and gardens.

Peter Loewer

Editor of the flower descriptions, Peter Loewer has written and illustrated many books, including *Peter Loewer's Month-by-Month Garden Almanac, Bringing the Outdoors In,* and the forthcoming *Gardens by Design.* Articles by Loewer have appeared in *Horticulture, Women's Day, Green Scene,* and *The American Horticulturist.*

Jim Wilson

Author of the gardening essays and consultant for the how-to-grow descriptions, Jim Wilson is a co-host of the Victory Garden, a public television program. Along with his wife, he owns and operates Savory Farm, a nursery that supplies herbs to restaurants nationwide. He coauthored *How to Grow a Thriving Vegetable Garden.*

Katharine Widin

Author of the essay on pests and diseases, Katharine Widin holds an M.S. and Ph.D. in plant pathology. Currently she operates a private consulting firm, Plant Health Associates, in Stillwater, Minnesota.

Library of Congress
Cataloging-in-Publication Data
Main entry under title:
Taylor's guide to annuals.
(Taylor's guides to gardening)
Based on: Taylor's encyclopedia of gardening.
4th edition. 1961.
Includes index.
1. Annuals (Plants). I. Taylor's encyclopedia
of gardening. II. Title: Guide to annuals.
III. Series.
SB422.T39   1986   635.9'312   85-30496
ISBN 0-395-40447-9 (pbk.)

Prepared and produced by Chanticleer Press,
Inc., New York
Cover photograph: *Tagetes patula*
'Happy Days' by Charles Marden Fitch

Designed by Massimo Vignelli

Color reproductions by Reprocolor
International, s.r.l., Milan, Italy
Printed and bound by Dai Nippon, Tokyo, Japan
Typeset by American-Stratford Graphic Services, Inc.

First Edition.

DNP   10   9   8   7   6   5

Contents

Preface

Annual flowers are a boon to beginners, providing a profusion of shapes and colors at modest expense. Experienced gardeners love them because of their infinite variety; you can plant different annuals year after year, yet never run out of choices.

Annuals are usually planted alongside perennials, bulbs, shrubs, or ornamental vegetables, yet their grace and stunning color allow them to stand alone, too. Many gardeners plant them especially for cutting, placing them at the back of the garden where snipped stems will be camouflaged by other flowers.

All gardens have areas that are perfect for annuals. A multicolor island of verbenas or zinnias is handsome in the front or back yard, enlivening the green expanse of a lawn.

A small bed of pansies near the entrance to a house adds a cheerful touch in late spring before most other annuals start to bloom. A clump of ornamental grasses planted next to a pool or a small group of candytufts grown near a stone wall can add interest to an area that might otherwise seem dull.

As with music, familiarity with annual flowers deepens your enjoyment of them. Once you have grown a flower, you will always know it. Some you will love; these you will replant, along with new kinds. One day someone may say: "I like the way you use flowers. Mind if I come over so you can show me how to do it?" On that day you will know that you have arrived—your hobby has evolved into an art form, and you have become an expert.

Whether you are interested in border plantings, cutting gardens, ground covers, rock gardens, container plantings, or gardens for sun or for shade, this book will introduce you to a wonderful family of garden plants and show you exactly how to grow them.

How to Use

Loved for their abundant blossoms throughout the summer, annuals are some of the easiest flowers to grow. They provide instant color in a single growing season and make excellent cut flowers. Annuals richly reward the time and effort you invest in planning and planting your garden.

There is no mystery to growing annuals—all that you need to know can be found in this guide. Designed to answer the needs of both amateurs and seasoned gardeners, this book makes it easy to cultivate a garden that suits your individual tastes and needs. It can also help you identify plants that you see when you visit gardens and nurseries.

If you have never planted a garden before, you will find practical tips that will get you started and keep you going. If you have been growing annuals for years, you will discover new plants and fresh ways to use old favorites.

How This Book Is Organized

This guide contains three types of material: color plates, flower descriptions, and expert articles that guide you through every aspect of growing annuals.

Color Plates

More than 300 of the most popular and interesting annuals in cultivation today are illustrated in the color plates. Each plate is accompanied by a drawing; together, they clearly illustrate the plant's flowers and its overall shape. The plates are arranged according to color, and within each color group, by shape. Plants that are grown primarily for their foliage or fruit appear together in a separate section.

If you are a beginner, browse through the color plates looking for plants that appeal to you. Even if you are unfamiliar with their common and scientific names, you will no doubt encounter many that you have seen before. To find out more about these familiar annuals, turn to the page numbers provided in the captions.

Color Key

A color key introduces the color plates and explains the variations in hue that occur within each group. For example, the group white flowers includes some flowers that appear white but may, in fact, be cream-colored, pale yellow, or pale pink.

Flower Chart

The chart that begins on page 54 makes it simple to select plants that are right for you. The chart presents the most important characteristics of each flower: its hardiness to frost, preference for warm or cool weather, suitability for cut or dried flowers, soil and light requirements, and plant height.

Like the color plates, the flower chart is divided into six groups;

This Guide

within each group, the plants are arranged alphabetically by scientific name.

Captions
The captions that accompany the color plates provide essential information at a glance: the kind of soil a plant needs and how much sunlight it can tolerate. The captions also give the scientific name of the plant, its height, and the length or width of individual flowers or flower clusters. Finally, a page reference directs you to the description of your plant in the Encyclopedia of Annuals.

Encyclopedia of Annuals
Here you will find a full description of each flower featured in the color plates. These flower descriptions are based on the authoritative *Taylor's Encyclopedia of Gardening,* revised and updated for this guide. The descriptions are arranged alphabetically by genus and cross-referenced by page number to the color plates. If you are unfamiliar with scientific names, turn to the index on page 469 and look for your plant's common name.
Each description begins with a heading indicating the genus name, followed by the common and scientific family names. Pronunciation of the scientific name precedes a brief overview of the genus.

Genus
This section presents the general characteristics of the garden plants in the genus. The How to Grow section outlines broad growing requirements for the genus, including preference for warm or cool weather.

Species and Hybrids
After the genus description, you will find detailed information on the flowers included in the color plates and additional information about popular cultivars. Each species description includes the plant's country of origin, its hardiness to frost, and any growing tips that differ from the genus requirements, such as the need for enriched soil or a special pH. Because most annuals bloom in summer, the bloming period is mentioned only if exceptionally long or another season. Next to the species description, you will find a black-and-white illustration depicting the mature plant.

Gardening Articles
Written by experts, these articles explain every aspect of gardening with annuals—how to prepare the soil, when to plant, and other important cultivation information, as well as tips on designing your garden. The article on choosing the best annuals tells you what factors influence gardening success and how to select the right annuals for your area. The frost date map tells you the frost zone in which you live; it is important to know your zone so you can make

a planting schedule based on the spring frost date in your particular location. You can fine-tune these planting dates by consulting the planting schedule on page 28.

In the section on botany, beginners will learn how to distinguish different kinds of annuals and the importance of scientific names. The illustrations of basic flower types show how to identify the parts of a flower. The article on writing a garden diary offers practical advice on keeping track of what you plant, when you plant it, and seasonal weather variations. Tips on working with cut flowers will help you become an expert in flower arranging and will tell you what to do to prepare dried flowers.

The garden calendar provides a practical schedule for maintenance activities throughout the year. Should you run into difficulty, the pest and disease chart will help you identify your problem, then cure it. The list of major nurseries and seed suppliers tells you the best sources for ordering annuals by mail. Finally, all the technical terms you may encounter are defined in the glossary.

Using the Flower Chart

The chart is a short-cut way of selecting annuals. For example, you want to make a free-standing circular bed using only purple and white flowers. In the center, you want purple flowers up to 18 inches high and for the edging, low-growing white flowers—no more than 12 inches or they will spoil the graduated effect.

Starting with the purple flowers, turn to the section of the chart that deals with blue to purple flowers. Scan the chart looking for plants that are 12 to 24 inches in height. Next, since your site is in the shade for part of the day, find those that can tolerate partial shade.

Twelve blue to purple flowers meet your height and shade requirements. Because you often take four to five day vacations in summer, you eliminate flowers that require moist soil. Now you are left with seven choices: *Ageratum Houstonianum* 'North Sea', *Collinsia grandiflora, Consolida ambigua, Consolida orientalis, Machaeranthera tanacetifolia, Myosotis sylvatica,* and *Trachelium caeruleum.*

Turning to the color plates, you look for flowers that will look good massed together. You select *Ageratum, Machaeranthera,* and *Myosotis.* Now read the descriptions of these plants, then choose the one that most appeals to you. When selecting white flowers, follow the same procedure.

Although most annuals will bloom in your area, if you want to choose those that will bloom the longest, also check the plant's warm- or cool-weather preference. Select those whose preference matches your growing season. Since you live in an area with a medium-length cool growing season, you find that two of the blue flowers prefer cool weather, *Machaeranthera* and *Myosotis.*

You can also use the flower chart to help you draw up a planting schedule. Simply check the hardiness listing and the warm- or cool-weather preference. Then, turn to the schedule on page 28. Here you will learn when to plant seeds outdoors, when to transplant seedlings, and how to account for the annual's warm- or cool-weather preference.

Using the Color Plates to Plan Your Garden

Annuals come in a wide array of colors, and today it is almost impossible to learn about every new cultivar that is introduced. In this guide, typical color varieties are illustrated. As you plan your garden, you can narrow your choices by referring to these typical garden plants. First, decide what colors you want in your garden and how tall the plants should be. You may, for example, design a bed composed chiefly of warm hues—reds, yellows, and oranges. Turn to the plates that feature red to orange flowers (pages 232-271) and choose those that appeal to you and that are the right height. Follow the same procedure in selecting your yellow flowers. Once you have made your selection, turn to the corresponding flower descriptions and make sure that the plants are good choices for your area and that the recommended planting times are convenient.

If you are unable to find exactly what you are looking for, or want a broader range of choices, turn to the other color sections and look for shapes that you like. Check the appropriate flower descriptions, which will tell you if these flowers also come in the warm tones that you want for your garden.

Basic Botany

Beginning gardeners are often unfamiliar with botanical terms, and even scientists may find that plants are difficult to categorize. Many garden writers attempt to arrange plants by their life cycles—annual, perennial, or biennial—but exceptions abound. Seedsmen get around the problem by deferring to the generally accepted use. If the plant is used as an annual, it is often lumped with annuals, even though technically it is called a biennial or perennial. This book follows the same functional classifications—in addition to true annuals, the coverage includes biennials and perennials that act like annuals.

What Is an Annual Flower?

In the classic sense, an annual flower is one that will complete its life cycle—from planting through flowering, seed formation, and death—in one growing season. Annual flowers bloom quickly and are beloved for providing "instant color." Their bloom span, ranging from one to five months, is longer than that of most perennials. Annuals include three classes of plants, depending on their tolerance for heat or cold: warm-weather annuals, cool-weather annuals, and frost-hardy annuals.

Warm-weather Annuals

True warm-weather annuals are frost tender and are usually planted in warm soil in late spring after the danger of frost is past. In the Deep South, second plantings are often made after midsummer. This group includes zinnias, cosmos, and celosia. The warm-weather annuals include not only the true annuals, but also kinds that in mild areas survive the winter and regrow the following year. Technically, these are biennials, tender perennials, or half-hardy perennials. Since they grow and are used like annuals over most of the United States, this book lumps them with the true annuals.

Cool-weather Annuals

The cool-weather annuals include two classes: half-hardy kinds that will tolerate a few degrees of frost and tender kinds that are killed by light frost. Half-hardy kinds can be planted somewhat earlier than the tender kinds. Cool-weather annuals do best in temperate coastal climates, high altitude gardens, and states in the northern third of the country. These plants can be grown successfully elsewhere but the bloom span is short. Among these flowers are schizanthus, dimorphotheca, nemesia, and calceolaria.

Frost-hardy Annuals

Since they can withstand several degrees of frost, the frost-hardy annuals, such as larkspur, stock, pansies, and calendula, are planted in the fall in mild-climate areas for winter and early spring bloom. Farther north, some kinds can be sown outdoors in late fall and will survive hard winters as tiny seedlings if protected with a light mulch. Larger seedlings, grown from earlier fall plantings, would probably be killed by severe cold. If such perilous plantings are not for you, plant in very early spring instead.

The frost-hardy annuals are sometimes confused with biennials because both, when planted in early fall in mild climates, will survive the winter and bloom the next spring. However, planted in spring, biennials will usually go through the first season as vegetative rosettes without blooms, while spring-planted hardy annuals will flower reliably within a few weeks.

Biennial and Perennial Plants

In addition to true annuals, this book includes certain biennials and perennials. Their inclusion depends on the relative earliness of their bloom; the plants must develop good color in the length of time required by true annuals when started in the spring from seeds.

Biennials require two seasons to complete their life cycle. During the first season only their leaves appear. They survive the winter, then flower and die in the second season. Certain biennials may perform like short-lived perennials. Others may fool you into believing they are perennials because they endure for a long time. This is due to a succession of volunteer seedlings that sprout from seeds formed the previous year.

Perennials are long-lived plants that regrow each year from a persistent rootstock. Some qualify as annuals because they have been specially bred for rapid bloom. For example, all foxglove and hollyhock varieties were once considered perennials. Today plant breeders have produced precocious plants that bloom within five to seven months after seeding; these cultivars are sold as annuals for first-year bloom.

Some quick-blooming tropical perennials are now sold as annuals, particularly in the Deep South and warm West. The latest of these tropical species is the New Guinea impatiens, a sun-tolerant, heat-resistant flower. We can expect to see other introductions of species now grown principally as pot plants.

Common and Scientific Names

As you begin to identify annual flowers, you will enter the arcane world of taxonomy, a system of organizing related plants into smaller and smaller groups. This indexing is more than merely an exercise for scientists, for it produces Latin names that are accepted internationally. Common names, on the other hand, can vary from country to country or, in extreme instances, between neighborhoods in the same town. Depending on one's taste (scientific, romantic, or macabre), *Amaranthus caudatus* may be known to one neighbor as "Kiss-Me-Over-the-Garden-Gate" and to another as "Love-Lies-Bleeding."

In books and seed catalogues, and at nurseries, annuals are usually listed by their most popular common names or by shortened Latin

Basic Botany

names. For example, Four O'Clock is the preferred common name for *Mirabilis Jalapa* and, since the Latin name is difficult, you will rarely see it used. On the other hand, since zinnia is easy to pronounce, it has become the accepted common name for all garden species of the genus *Zinnia*. Many catalogues carry cross-references of common and botanical names.

Cultivars
The term "cultivar," short for cultivated variety, was coined rather recently and has created about as much confusion as enlightenment. It should be applied only to plants that are vegetatively propagated (cloned) to produce virtual carbon copies of the original. Therefore, it has little application to annuals, which are usually propagated from seeds and are more variable. Nurseries and seed suppliers use the terms "cultivar" or "variety" interchangeably.

Varieties
With seed propagation comes a certain degree of variation in plants. Although seed breeders can at first reproduce "true" selections of a given species, after a while the inbreeding weakens the resulting plant population.
Varieties may seem remarkably uniform. However, a trained eye can usually discern variations from plant to plant. The variation ranges from virtually none in hybrids to a considerable difference in seed stocks that have been neglected for several years. For this reason, it is customary to renew seed lines every seven years or less by selecting several choice representatives (as similar as possible) from each given variety to serve as seed parents. The seeds from these are combined and increased to replace the old line. Saving seeds from only one plant might be risky because it could narrow the gene pool and lead to loss of vigor and to the intensification of undesirable characteristics.

The Importance of Scientific Names
Plant scientists are scrupulous about using internationally accepted Latin nomenclature in their technical literature. However, those who market seeds and plants are usually less concerned with "official" names. Instead they use what they perceive to be the most popular common names.
The amateur can be forgiven for asking "Why bother?" when faced with learning strange and sometimes unpronounceable Latin names. You can even get along reasonably well with only common names, but just for a while. As your gardening skill advances and you begin reaching for unusual plants, a knowledge of the rudiments of scientific nomenclature becomes useful. Often, for example, if you know that two annuals are of the same genus, you can estimate their environmental needs and growing requirements with a fair degree of accuracy. *Zinnia elegans,* the large-flowered zinnia, has much the same

growing requirements as *Zinnia angustifolia,* a very different zinnia with narrow, willowlike leaves and small flowers.

Marigolds provide a good example of the usefulness of scientific names. Marigolds belong to the genus *Tagetes* (the "g" is hard, as in "go"). Were you to mention marigolds in England, a gardener there might think you were referring to calendulas, which they call marigolds. But mention *Tagetes* and some of the confusion will clear. Go on and name the species *patula* and they will know that you are speaking of what we call "French Marigolds." Finally, give a variety name such as 'Queen Sophia' and you and your fellow gardener will understand one another completely.

Genus and Species

You are working with what taxonomists call a binomial—a name made up of two parts, the first identifying the genus to which the plant belongs, the second identifying a particular species within that genus. Every garden flower has a binomial designation. Sometimes this binomial is followed by another name enclosed in a single quotation mark: for example, *Tagetes patula* 'Queen Sophia'. The words enclosed within the quotation mark indicate the specific variety (cultivar) with which you are dealing.

Hybrids

Only a decade or so ago, hybrids between species or genera were unthinkable, and the hybrids accidentally produced in nature were usually sterile. Now scientists are introducing intergeneric and interspecific hybrids to create disease- or insect-resistant plants. In some cases, they are even restoring fragrances that have been lost in cultivation. The symbol "×" in a Latin name means that the plant is a hybrid.

Learning Scientific Names

Gardeners are often caught in a web of descriptive words that taxonomists deplore. Such words are semantically sloppy. Consider the class name, "Giant Zinnia." What is gigantic, the plant or the blossoms? Today you can buy dwarf zinnias with giant flowers or tall zinnias with small blossoms. The label "double blossoms" is equally unclear. Are the flowers born in twos side by side or over and under? Neither. Doubleness in flowers refers to multiple layers of petals. The label "mixed" is often erroneously used in lieu of "mixed colors."

Because trade jargon is often confusing, following scientific names is far safer. Although it may take some effort at first to translate these specialized terms, you will be pleasantly surprised at how easily it actually goes once you get started.

Anatomy

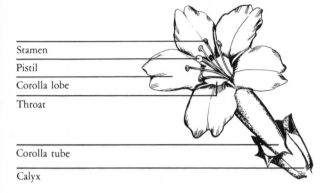

Stamen

Pistil

Corolla lobe

Throat

Corolla tube

Calyx

Involucre

Disk flowers

Ray flower

*These drawings show
the most common
anatomical parts of
flowers.*

Banner

Keel

Wing

Sepal

Pedicel

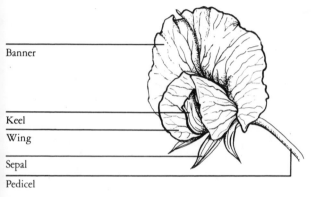

Petal

Stamen

Pistil

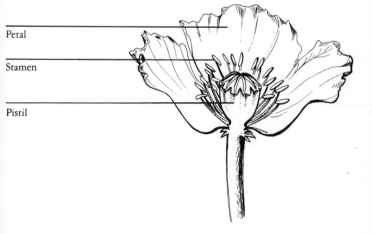

Clusters

Umbel	A flower cluster in which the individual flower stalks grow from the same point	
Corymb	A flattened cluster in which stalks grow from the axis at different points and flowers bloom from the edges toward the center	
Cyme	A branching cluster in which the flowers bloom from the center toward the edges, and in which the tip of the axis always bears a flower	
Panicle	An open flower cluster, blooming from bottom to top, and never ending in a flower	
Raceme	A long, tall cluster in which individual flowers are born on short stalks	

Leaves

Alternate	Arranged singly along a twig or shoot, and not in whorls or opposite pairs	
Opposite	Arranged along a twig or shoot in pairs, with one on each side	
Whorled	Arranged along a twig or shoot in groups of three or more at each node	
Pinnate	Having leaflets arranged in two rows along an axis	
Palmate	Having leaflets arranged like the fingers on a hand, arising from a single point	

Choosing Your

Some annuals can be grown anywhere in the country, but others have limitations on their geographic adaptability. These limitations are imposed by three factors that every gardener should keep in mind when choosing flowers: tolerance for cold or heat, preference for a warm or cool growing season, and the length of time plants take to reach maturity, that is, the number of days from planting to full bloom.

Tolerance for Cold or Heat

Because many annuals die in cold weather, they are traditionally divided into three groups, according to their tolerance for cold. Frost-tender annuals cannot withstand the cold and are killed by even a light frost. Half-hardy annuals can tolerate light frost, but are killed by hard frost. Finally, frost-hardy annuals can survive the winter as small seedlings except under the most extreme weather conditions.

No matter where you live, you can grow all three kinds of annuals as long as you plant them at the right time. However, if you live in an area where frosts persist until late spring, and you do not want to bother starting seedlings indoors, some annuals will not be suitable for you.

Although many gardeners do not take it into consideration, an annual's tolerance for heat also influences its suitability for certain regions. Some annuals cannot tolerate heat, while others are notably heat-resistant. Heat-resistant annuals bloom right through the summer in the warmest areas of the country, except in a few extremely stressful, very hot climates. Although many seed catalogues publish lists of heat-resistant flowers, these lists are often too inclusive. Many reliable heat-resistant flowers are noted in the flower descriptions. However, if you live in a very warm climate, consult a landscaper in your local parks department, a state botanical garden, or town nurseries for the best heat-tolerant varieties for your area.

Preference for a Warm or Cool Growing Season

Many gardening failures are caused by planting cool-weather flowers too late. Consequently, these annuals don't begin to bloom until hot weather has arrived, and their show of color is shortened.

Conversely, planting warm-weather annuals too early can bring disappointment. Seeds can rot in cold soil; seedlings can be shocked by exposure to cold rain and be set back or killed by frost.

Gardeners often overlook the potential of late-season plantings. In areas that have long summers, it is usually possible to grow two crops of warm-weather annuals. The second crop is planted just after the heat has sapped the vitality of the first crop. Farther north, cool-weather annuals make up the late crop; they will bloom about 30 days before the first light frost in autumn.

By paying attention to warm- and cool-weather preferences, you can

Annuals

select the annuals that will bloom the longest in your area. For example, if your summers are long and warm, a cool-weather annual, such as China Pink, must be planted early and will only bloom briefly before it burns out with midsummer heat. Cosmos would be a better choice for your climate. If you live in an area with cool summers, China Pink will bloom just fine most of the season; Cosmos, on the other hand, would bloom relatively late because it needs warm temperatures to perform well.

Days to Maturity
A final consideration should influence your flower selection, especially if you want flowers for fall bloom. Flowers are affected by the number of hours of sunlight they receive. Day length influences the number of days certain annuals require to mature. This explains why annuals seem to develop and bloom so rapidly in northern areas where summer days are long. In the Deep South, where midsummer days are relatively short and the nights long, plants may grow more slowly.
Soil temperature is even more critical to flower growth than day length. Little plant growth takes place at soil temperatures below 40° F. During the growing season soil temperatures must range from 40° to 100° F for plants to flourish.
Because of day length and soil temperature, flowers planted in the summer generally will mature faster than those planted in the spring—you can expect blooms within 45 to 60 days. Spring-planted flowers require about 60 to 90 days to mature, while those planted in late summer mature in fall and may take 90 to 120 days before blooming.
When choosing annuals, keep in mind the time you want to plant them. Will the days be long enough and sufficiently warm for them to mature?

When to Plant

Before you can make a planting schedule, you need to know the length of the growing season in your area. The frost date map on page 26 divides the country into seven zones based on the average number of days between the last killing frost in the spring and the first killing frost in the fall. The period between the spring and fall frosts (often referred to as the frost-free days) represents the growing season. Looking at the map, you will see that growing seasons in the United States vary from less than 120 days in the far North to more than 320 days in subtropical and desert regions of the South, Southwest, and West. Knowing the number of frost-free days will help you estimate how long you can expect to grow annuals in your region.

Using Frost Dates

Look at the frost date map to find the average date for the last killing spring frost in your area. The how-to-grow section of each flower description will tell you when to sow seeds or transplant seedlings based on the spring frost date.

If you want to plan a second late-season planting before the fall frost, you can roughly gauge the proper planting time by subtracting 90 to 120 days from the total number of frost-free days. For example, if you live in an area with 200 to 240 frost-free days, you will have to start your second planting approximately 100 days after your first planting. Unlike the spring-frost date, the fall-frost date cannot be generalized on a national basis because dates can vary by as much as 30 days even within a given zone. For more precise information on the fall-frost date in your local area, contact your local Cooperative Extension Service.

In using frost dates, keep in mind that the spring and fall dates are averages; frost could occur earlier or later than predicted. You may have to adjust the spring and fall dates to compensate for local factors that influence temperature—nearby bodies of water, urban warmth, altitude, fog, and winds.

Gardening Like a Pro

Because the prevailing temperature can vary substantially within a single frost zone, experienced gardeners often fine-tune their planting dates according to the relative warmth or coolness of their growing season. For example, even though both Seattle and the South Carolina highlands are in the same zone and have 220-day growing seasons, South Carolina is considerably warmer than Seattle. Different kinds of annuals flourish in each area and must be planted at different times.

The schedule on the following pages presents the seven types of growing seasons found in the United States. These seven types do not correspond to frost zones: a single zone may have both warm and cool growing seasons in different parts of its range.

To use the planting schedule, first find the season length that best describes your area: short (less than 120 days to 160 days), medium-length (160 to 240 days), long (240 to 320 days), and very long (more than 320 days). Next, choose the prevailing midsummer climate: cool (70° to 80°F), warm (80° to 90°F and sometimes higher), or hot (95° to 105°F in the late afternoon).

How to Evaluate Information
Now you are ready to establish planting dates. List the annuals you wish to grow. Note whether each is hardy, half-hardy, tender, or notably heat-resistant. Also indicate the annual's preference for warm or cool weather. On the schedule select your growing season category. Then for each flower, select the column defining its hardiness. Reading across the chart you will learn when to plant seeds outdoors (direct seeding) and when to transplant the seedlings that you have begun indoors.

Interpreting Planting Times
The chart refers to nine periods. To figure out the correct time for your area, refer to the definitions listed below:

Early spring: 45 to 60 days before the average spring frost-free date
Mid-spring: from 45 days before the spring frost-free date until the date itself
Late spring: 15 to 30 days after the frost-free date
Early summer: the period when late trees leaf-out
Midsummer: the warm weather midpoint
Late summer: the period with the warmest days and nights
Early fall: 30 days before the average killing frost
Late fall: the period after most annuals are worn out or killed by light frost
Winter: the period after heavy killing frost and beginning of freezing weather

Preparing Your Schedule
Next to each annual on your list, write down the season or seasons for planting seeds and transplanting seedlings. You can adjust these dates according to the annual's preference for cool or warm weather. Even if your area's growing-season temperature (cool or warm) is not compatible with the plant's temperature preference, you can still grow the annual by adjusting your planting times: If the annual prefers cool weather, plant at the earliest time in spring; for second crops, plant as late as you can in summer or fall. Annuals that prefer warm weather should be planted at the latest time in spring and the earliest option in summer or fall. You can easily translate these approximate times into actual planting dates as the seasons take shape. By logging these dates in your garden diary you can make adjustments from season to season.

Frost Date Map

This map is based on freeze data tabulations made by the United States Weather Bureau.

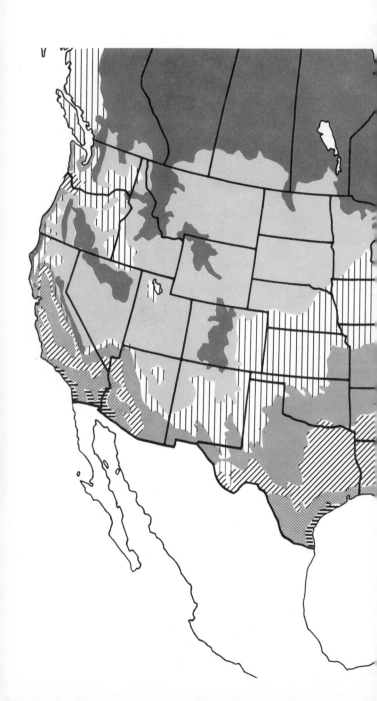

The key below shows the average dates of the last spring frost and the average length of the growing season in seven frost zones. The growing season is the period between the spring and fall frosts, often referred to as the frost-free days.

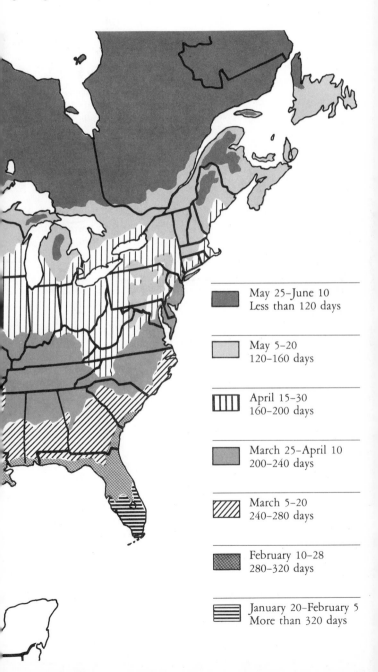

May 25–June 10
Less than 120 days

May 5–20
120–160 days

April 15–30
160–200 days

March 25–April 10
200–240 days

March 5–20
240–280 days

February 10–28
280–320 days

January 20–February 5
More than 320 days

Schedule

Hardy
Extremely hardy to
frost; not heat-resistant

Growing Season	How to Plant	Hardy
Short, cool	Direct seeding	Early spring through late spring
	Transplanting	Early spring through midsummer
Short, warm	Direct seeding	Early spring through mid-spring
	Transplanting	Early spring through late spring
Medium-length, cool	Direct seeding	Early spring through late spring
	Transplanting	Early spring through midsummer
Medium-length, warm	Direct seeding	Early spring
	Transplanting	Early spring
Long, cool	Direct seeding	Early spring. Again in early fall
	Transplanting	Early spring through spring. Again in late summer

| Half-hardy
Hardy to light frosts but injured or killed by freezes; not heat-resistant | Tender
Tender to frost; moderately tolerant of heat | Heat-resistant
Very tolerant of heat; requires warm soil |
| --- | --- | --- |
| *Half-hardy* | *Tender* | *Heat-resistant* |
| Mid-spring through late spring | Late spring | Not adapted |
| Mid-spring through midsummer | Late spring through midsummer | Not adapted |
| Mid-spring | Late spring through midsummer | Not adapted |
| Mid-spring through late spring | Late spring through midsummer | Chancy late spring |
| Early spring through late spring | Late spring through midsummer | Late spring |
| Mid-spring through late spring | Late spring through midsummer | Late spring |
| Early spring | Late spring through late summer | Late spring through early summer |
| Early spring through mid-spring | Late spring through late summer | Late spring through early summer |
| Early spring. Again in late summer | Late spring through midsummer | Late spring through midsummer |
| Early spring. Again in late summer | Late spring through midsummer | Late spring through midsummer |

Schedule

Hardy
Extremely hardy to
frost; not heat-resistant

Growing Season	How to Plant	Hardy
Long, warm	Direct seeding	Early spring. Again in early fall
	Transplanting	Early spring. Again in late fall
Very long, hot	Direct seeding	Late fall or winter. Chancy in early spring
	Transplanting	Late fall or winter. Again in early spring

Half-hardy Hardy to light frosts but injured or killed by freezes; not heat-resistant	*Tender* Tender to frost; moderately tolerant of heat	*Heat-resistant* Very tolerant of heat; requires warm soil
Half-hardy	*Tender*	*Heat-resistant*
Early spring. Again in early fall	Mid-spring. Again in late summer	Late spring through midsummer
Early spring. Again in late fall	Mid-spring through late spring. Again in late summer	Late spring. Chancy in midsummer
Fall or winter through early spring	Mid-spring. Again in late summer	Late spring. Again in late summer
Fall or winter through early spring	Mid-spring. Again in late summer	Late spring. Again in late summer

Getting Started

You can easily go down to a garden center, purchase a few plants or seed packets of annual flowers, dig up the soil, and plant them. With luck you might get a good show of color in return for your time and expense, for despite an avalanche of "do's" and "don'ts" in gardening, there is much room for experimentation. However, you will have consistently better results if you use the following suggestions as a guide.

How the Environment Affects Your Choice of Flowers

Most annuals can be considered as either cool-weather or warm-weather flowers. Cool-weather annuals include some that will bloom through the winter in mild climates or survive as seedlings through northern winters. These bloom early, sometimes before the last spring frost. Warm-weather annuals are durable plants that will continue to bloom for months in heat that drives people indoors. To choose suitable kinds for your garden, you must be aware of the temperature changes throughout the year for your area.

Many garden books and seed catalogues provide zone maps, which advise the best time to plant outdoors. Some of these maps are useless for selecting annuals because their hardiness zones are designed for perennials and woody plants. The most appropriate maps for annuals are those based on the average dates for the last killing frost in the spring and the first killing frost in the fall. (Refer to the map on page 26.) You can locate your area on the map and determine with a fair degree of accuracy when it is safe to plant warm-weather frost-tender flowers and when you can expect these flowers to be cut down by fall frost. Frost-hardy plants can be planted 30 to 60 days before your average frost-free date; in fact, the cool-weather annuals must be planted early to start blossoming in the spring.

Each garden also has its own microclimates—warm, cold, or drafty situations within which certain kinds of plants will do better than others. Identifying such potential trouble spots is basic to successful gardening. Some gardens are so beset by frequent strong winds that windbreaks and low-growing flowers are advisable. It is important to assess your garden environment before choosing the annuals you want to grow.

Understanding Light Requirements

Beginning gardeners are often placed in a quandary by instructions that read "Plant in full sun" or "Prefers full sun." What do you do when a flower bed gets only six to eight hours of sun during the summer, and sunup to sundown may span sixteen hours or more? Go ahead and plant sun-loving annuals. Assisted by reflected light, they will probably do well.

In the humid South and East, many flowers listed as "shade tolerant" will do all right in full sun; coleus and impatiens are just two examples. However, these plants will stay in better condition on hot days if they are in light shade. The same plants would burn out in midsummer in the hot, dry West and Southwest unless given light, daylong shade or moderate afternoon shade. For example, salvia—a sun-loving annual—can be affected by too much light in certain environments. With a little experience, you will soon know how to assess the sunlight in various parts of your yard.

Home gardeners pay little attention to the effect of latitude on day length and on the speed of plant growth because they are concerned with their own home grounds, not a national overview. But bear in mind that in the Deep South, midsummer days are relatively short and nights are long, while in the far North, midsummer days are very long. This extra light is one reason annuals grow and flower so rapidly in the northern states. Conversely, it might explain why certain annuals "blank"—refuse to blossom—during midsummer in parts of the South. Excessive heat can also be a contributing factor, of course.

Although no blanket rule of light requirements can be applied to fit all situations and regions, in general, you will do well to follow the light requirements given on your seed packets or plant tags. Very few annual flowers will bloom in moderate to dense shade. Most prefer direct sun all day except in the Deep South and warm West, where afternoon shade keeps annuals from drying up prematurely in the extreme heat.

Water Requirements

Except for desert climates, many annuals can survive without supplementary irrigation, yet they won't look good during dry spells. Annuals with large leaves that droop when dry are especially conspicuous.

Between rains, watering every seven to ten days will keep established plants thriving. Effective irrigation is more than just a token sprinkling with a water hose. The soil should be wet to a depth of ten inches or more, which would require two inches of water, more or less. If you use a sprinkler head, set a water glass within the spray pattern and move the sprinkler when two inches of water has accumulated in the tumbler.

Frequent sprinklings may be required to sprout seeds or to establish transplants. On windy, dry days as many as three or four daily sprinklings may be needed.

Western gardeners find that furrow or flood irrigation works well. They surround raised beds or raised rows with ditches or furrows and flood them with water. The raised areas absorb the water, which slowly moves up toward the surface.

In the East, where water isn't so expensive, sprinkler irrigation is the standard. By attaching a bubbler to your hose, you can decrease problems with foliage diseases and minimize the washing away of soil.

Drip or trickle irrigation makes efficient use of water and promotes faster growth than either sprinkling or flooding. Inexpensive kits of drip tubing and accessories are becoming widely available. You can hide the tubing under a mulch.

Either furrow or drip irrigation is preferred to overhead sprinkling because they do not wet the foliage. Sprinkling leaves encourages the spread of foliage diseases such as mildew and fungal leafspots, common diseases of zinnias and grandiflora petunias.

The water requirements of plant species vary widely. As a rule of thumb, you can equate water requirements to the size and color of leaves. Narrow or needlelike leaves, especially those that are gray, silvery, or furry, indicate that the plant may be of dryland origin and needs relatively little water. On the other hand, flowers with big, dark green leaves usually require generous amounts of water. During dry spells, a two-hour watering every seven to ten days should be sufficient, but newly transplanted seedlings may require twice-daily watering. Watch the foliage of flowers; the leaves may droop during the day but should perk up at night. If foliage is still limp come morning, water without delay.

Soil Requirements
Some gardening manuals do a disservice to gardeners by instructing them to grow annuals in rather poor soil to "encourage bloom." While it is true that most flowers don't need as high a level of plant nutrients as do vegetables, it is also true that they require enough to produce the sturdy vegetative frame needed to sustain blooming.

Organic Matter
When preparing soil for flower beds, always incorporate a generous amount of organic matter, such as garden compost, peat moss, or pulverized pine bark. Organic matter helps water penetrate the soil and stores nutrients. It also activates beneficial soil organisms, which break down soil particles and fertilizers to release the plant nutrients. The how-to-grow information in the flower descriptions indicates whether the species must have enriched soil.

Phosphate, Potash, and Nitrogen
Add to the soil moderate amounts of phosphate and potash, but apply nitrogen sparingly, because too much of it can encourage excessive vegetative growth. The same effect can be achieved by occasional light applications of low-nitrogen complete fertilizer blended for garden flowers or vegetables. A granular fertilizer, such as one with a 5-10-10 analysis, would work well. In high-rainfall areas with sandy soils, the modern controlled-release fertilizers are gaining favor.

pH Levels
Garden experts judge the acidity or alkalinity of soil by measuring the pH level—the hydrogen-ion concentration. A pH of 7.0 is

neutral, the value of pure water. A higher number (8.0 or 9.0) indicates that the soil is alkaline, and a lower number (6.0 or 5.0) that the soil is acid. Most flowers thrive at soil pH ranges of 5.5 to 7.0. Soils acid enough to grow azaleas need lime to produce most garden flowers. Soils in the arid West and Southwest, and in other areas where they are derived from limestone, seldom need liming. The pH of the soil also affects plant growth in ways other than measuring relative acidity or alkalinity. It indirectly regulates the availability of secondary nutrients such as calcium and magnesium and micronutrients such as iron, copper, and zinc.

If you want to know the soil pH of your garden, take or send a soil sample to the Cooperative Extension Service in your county or buy an inexpensive test kit. It sure beats guessing!

Preparing the Soil
Well-prepared soil can greatly improve plant growth, flower size, and the duration of color. Ideally, soil preparation should begin the summer or fall prior to your first plantings.

Tenacious, deep-rooted perennial grasses, such as Bermuda grass in mild climates and quack grass in the North, need to be eradicated with special herbicides or repeated digging with a spading fork. Neither method is foolproof. Bits of roots will sprout and proliferate. There is no coexistence with these grasses; you need to clean them out entirely before you plant, and it takes time.

Northern lawn grasses, such as bluegrass and creeping red fescue, are easier to eradicate than deep-rooted grasses. You can strip off the sod by running a flat shovel underneath it. Then invert the slabs of sod, pile them out of the way, and let them decompose to compost. If this sounds like a lot of work, it is nothing compared to struggling with tufts of grass that sprout after being turned under.

Testing for Moisture
Before you work the soil, dig a spadeful and test it for moisture. Squeeze a handful. If it compresses into a moist, sticky ball instead of crumbling when you release pressure, it is too wet to work. Wet soil will roll up into clods or large pills if you till it; breaking down such particles to a desirable texture will take years of root action and weathering. On the other hand, extremely dry, hard soil can be ruined by tilling, which reduces it to dust. Either soak the soil deeply and wait three to four days before working it or wait for a good rain, as farmers do.

Adding Organic Matter
Be sure to lay in the materials you will need for soil improvement. Provide 8 to 16 cubic feet of organic matter per 100 square feet of bed. This is equivalent to two to four bags of peat moss, or pulverized pine bark, in four cubic-foot-size bags. Use the lesser amount on dark-colored loamy soils and the greater amount on

either heavy clay or light sandy soil. This volume of organic matter will raise the level of soil in the bed and help it drain better while improving water penetration and biological activity. If you use raw sawdust or shavings for organic matter, you will need to add three to five pounds of high-nitrogen fertilizer per 100 square feet to promote its rapid conversion to humus.

Incorporating Phosphate Sources
Only a few soil types in the United States are naturally high in phosphorus. A phone call to your Cooperative Extension agent will tell you if supplementary applications of phosphate are customary for your area. Although you can have your soil tested, most gardeners simply mix five pounds of 0-46-0 treble superphosphate per 100 square feet of garden. Because phosphate stays where you place it, be sure to mix it thoroughly into the deep layers of soil. On acid soils, you can substitute ten pounds of rock phosphate; if used on high pH alkaline soils, this natural compound breaks down too slowly. Bone meal is an alternative phosphate source, but it is very expensive per pound of nutrients and also releases phosphorus slowly. However, both bone meal and rock phosphate appeal to organic gardeners.

Regulating Acidity or Alkalinity
In most regions except arid, high pH western soils, lime should be worked into the soil at the time of preparation. Lime neutralizes soil acidity, supplies calcium, makes certain micronutrients more available to plants, and, in addition, improves soil structure. Dolomitic limestone is preferable, because it contains magnesium as well as calcium. Slaked or pelleted limestones both work faster than ground limestone to correct acidity, but they are more expensive.
For clay or clay loam soils, you should work in gypsum to loosen the structure. Gypsum is calcium sulphate, and it is most effective when organic matter is also added. Because gypsum does not change the soil pH, it is especially useful where edgings of annuals are to be planted next to acid-loving azaleas.
Use the agricultural grade of sulfur to make alkaline soils more acid. The effect is rather short term, and application rates are difficult to judge. The incorporation of a generous amount of sphagnum peat moss will slightly acidify the soil.

Mixing in Soil Additives
The first time you dig an area of soil, go deeper than just a surface tilling. Spade or mechanically till a six- to eight-inch layer and then shovel it aside. Next, till the exposed lower layer and mix in organic matter, as well as lime and phosphate, if needed. Replace the top layer and mix in more of the additives. Set a sprinkler on the bed and let it run for two to three hours to settle the soil. Wait three to four days for it to dry and then rake it level. This extra effort and

the slight extra expense of careful preparation will pay off in improved plant growth and ease of cultivation.

Buying Annuals
Prior to about 1950, greenhouse growers sold well-hardened annual plants at a young green stage, without flower buds or blossoms. They knew that very young plants suffer less transplanting shock, adjust and resume growth quicker, and soon catch up with older transplanted flowers. Then, to satisfy a new generation of buyers who wanted instant color, growers began delivering older plants that were already in bloom. Soon any variety of flowers that was slow to bloom in pots or market packs disappeared from garden-center shelves. Today, gardeners buy flats, packs, or pots of annuals in early or full bloom.
Some kinds of flowers—petunias, dwarf marigolds, impatiens, and the like—are so vigorous that they hardly slow down when transplanted in full bloom. But others, such as celosia, put so much of their strength into forming large flowerheads that once in bloom, they will often barely survive when transplanted.

What to Look for in Container Plants
Choose the youngest plants available. Avoid tall, wiry plants that have been growing in a container so long that they are shedding their lower leaves. Yellowed or discolored plants are suffering from starvation. If you can pop a small seedling out of a plastic flat or tap a larger plant out of a pot, do it carefully and look at the root ball. See if it has a mass of roots spiraling around the container. If so, the plant is pot-bound; it will adjust slowly when you transplant it, no matter how carefully you untangle and spread out the roots. Seedlings grown in peat pots rarely have this problem.
Try to find fresh-looking plants. Growers deliver plants to retailers very early in the year. Prolonged bad weather may set in, and the plants will languish on the shelves for weeks, becoming root-bound, wiry, and starved. You may have to look around for a shop with a new shipment.
Annuals grown in pots four to six inches in diameter are becoming popular for creating a mature-looking garden in a hurry. These are fine for small color spots but expensive for large areas.

Direct Seeding in the Garden
Many gardeners regularly grow large spreads of color by planting seeds directly in their flower beds. Excess seedlings are either thinned out and discarded, or transplanted to fill up skipped spaces. This method works especially well with large-seeded flower varieties that sprout and grow quickly. Some flowers that have a distinct taproot, such as larkspurs, do best when direct seeded rather than when started indoors and later transplanted outdoors.
An old but good method of getting a good stand of flowers from

direct seeding is to work up the soil well and then rake it level. If it is early in the season and the level of soil moisture is good, take the edge of a board and press it into the soil to make furrows. Scatter the seeds in the furrow, then cover them lightly with sand or potting soil. Press the cover down with the flat side of the board; water with a fine spray daily until the seeds emerge. Flower seedlings growing in rows are easy to distinguish from weeds; distinguishing between the two is much more difficult when the seeds have been randomly scattered.

If you are starting in midseason when the soil is dry, first make a furrow in the prepared soil. Use a pointed hoe to dig three or four inches deep. Flood the furrow with water until it won't take any more. Leave it alone for a while, then flood it again. When the water has soaked in, scatter the seeds thinly, cover to a depth of three times the diameter of the seeds, and press down lightly with the flat side of a slat. The purpose of firming the seeds into the moist soil is to establish a bond between the seeds and the soil so that soil moisture can be transferred to the seeds.

Almost all tall or bushy large annuals grow best from direct seeding. However, in the North, the kinds that require warm soil for sprouting are often started indoors and transplanted while small in order to get a longer show of color.

Starting Plants from Seeds Indoors

A sure way to get just the flower varieties you want when you want them is to grow your own from seeds under controlled conditions. This gives you an early start so that sturdy seedlings will be ready for transplanting at the proper time.

Starting seeds indoors is not difficult, even for novices, if you follow these simple steps:

1. Install fluorescent lights.
2. Use seed-starting mixtures.
3. Observe the recommended sprouting and growing temperatures.
4. Use common sense in selecting containers for sprouting seeds.
5. Avoid overwatering.

Using Fluorescent Lights

Fluorescent lights—two 40-watt daylight-type tubes in a reflecting fixture—will cast the equivalent of strong sunlight on an area of 12 by 40 inches. During winter and early spring when you are planting many seeds indoors, there just isn't enough strong sunlight. In northern cities, a windowsill can be an inhospitable place for plants, with intense cold penetrating through the glass and with a weak sun entering at a low angle, if the sun shines at all.

The trick to using fluorescent lights properly is to hang them in a cool spot, 50° to 65° F, where plants are protected from cold and drafts. Warm rooms, 65° to 75° F or more, can cause plants to grow

When you start seeds under lights, lower the chains so the light tubes are within two inches of the top of the seeded pots. Raise the lights to six inches as soon as seedlings sprout.

If seedlings start to stretch, lower the lights again. Place shallow trays under the pots. To prevent root rot, do not allow water to stand in trays.

Getting Started

tall and spindly. Cool growing temperatures and strong light make the best combination.

In a cool room, how can you raise the temperature of the growing medium to the 65° to 80°F recommended for sprouting many species? You can either use a heating cable or place the seeded pots, covered with clear plastic, in a warm spot, such as the top of a refrigerator or on top of a water heater, until the seeds sprout. Then, at the first hint of green sprouts, move the pots to a cool room and put them under fluorescent lights.

Hang your lights on chains so that they can be lowered to within two inches of the top of seeded pots. The slight warmth and strong light from the tubes will make seedlings grow in a hurry. When the seedlings are the size of a dime, raise the lights so that they hang about six inches above the seedlings. If you start some seed containers late, you can still use the same light distance by setting the new containers on empty pots, thereby raising the individual pots closer to the tubes. If seedlings start to stretch, lower the lights and, if possible, the room temperature as well.

In late spring, windowsills become good places to start seeds. West- or south-facing windows get strong light and radiated warmth. But when a late cold snap comes, you will still need to pull seedlings back from cold windows, as you would during the winter.

Special Seed-starting Mixtures

Garden soils are not satisfactory for starting seeds in containers. Plant diseases can flourish in garden soil, especially damping-off, a malady that can run through seedlings like wildfire. It is particularly serious under cool, damp, low-light conditions. Nor are all potting soils pasteurized to kill harmful fungi and bacteria.

If you have had trouble with damping-off disease in seedlings, you can pasteurize soil to kill the harmful elements. Place two and one-quarter pounds of moistened soil in a plastic bag. Prick four or five holes in the bag, then place it in a microwave oven at full power for exactly two and one-half minutes. Store the soil in a clean, sealed container.

The best seed-starting medium is one of the special mixes composed principally of high-grade sphagnum peat moss and vermiculite, or horticultural vermiculite alone. Using these mixes substantially lessens the chances of damping-off disease. In addition, a topping of shredded, milled sphagnum moss can prevent most disease pathogens from developing. This material is a light greenish-buff substance that still looks like moss, not the brown peat moss from a bale.

Do not use fertilizer on seedlings until after they have been transplanted outdoors and have formed new feeder roots. Seedlings cannot tolerate much plant food.

Recommended Sprouting and Growing Temperatures

Seed packets and catalogues will give you the recommended range of temperatures for seed sprouting. Some seeds will sprout at relatively low temperatures, 50° to 60° F. A few, such as coleus, prefer temperatures of 75° to 85° F. You can use a number of devices and approaches to give seeds what they need: heating cables or pads, sprouting boxes heated by grounded incandescent lights, warm spots around the house, or, in late spring, a hotbed outdoors.

A fact that escapes many gardeners is that certain flower seeds sprout best in complete darkness. Seed packets may not tell you this, but the better seed catalogues will.

As a rule, optimum growing temperatures are 10° to 15° F below sprouting temperatures. If you fail to lower the temperature as soon as the seeds have sprouted, the seedlings may stretch, become leggy, and succumb to disease. It is almost impossible to make leggy seedlings grow normally.

Planting Procedure for Indoor Seeding

Most gardeners use shallow four- to six-inch clean-washed plastic pots for sprouting seeds. Fill each pot to the brim with seed-starting mix just as it comes from the package, then tamp it down with the bottom of another clean pot. Next, set the filled pots in a tray of warm water and let the water soak up from the bottom through the essential drainage holes. Once the surface is moist, scatter the seeds evenly over the surface and cover lightly with vermiculite, milled sphagnum moss, or sharp, gritty sand that has been heated at 150° F for an hour to kill disease organisms and weed seeds.

Now, place your seed pots under the fluorescent light fixture, which is adjusted to the proper height. Under a two-tube fluorescent light fixture, consisting of 40 watts per tube, you can fit 12 six-inch pots. (You should rotate the pots occasionally because the end position receives less intense light than the center.) When the tiny seedlings have sprouted, you will need to transplant them to two-inch plastic or peat pots. Place one or two seedlings in each pot. This will expand your space requirements, and you will soon run out of room, even if you shift pots to windowsills and heated porches.

Another option is to grow fewer kinds of flowers and to seed them directly into peat pots or peat wafers. The space requirements are then the same at the start and finish, and transplanting is avoided. However, far fewer plants can be started in a given area.

When seeding a large number of flowers, transplanting seedlings from seeded flats or pots is virtually essential. The seedlings are growing close together and have sparse root systems. Although individual plants can be carefully pricked out and reset into small pots indoors, attempting to transplant them directly into the garden usually fails because the root system is not yet strong enough. Indoor transplanting permits a dense, compact root system to form, which will support the little plant through the rigors of adjustment to the garden.

Avoid Overwatering

The best way to water seeded pots or flats is from the bottom, or by spraying them from above using a very fine, low-pressure spray of tepid water. A rubber squeeze bulb with a small sprinkler head is ideal for this purpose: It will not dislodge seeds or knock over seedlings.

If the containers feel light when lifted, set them in a dish and water them from below. Evening watering should be done early enough to let the foliage dry before nightfall.

Keeping seeded containers and seedlings too wet will encourage the outbreak of damping-off. This plant disease causes problems beneath the soil surface as well as above it. Beneath the surface it invades seeds and kills them just as they are sprouting or just before they emerge. Above, it girdles and topples seedlings.

Cold Frames and Hotbeds

A cold frame is a homemade or ready-made structure covered with a glass sash, clear fiberglass sheet, or clear plastic film. The frames are designed to seal out cold while admitting sunlight, and their cover is pitched or arched to shed rain. Some cold frames have reliable heat-actuated opening and closing devices. Do-it-yourself frames can have a lining of rigid plastic foam insulation, painted black for heat absorption. All frames should drain well if sunk into the ground, to prevent their becoming a bathtub when it rains. Moreover, the cover should prop open securely. Perhaps the most common weak spot in cold frames is a poorly attached cover that slams shut when propped open for cooling or that rips off when strong winds work it loose.

Gardeners use cold frames for several purposes. Early in the spring, the cold frame acts as a halfway house and parking lot for indoor-started, transplanted seedlings of frost-hardy species. Later in spring, the frost-tender species can be moved to the cold frame.

Always keep a weather eye out for cold or windy nights and cover the frame to prevent drastic drops in temperature or freezing inside the frame. In the fall, the frame can be filled with pansies, stock, or calendulas and left open during the day but closed at night to prolong the growing season.

If cold frames are heated with electric cables or a grid of hot-water pipes, they are called hotbeds and act as small greenhouses.

Electricity for heating can be expensive, so hotbeds are usually well insulated. They should not be bottled up too tight or condensation will occur, which can encourage the spread of plant diseases.

Caring for Indoor Seedlings

Beginning gardeners have a tendency to kill seedlings with kindness. Plants should be inspected daily and watered only when the container feels light, not when the soil surface looks a little dry. If seeds fail to emerge and seedlings pinch off at the base or topple

The lid of a cold frame should prop open securely to three positions: slightly open, half-open, and fully open. Sink the frame into the ground or build a bank of soil part way up the sides. Many cold frames also have rubber insulation around the inner rim.

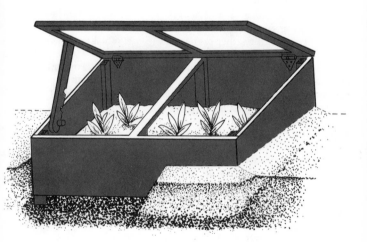

over, damping-off has occurred. Move the seeded pots into strong, direct sunlight, reduce the watering frequency, and drench with a special seedling fungicide.

As a rule, seedlings should not be fed while growing in a seeded pot or flat; nor should they be fed at the time of transplanting. Even indoor transplanting shocks seedlings, and they must develop new feeder roots before being fed. The regular potting soils formulated for transplanting contain enough plant nutrients to sustain seedlings for three to four weeks.

Slow-growing species are usually kept in seeded pots for five to six weeks and small individual pots for another six weeks before they are set into the garden. Only one or two feedings would be needed during this procedure, and these only near the end of the indoor period. Fast-growing kinds may spend as little as three to four weeks in seeded pots and another four weeks in individual pots. Two feedings would suffice for them. Soluble plant foods with a 1:2:1 ratio of nitrogen, phosphate, and potash (10-20-10, for example) are good for seedlings, especially if the formulation also contains micronutrients. Use fertilizers at only one-quarter to one-half the rates recommended for mature plants.

Hardening Off Seedlings

The last step in preparing flower seedlings for the harsh outdoor environment is to harden off, or acclimatize them. Their major adjustment will be against drying winds, more so than to cold or to strong sunlight. The tissues of seedlings grown indoors are soft and succulent, and the cell walls thin. Thrusting seedlings into the garden at such a vulnerable stage is asking for damage or loss. Hardening off is simple. A week before the safe transplanting date, find a corner of a porch, patio, or garage that is protected from strong winds yet open to sunlight and temperature changes. Move your transplants there. Watch them closely; they may need twice-daily watering, depending on the ratio of top growth to root-ball size. After three to five days, set them in a fully exposed outdoor location but still in their pots. Be wary of cold nights; even though it may not frost, a warm-weather species can be severely shocked by near-freezing temperatures. Move the plants back inside at night rather than risk such damage or loss.

A cold frame is an ideal hardening off site because the cover can be propped open by degrees to gradually accustom plants to wind, dryness, and cold.

Transplanting Flower Seedlings

Seed packets and catalogues will suggest the necessary spacing between plants. It may seem like a lot of room at first, but the plants will spread or billow out to nearly touch each other at maturity. If you cram plants, the result may be poor performance as well as problems with diseases and insects.

Prepare the soil and work phosphate and lime into it, if needed. A low-nitrogen complete fertilizer, such as 5-10-10, can be substituted for the phosphate. Some gardeners swear by high-phosphate starter fertilizers, which are dissolved in water and then used to water-in the transplants. These are most effective on soils with adequate nitrogen, for neither phosphorus nor nitrogen works well alone. Although some gardeners claim vitamin concoctions help in transplanting, no scientific data support their use. Fish emulsion, dissolved at half the normal rate, gets transplants off to a fast start.

A tried and true method of transplanting is to dig planting holes and fill them with water. Let the water soak in, and then add more. It is much easier to supply a reservoir of soil moisture before transplanting than after, because many types of soils seal over and shed water.

Inspect your seedlings as you take them out of individual pots. Ordinarily, seedlings have enough vigor to outgrow a minor pot-bound condition. But if roots circle around and create a mat, take a sharp knife and draw it up one side, across the bottom, and down the other side. New feeder roots will form at the cut line. They will grow out into the surrounding soil instead of being trapped inside the cage of girdling roots.

Many garden books, especially European ones, will instruct you to pinch out the leader, or central, stem of flower seedlings to a height of six to nine inches when transplanting them or shortly thereafter. Modern research indicates no advantage to this procedure; in fact, it usually delays blooming. An exception might be made when transplanting large seedlings with very small root balls. You might snip a few of the branches off to half length. By decreasing plant size, you would reduce the severity of wilting on dry, windy days.

Routine Maintenance

Weeding is a major chore in flower gardening, but it can be reduced by mulching with pine needles or dried grass clippings. Get after weed seedlings early, before they flower and drop seeds, and the weed problem will diminish each succeeding year. Weed pulling goes quickly if done after a rain, or you can cultivate dry soil to a shallow depth to kill emerging weeds. Weeds may regrow if you cultivate moist soil.

Spraying for insects is seldom needed in the North but is routine in mild climates. Small sucking insects, such as whiteflies, aphids, thrips, and leafhoppers, can be controlled with insecticidal soaps or mild chemicals. Red spider mites usually need a specific control, a chemical called a miticide. Gardeners seldom bother with spraying for foliage diseases, preferring, rather, to select trouble-free species. Sprays wash off with every rain or sprinkling.

Over much of the country, the chrysanthemum leaf miner has escaped from greenhouse crops and is attacking certain species of

Getting Started

annuals with thick leaves. If you notice tunneling between the bottom and top surfaces of leaves, strip off and dispose of the affected parts. Control is quite difficult, requiring toxic chemicals. It is better to discontinue growing susceptible plants.
Japanese beetle attacks on many kinds of flowers are a summer plague in the eastern third of the United States. Sex-attractant traps and milky spore disease offer a degree of biological control. Concentrate on the kinds of flowers that don't appeal to beetles in your garden.

Dead-heading and Shearing
For annuals, pruning consists mainly of dead-heading, or pinching off faded blossoms to promote more flowering, and of shearing off ungainly branches. The object of dead-heading is to prevent the development of unsightly seed heads that drain energy from the plant. The object of shearing, and then feeding and watering, is to replace thin, spindly, nonproductive branches with vigorous new growth. Do this once or twice during the growing season. Plants with large leaves, such as zinnias, don't take kindly to shearing, but marigolds and petunias thrive on it. Certain modern varieties are self-covering; new growth forms a canopy that hides unsightly weathered leaves and spent blossoms. Some hybrids, such as triploid marigolds, don't set seeds and need not be sheared; spent blossoms drop off.

Stem Cuttings
Certain kinds of annuals, such as coleus and impatiens, can be easily propagated by taking stem cuttings. The plant must be in the middle of its growth cycle at the time the cuttings are made. Choose a healthy side shoot that is not in flower. With a razor or a sharp knife, cut the stem about one-half inch below a pair of leaves. The cuttings should be at least two to three nodes long. The new roots will arise below the nodes where the stem buds are located in the axils of the leaves.
Insert the cuttings in moist sand, spacing them so their leaves barely touch. Remove the lowest leaves and push the stem gently down; this prevents the development of air spaces around the cutting. Cover the flat with plastic film, using a wire frame or wooden stakes to keep the bag from touching the cuttings. Place the container in indirect light, never in sunlight. Watch for signs of discoloration or disease, and remove any plants with these symptoms. After the plants are rooted, remove the bag. You will know that roots have formed when you see new growth and when the cuttings resist a gentle tug.

The End of the Season
After the first frost, annuals should be pulled and composted to prevent insects from proliferating and to reduce the spread of

To propagate new annuals from stem cuttings, cut off the uppermost part of the stem just below a leaf joint, then remove the leaves at the base.

diseases. Flowers whose seeds attract wild birds can be pulled after the seeds have been gleaned. In warm climates where frost-hardy annuals survive the winter, old plants should be removed prior to spring planting. Otherwise, the insects harboring on the old plants will infest transplants as they are set into the garden.

Gardening Tools

You don't need to invest a fortune in tools to grow flowers, but it helps to start with the best you can afford. Some of the bargain-priced garden tools sold today are constructed of lightweight, soft metal, and have handles of shoddy imported wood. These can break or bend at first use. Ask your dealer for the grade of tools sold to commercial landscapers. You will get top-of-the-line pieces that should hold up for many years.

Some gardeners prefer to order from mail-order tool specialists. These businesses offer small, strong, lightweight tools as well as heavy, ultra-strong tools of forged steel. Beware of the heavy equipment, however, unless you are a weight lifter.

A recommended starter set of tools consists of only five items:

1. Round-point shovel with a "D" handle or a long handle
2. Iron rake for leveling soil
3. Convertible hoe; the blade has a straight cutting edge on one side for weeding and a pronged or pointed tool on the other for cultivating
4. Hand trowel
5. Pump-sprayer, either one-gallon or two-gallon capacity, depending on your strength and the size of the job.

Storing Extra Seeds

If you have leftover seeds, they will store best under cool, dry conditions. An ideal container is a fruit jar with a rubber seal, plus desiccant capsules. Drop in the capsules, then a wad of paper, then the seed packets with the tops folded over and taped down. Seal the jar and place in a refrigerator. This procedure is especially valuable for short-lived seeds, such as larkspurs, and tiny, fragile, valuable seeds, such as begonias and hybrid petunias.

The Color Plates

The plates on the following pages are divided into six groups: pink flowers; blue to purple flowers; white flowers; grasses, fruit, and foliage; yellow flowers; and red to orange flowers (which also includes multicolors). Preceding the color plates, there is a Color Key, which shows the range of hues included in each color group. To help you select the right flower for the right place, the Flower Chart indicates important characteristics of each plant.

Color Key

Everyone sees color somewhat differently; what appears cream-colored to one gardener may seem pale yellow to another. Even pink and blue tones can seem quite similar, especially if viewed at different times of the day. The Color Key presents the variations in intensity and tone included in each color group.

When you purchase seeds or seedlings, be aware that the color indicated in the catalogue or on the package and identification tag may differ from the way you interpret that color. For example, nurseries and horticulturists use the term "blue" to describe colors ranging from lavender to blue to dark purple or even magenta.

Flower Chart

The Flower Chart is divided into six groups. Within each group, the scientific names of the flowers are listed in alphabetical order, and the names are followed by the page numbers of the color plates. The flowers are evaluated in six ways: hardiness to frost, preference for warm or cool weather, suitability for cut or dried flowers, soil requirements, light requirements, and plant height. Three hardiness ratings are indicated: hardy annuals (HA), half-hardy annuals (HHA), and tender annuals (TA).

Color Key

Pink Flowers

Blue to Purple Flowers

White Flowers

This chart shows the
range of hues in each
group of color plates.

Color Key

**Grasses, Fruit and
Foliage**

Yellow Flowers

**Red to Orange
Flowers**

Flower Chart

	Page Numbers	Hardiness
Pink Flowers		
Abronia umbellata	117	TA
Agrostemma Githago	84	HHA
Alcea rosea 'Majorette'	109	HA
Antirrhinum majus 'Little Darling'	111	HHA
Arctotis stoechadifolia	103	TA
Begonia × semperflorens-cultorum	80	TA
Bellis perennis	101	HA
Calandrinia umbellata	84	HHA
Callistephus chinensis 'Early Charm Choice'	102	TA
Catharanthus roseus	81	TA
Centaurea americana	99	HA
Centaurium Erythraea	90	HA
Clarkia amoena	86	HA
Clarkia purpurea	85	HA
Clarkia unguiculata	93	HA
Cleome Hasslerana	118	HHA
Coriandrum sativum	119	HA
Cosmos bipinnatus	105	TA
Crepis rubra	99	HA
Cymbalaria muralis	91	TA
Cynoglossum officinale	91	HA
Dahlia 'Flashlight'	103	TA
Dahlia hybrids	102	TA
Dianthus Armeria	110	HA
Dianthus barbatus	114	HA
Diascia Barberae	111	HHA
Digitalis purpurea 'Campanulata'	97	HA
Digitalis purpurea 'Foxy'	95, 96	HA
Dolichos Lablab	97	HHA
Dorotheanthus bellidiformis	100	TA
Erodium cicutarium	88	HA

| Warm Weather | Cool Weather | Cut Flowers | Dried Flowers | Dry Soil | Average Soil | Moist Soil | Sun | Partial Shade | Shade | Under 12 in. | 12–24 in. | Over 24 in. | Creeper |

Flower Chart

	Page Numbers	Hardiness
Pink Flowers continued		
Erysimum linifolium 'Variegatum'	113	HA
Gomphrena globosa 'Buddy'	108	TA
Helipterum roseum	100	TA
Iberis umbellata	115	HA
Impatiens 'New Guinea'	81	TA
Impatiens Wallerana	80	TA
Ionopsidium acaule	90	HA
Ipomoea Nil	83	TA
Lantana montevidensis	116	HHA
Lathyrus odoratus 'Mammoth Mixed'	109	HA
Lavatera arborea	86	HA
Lavatera trimestris	87	HA
Linaria maroccana 'Fairy Bouquet Improved'	110	HA
Linum grandiflorum	83	HA
Lobularia maritima 'Rosie O'Day'	116	HA
Lopezia hirsuta	89	TA
Lunaria annua	88	HA
Lychnis Coeli-rosa 'Love'	113	HHA
Malcolmia maritima	112	HA
Malope trifida	89	HA
Matthiola incana 'Annua'	107	HA
Matthiola longipetala	92	HA
Mesembryanthemum crystallinum	101	TA
Mirabilis Jalapa	82	HHA
Nemesia strumosa	106	TA
Nicotiana alata	92	TA
Nicotiana Tabacum	93	TA
Oenothera speciosa	87	HA
Orthocarpus purpurascens	94	HA
Pelargonium × domesticum	108	TA
Petunia × hybrida 'Pink Satin'	82	HHA

Warm Weather	Cool Weather	Cut Flowers	Dried Flowers	Dry Soil	Average Soil	Moist Soil	Sun	Partial Shade	Shade	Under 12 in.	12–24 in.	Over 24 in.	Creeper
■	■	■	■	■	■	■	■	■	■	■	■	■	■
	■		■		■		■			■	■		
■	■	■	■	■	■		■			■	■		
	■	■	■	■	■		■				■		
■	■				■		■			■	■		
■						■	■	■		■			
■						■	■	■		■			
	■				■		■	■		■			
■					■		■						■
■					■		■						■
	■				■	■	■						■
■	■				■		■					■	
■	■			■			■					■	
■	■				■		■			■			
■					■		■			■			
■					■		■	■		■			
■						■	■			■	■		
■	■	■	■		■	■	■		■	■	■		
■					■		■			■			
	■				■		■	■		■			
	■				■		■				■		
■					■		■			■	■		
	■				■		■	■		■			
■			■		■		■						■
■					■		■			■	■		
■	■					■	■			■			
■	■				■		■	■			■		
■					■		■				■		
■					■		■			■			
■			■		■		■			■			
■					■		■	■		■			
■	■				■	■	■			■	■		

Flower Chart

	Page Numbers	Hardiness
Pink Flowers continued		
Polygonum capitatum 'Magic Carpet'	117	HHA
Polygonum orientale	94	HA
Portulaca pilosa	85	TA
Primula malacoides	114	HHA
Primula obconica	115	HHA
Pueraria lobata	96	HHA
Salvia Sclarea	95	HHA
Scabiosa atropurpurea	119	HHA
Scabiosa stellata	118	HHA
Schizanthus pinnatus	105	TA
Schizanthus × wisetonensis	104	TA
Senecio elegans	104	HHA
Silene Armeria	112	HA
Silybum Marianum	98	HA
Verbena × hybrida	107	TA
Verbena × hybrida 'Pink Bouquet'	106	TA
Xeranthemum annuum	98	HA
Blue to Purple Flowers		
Ageratum Houstonianum 'North Sea'	123	TA
Anagallis Monellii linifolia	129	TA
Anchusa capensis	146	TA
Asarina Barclaiana	139	TA
Asperula orientalis	125	HA
Borago officinalis	140	HA
Brachycome iberidifolia	127	HHA
Browallia speciosa 'Blue Bells'	128	TA
Browallia viscosa	130	TA
Campanula Medium	138	HA
Catananche caerulea	125	HA
Centaurea Cyanus	124	HA
Cobaea scandens	138	TA

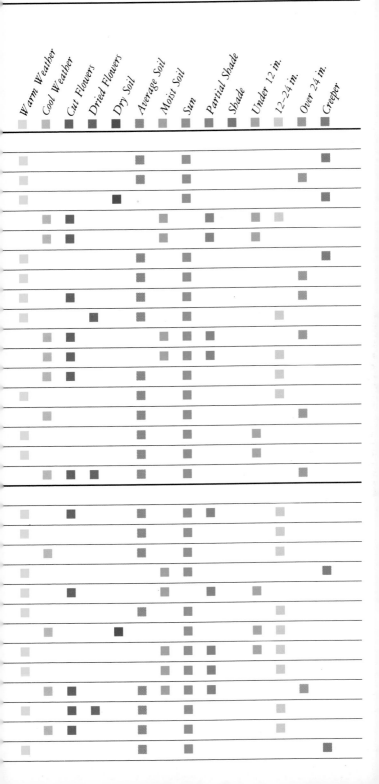

Flower Chart

	Page Numbers	Hardiness
Blue to Purple Flowers continued		
Collinsia grandiflora	133	HHA
Consolida ambigua	143	HA
Consolida orientalis	143	HA
Convolvulus tricolor	134	TA
Cynoglossum amabile 'Blanche Burpee'	144	HA
Echium Lycopsis	139	HA
Erysimum linifolium	144	HA
Eustoma grandiflorum	137	HHA
Exacum affine	147	TA
Felicia amelloides	126	HHA
Felicia Bergerana	126	HHA
Gilia capitata	123	HA
Heliotropium arborescens 'Marine'	145	TA
Ipomoea purpurea	134	TA
Ipomoea tricolor 'Heavenly Blue'	135	TA
Lavatera arborea 'Variegata'	137	HA
Linum usitatissimum	136	HA
Lobelia Erinus	129	HA
Lupinus subcarnosus	142	HA
Lupinus texensis	141	HA
Machaeranthera tanacetifolia	127	HHA
Mimosa pudica	122	HHA
Myosotis sylvatica	145	HA
Nemophila maculata	131	HA
Nemophila Menziesii	130	HA
Nicandra Physalodes	136	HHA
Nierembergia hippomanica var. *violacea*	135	HHA
Nigella damascena	124	HA
Oxypetalum caeruleum	146	TA
Phacelia campanularia	131	HA
Salvia farinacea 'Victoria'	142	HHA

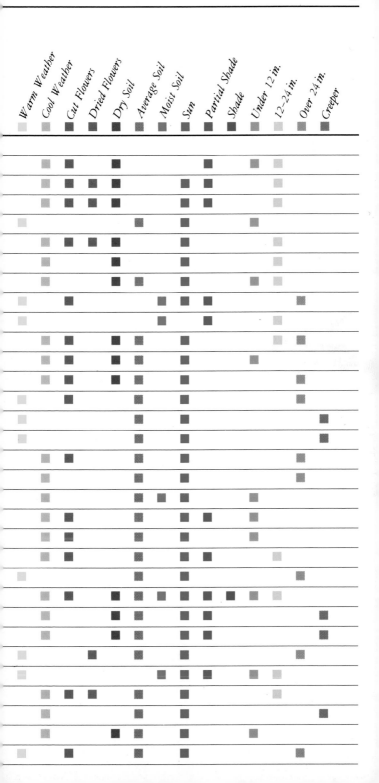

Flower Chart

	Page Numbers	Hardiness
Blue to Purple Flowers continued		
Salvia patens	140	HHA
Salvia viridis	141	HHA
Senecio × *hybridus*	128	TA
Torenia Fournieri	133	TA
Trachelium caeruleum	147	TA
Trachymene coerulea	122	HA
Viola tricolor	132	HA
Viola × *Wittrockiana*	132	HA
White Flowers		
Actinotus helianthi	156	TA
Ageratum Houstonianum	154	TA
Ammobium alatum 'Chelsea Physic'	158	TA
Androsace lactiflora	151	HA
Androsace septentrionalis	152	HA
Argemone munita	159	HHA
Carum Carvi	152	HA
Catharanthus roseus 'Albus'	162	TA
Chrysanthemum Parthenium 'Golden Feather'	158	HHA
Chrysanthemum Parthenium 'White Stars'	157	HHA
Datura inoxia	162	TA
Dimorphotheca pluvialis	157	TA
Dimorphotheca sinuata	156	TA
Echinocystis lobata	169	HHA
Fragaria vesca 'Alpine'	160	HA
Gaura Lindheimeri	166	HHA
Gypsophila elegans 'Golden Garden Market'	167	HA
Helianthus annuus 'Italian White'	155	HA
Hibiscus Moscheutos	163	HHA
Hyoscyamus niger	164	HA
Iberis amara	166	HA
Iberis pinnata	153	HA

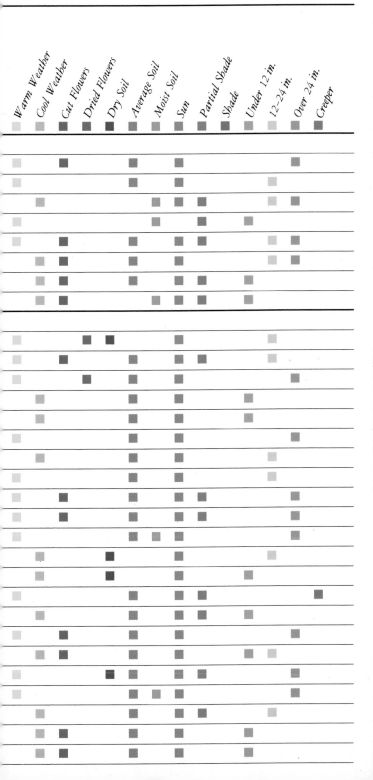

Flower Chart

	Page Numbers	Hardiness
White Flowers continued		
Ipomoea alba	163	TA
Ipomopsis aggregata	168	HA
Lobularia maritima	150	HA
Malva verticillata var. *crispa*	165	HA
Martynia annua	164	TA
Matricaria recutita	159	HA
Mesembryanthemum crystallinum	155	TA
Nicotiana alata 'Lime Green'	168	TA
Nicotiana alata 'Niki White'	169	TA
Oenothera deltoides	161	HHA
Omphalodes linifolia	150	HA
Osteospermum 'Buttermilk'	154	HHA
Proboscidea louisianica	165	TA
Reseda alba	167	HA
Sabatia angularis	153	HA
Satureja hortensis	151	HA
Viola cornuta 'White Perfection'	161	HA
Viola Rafinesquii	160	HA
Grasses, Fruit, and Foliage		
Agrostis nebulosa	179	HA
Alternanthera ficoidea	188	TA
Amaranthus tricolor 'Illumination'	189	TA
Atriplex hortensis 'Rubra'	184	HHA
Benincasa hispida	192	TA
Beta vulgaris 'Ruby Chard'	187	HHA
Brassica oleracea: Acephala Group	181	HA
Brassica oleracea: Acephala Group 'Dynasty Pink'	180	HA
Briza maxima	177	HA
Capsicum annuum 'Holiday Cheer'	191	TA
Capsicum annuum 'Red Missile'	190	TA
Cardiospermum Halicacabum	195	TA

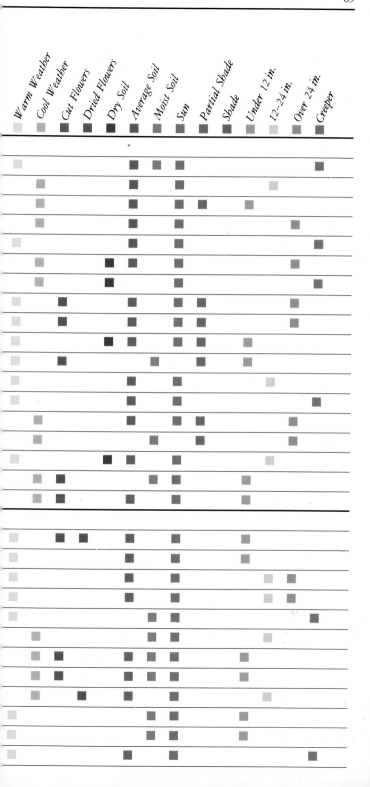

	Page Numbers	Hardiness
Grasses, Fruit, and Foliage continued		
Centaurea Cineraria	180	HHA
Coix Lacryma-Jobi	197	HHA
Coleus × hybridus	186, 187	TA
Cucurbita ficifolia	193	TA
Cynara cardunculus	182	HHA
Dolichos Lablab	195	HHA
Euphorbia cyathophora	186	HHA
Euphorbia Lathyris	194	HA
Euphorbia marginata 'Summer Icicle'	182	HHA
Foeniculum vulgare	178	HA
Helichrysum petiolatum	183	HHA
Hibiscus Acetosella 'Red Shield'	189	HHA
Hordeum jubatum	173	HA
Humulus japonicus	196	HHA
Iresine Herbstii 'Jepson'	188	TA
Kochia scoparia var. *tricophylla* 'Childsii'	179	HHA
Lagenaria siceraria	192	TA
Lagurus ovatus var. *nanus*	172	HA
Lamarckia aurea	174	HA
Luffa acutangula	193	TA
Luffa aegyptiaca	194	TA
Moluccella laevis	197	HHA
Momordica Charantia	191	TA
Ocimum Basilicum 'Dark Opal'	185	TA
Origanum Majorana	196	TA
Panicum miliaceum	178	HA
Panicum miliaceum 'Violaceum'	175	HA
Pennisetum setaceum	172	HHA
Pennisetum setaceum 'Cupreum'	177	HHA
Pennisetum villosum	173	HHA
Perilla frutescens 'Atropurpurea'	184	TA

Warm Weather	Cool Weather	Cut Flowers	Dried Flowers	Dry Soil	Average Soil	Moist Soil	Sun	Partial Shade	Shade	Under 12 in.	12–24 in.	Over 24 in.	Creeper

Flower Chart

	Page Numbers	Hardiness
Grasses, Fruit, and Foliage continued		
Perilla frutescens 'Crispa'	185	TA
Phalaris canariensis	176	HA
Polypogon monspeliensis	175	HA
Salvia argentea	183	HHA
Senecio Cineraria 'Silver Dust'	181	HHA
Setaria italica	176	HA
Solanum Melongena 'Golden Eggplant'	190	TA
Triticum aestivum	174	HA
Yellow Flowers		
Abelmoschus esculentus	219	TA
Anethum graveolens	212	HHA
Arachis hypogaea	210	TA
Argemone mexicana	202	HHA
Baileya multiradiata	231	HHA
Barbarea verna	214	HA
Barbarea vulgaris	215	HA
Calceolaria crenatiflora	211	HHA
Calceolaria integrifolia	210	HHA
Calceolaria mexicana	211	TA
Cassia fasciculata	218	HA
Cerinthe major	216	HA
Cheiranthus Cheiri	205	HHA
Chrysanthemum coronarium	223	HA
Chrysanthemum Parthenium	213	HHA
Coreopsis tinctoria	226, 227	HA
Dahlia hybrids	220	TA
Datura Metel	217	TA
Dyssodia tenuiloba	228	HA
Erysimum Perofskianum	204	HA
Eschscholzia californica	208	HA
Gaillardia pulchella	224	HA

Warm Weather	Cool Weather	Cut Flowers	Dried Flowers	Dry Soil	Average Soil	Moist Soil	Sun	Partial Shade	Shade	Under 12 in.	12–24 in.	Over 24 in.	Creeper
■	■	■	■	■	■	■	■	■	■	■	■	■	■
■			■		■		■					■	
■		■			■		■				■		
■	■	■	■		■		■				■		
■					■		■					■	
■					■		■					■	
■			■		■		■					■	
■						■	■				■		
■			■		■		■					■	
■					■		■					■	
	■				■		■					■	
■					■		■						■
■					■		■					■	
	■		■		■		■			■			
	■				■		■			■			
	■				■		■					■	
	■					■		■		■			
	■				■	■	■	■				■	
	■				■	■	■	■		■			
■			■	■	■		■			■			
	■				■		■			■			
	■	■			■		■	■				■	
	■	■			■		■	■				■	
■		■			■		■	■				■	
■		■			■		■					■	
■		■				■	■				■	■	
■						■	■					■	
	■			■			■		■				
	■			■	■		■				■		
	■	■		■	■		■			■			
	■	■		■	■		■				■		

Flower Chart

	Page Numbers	Hardiness
Yellow Flowers continued		
Gazania rigens	224, 225	TA
Glaucium flavum	202	HA
Helianthus annuus	230	HA
Helianthus annuus 'Teddy Bear'	230	HA
Hibiscus Moscheutos	218	HHA
Hibiscus Trionum	220	HHA
Hunnemannia fumariifolia	209	HHA
Layia platyglossa	229	HA
Limnanthes Douglasii	201	HA
Lonas annua	212	HHA
Mentzelia Lindleyi	201	HA
Mimulus guttatus	206	HHA
Nemesia strumosa	205	TA
Oenothera biennis	217	HA
Oenothera erythrosepala	216	HA
Oenothera laciniata	219	HA
Oenothera missourensis	203	HA
Oenothera primiveris	203	HA
Pimpinella Anisum	213	HA
Platystemon californicus	200	HA
Portulaca oleracea	208	TA
Reseda lutea	214	HA
Reseda odorata	215	HA
Rudbeckia hirta	223	HHA
Rudbeckia hirta 'Gloriosa Daisy Marmalade'	222	HHA
Sanvitalia procumbens	221	TA
Saxifraga Cymbalaria	200	HHA
Tagetes erecta	231	HHA
Tagetes tenuifolia 'Tangerine Gem'	204	HHA
Thelesperma Burridgeanum	227	HA
Thunbergia alata	221	TA

Warm Weather	Cool Weather	Cut Flowers	Dried Flowers	Dry Soil	Average Soil	Moist Soil	Sun	Partial Shade	Shade	Under 12 in.	12–24 in.	Over 24 in.	Creeper
■	■	■	■	■	■	■	■	■	■	■	■	■	■
■				■			■			■			
	■				■		■					■	
■				■	■		■	■				■	
■				■	■		■	■		■			
■					■	■	■					■	
■					■		■			■		■	
■				■	■		■			■			
	■	■			■		■			■			
■						■	■			■			
■		■			■		■			■			
■					■		■			■			
■						■	■	■		■			
	■	■				■	■			■			
■		■			■		■	■				■	
■					■		■	■				■	
■					■		■	■		■	■		
■					■		■	■		■			
■					■		■			■			
	■				■		■			■			
	■					■	■			■			
■			■				■						■
	■				■		■	■				■	
	■	■			■		■	■		■			
■		■	■	■	■		■	■				■	
■		■	■	■	■		■	■				■	
■					■		■						■
	■				■		■	■		■			
■		■			■		■			■	■		
■		■			■		■			■			
■		■			■		■			■			
■						■	■	■					■

Flower Chart

	Page Numbers	Hardiness
Yellow Flowers continued		
Tolpis barbata	228	TA
Tropaeolum peregrinum	209	TA
Ursinia anthemoides 'Sunshine Blend'	226	HHA
Venidium fastuosum	225	TA
Viola cornuta	207	HA
Viola × Wittrockiana	206, 207	HA
Xanthisma texana	222	HA
Zinnia angustifolia 'Classic'	229	TA
Red to Orange Flowers		
Abutilon hybridum	260	TA
Alcea rosea	254	HA
Alonsoa Warscewiczii	256	TA
Amaranthus caudatus	268	TA
Amaranthus hybridus var. *erythrostachys*	269	TA
Anagallis arvensis	250	HA
Antirrhinum majus	267	HHA
Asclepias curassavica	257	TA
Begonia × semperflorens-cultorum	250	TA
Bellis perennis	244, 245	HA
Calendula officinalis 'Orange Coronet'	236	HA
Celosia cristata	271	TA
Celosia cristata 'Century Mixed'	269	TA
Celosia cristata 'Golden Torch'	268	TA
Celosia cristata 'Jewel Box'	270	TA
Chrysanthemum carinatum	239	HA
Chrysanthemum carinatum 'Merry Mixture'	238	HA
Cirsium japonicum	271	HA
Cosmos sulphureus 'Bright Lights'	236	TA
Cuphea ignea 'Hidcote'	264	TA
Dianthus chinensis 'Telestar Mix'	252	HHA
Dorotheanthus bellidiformis 'El Cerrito'	243	TA

Warm Weather	Cool Weather	Cut Flowers	Dried Flowers	Dry Soil	Average Soil	Moist Soil	Sun	Partial Shade	Shade	Under 12 in.	12–24 in.	Over 24 in.	Creeper
■	■	■	■	■	■	■	■	■	■	■	■	■	■
■					■		■			■			
	■				■	■	■	■					■
■		■			■		■			■			
	■	■		■	■		■					■	
■		■				■	■			■			
■		■				■	■	■		■			
■		■		■	■		■					■	
■		■			■		■			■			
■					■	■	■	■			■	■	
■					■		■				■		
	■				■		■			■	■		
■			■		■		■				■		
■			■		■		■				■		
■					■		■						■
■	■					■	■				■		
■						■	■				■		
■						■	■	■	■	■			
■						■	■			■			
■	■				■		■			■			
■	■	■			■		■			■			
■	■	■			■		■			■			
■	■	■			■		■			■			
	■	■			■		■	■			■		
■	■				■		■	■			■		
	■				■		■	■			■		
■		■		■	■		■	■			■		
■		■			■		■	■		■	■		
■	■				■		■				■		
■			■			■			■				

Flower Chart

	Page Numbers	Hardiness
Red to Orange Flowers continued		
Eccremocarpus scaber	261	TA
Emilia javanica	270	HA
Gaillardia pulchella	239	HA
Gaillardia pulchella 'Gaiety'	240	HA
Gerbera Jamesonii 'Happipot'	242	HHA
Glaucium corniculatum	253	HA
Hedysarum coronarium	261	HA
Helianthus annuus hybrid	240	HA
Helichrysum bracteatum 'Bikini'	244	HHA
Impatiens Balsamina	255	TA
Impatiens 'New Guinea'	251	TA
Impatiens Wallerana	251	TA
Ipomoea coccinea	263	TA
Ipomoea × *multifida*	262	TA
Ipomoea Quamoclit	263	TA
Ipomopsis rubra	265	HA
Lantana Camara	259	HHA
Lantana Camara 'Radiation'	258	HHA
Limonium sinuatum	266	TA
Mimulus × *hybridus*	249	TA
Nicotiana alata 'Niki Red'	265	TA
Osteospermum hyoseroides	243	HHA
Papaver nudicaule	252	HHA
Papaver Rhoeas	255	HA
Papaver somniferum	254	HA
Pelargonium × *hortorum*	257	TA
Pelargonium peltatum	260	TA
Penstemon gloxinioides 'Scarlet and White'	256	HHA
Petunia × *hybrida* 'Flash Series'	247	HHA
Phaseolus coccineus	262	HHA
Phlox Drummondii	246	HA

Warm Weather	Cool Weather	Cut Flowers	Dried Flowers	Dry Soil	Average Soil	Moist Soil	Sun	Partial Shade	Shade	Under 12 in.	12–24 in.	Over 24 in.	Creeper
■	■	■	■	■	■	■	■	■	■	■	■	■	■
■						■	■						■
	■	■		■	■		■				■		
■		■		■	■		■				■		
■		■		■	■		■				■		
■					■		■				■		
	■				■		■				■		
	■	■			■		■					■	
■				■	■		■	■				■	
■		■	■	■	■		■			■			
■					■		■	■				■	
■					■		■	■		■			
■					■		■	■		■			
■					■		■						■
■					■		■						■
■		■			■		■						■
	■				■		■				■		
■					■		■				■		
■					■		■				■		
■		■	■		■		■			■	■		
	■				■			■		■			
■		■			■		■	■			■		
■				■	■		■			■			
	■	■		■	■		■			■			
■	■	■	■	■	■		■				■		
■	■	■	■	■	■		■			■	■		
■		■			■		■	■		■	■		
■					■		■	■					■
	■	■			■		■	■			■		
■		■			■	■	■			■	■		
■					■		■						■
	■	■			■		■				■		

Flower Chart

	Page Numbers	Hardiness
Red to Orange Flowers continued		
Portulaca grandiflora	253	TA
Primula × polyantha	247	HA
Ricinus communis	267	TA
Ricinus communis 'Gibsonii'	266	TA
Rudbeckia hirta 'Gloriosa Daisy'	241	HHA
Salpiglossis sinuata	248	TA
Salvia splendens 'Red Hussar'	264	TA
Senecio × hybridus	245	TA
Tagetes erecta	234	HHA
Tagetes patula 'Cinnabar'	237	HHA
Tagetes patula 'Queen Sophia'	235	HHA
Tagetes patula 'Tiger Eyes'	234	HHA
Tithonia rotundifolia	237	TA
Tropaeolum majus	249	TA
Verbena × hybrida 'Showtime Blaze'	259	TA
Verbena × hybrida 'Springtime'	246	TA
Verbena peruviana	258	TA
Viola × Wittrockiana 'Clear Crystal Mix'	248	HA
Zinnia elegans	235	TA
Zinnia elegans 'Peter Pan Mix'	242	TA
Zinnia Haageana 'Chippendale Daisy'	238	TA
Zinnia Haageana 'Old Mexico'	241	TA

Warm Weather	Cool Weather	Cut Flowers	Dried Flowers	Dry Soil	Average Soil	Moist Soil	Sun	Partial Shade	Shade	Under 12 in.	12–24 in.	Over 24 in.	Creeper
■			■				■						■
	■	■				■		■	■				
■						■	■					■	
■						■	■					■	
■		■		■	■		■	■				■	
	■	■				■	■					■	
■						■	■					■	
	■					■	■	■			■	■	
■		■				■	■				■	■	
■		■				■	■				■		
■		■				■	■				■		
■		■				■	■				■		
■		■				■	■					■	
	■	■		■	■		■	■					■
■						■	■			■			
■						■	■			■			
■						■	■						■
	■	■				■	■	■		■			
■		■				■	■					■	
■		■				■	■					■	
■		■				■	■				■		
■		■				■	■				■		

Pink Flowers

Begonia ×
semperflorens-
cultorum
'Gin'

Plant height: 8–12 in.
Flowers: 1 in. wide
Sun to shade
Moist soil
Wax Begonia
p. 290

Impatiens
Wallerana

Plant height: 1–2 ft.
Flowers: 1–2 in. wide
Sun to partial shade
Moist soil
Busy Lizzy
p. 346

Catharanthus roseus
Plant height: to 2 ft.
Flowers: 1½ in. wide
Full sun
Average soil
Madagascar Periwinkle
p. 302

Impatiens 'New Guinea'
Plant height: 1–2 ft.
Flowers:
2–2½ in. wide
Sun to partial shade
Moist soil
p. 346

82

Petunia × hybrida 'Pink Satin'
Plant height: 8–18 in.
Flowers: 2–4 in. wide
Full sun
Average to moist soil
Common Garden
Petunia
p. 387

Mirabilis Jalapa
Plant height: 1½–3 ft.
Flowers: 1 in. wide
Full sun
Average soil
Four-O'Clock
p. 370

Ipomoea Nil

Creeper: to 10 ft.
Flowers: 4 in. wide
Full sun
Average soil
Morning Glory
p. 347

Linum grandiflorum

Plant height: 1–2 ft.
Flowers: 1 in. wide
Full sun
Average soil
Flowering Flax
p. 357

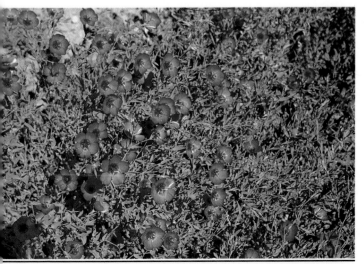

Agrostemma Githago

Plant height: 1–3 ft.
Flowers: 1 in. wide
Full sun
Average soil
Corn Cockle
p. 277

Calandrinia umbellata

Plant height: to 6 in.
Flowers: ¾ in. wide
Full sun
Dry soil
Rock Purslane
p. 296

Portulaca pilosa

Creeper: *to 12 in.*
Flowers: *½ in. wide*
Full sun
Dry soil
p. 393

Clarkia purpurea

Plant height: *to 3 ft.*
Flowers: *2 in. wide*
Full sun
Average soil
p. 307

Clarkia amoena

Plant height: 1–3 ft.
Flowers: 1–2 in. wide
Full sun
Average soil
Farewell-to-Spring
p. 307

Lavatera arborea

Plant height: 4–10 ft.
Flowers: 2 in. wide
Full sun
Average soil
Tree Mallow
p. 354

Oenothera speciosa   Plant height: 1–2 ft.
Flowers: 3 in. wide
Full sun
Average soil
Showy Evening
Primrose
p. 378

Lavatera trimestris   Plant height: 2–3 ft.
Flowers: 4 in. wide
Full sun
Dry soil
p. 354

Lunaria annua

Plant height: 1½–3 ft.
Flowers: 1 in. long
Partial shade
Average to moist soil
Honesty
p. 361

Erodium cicutarium

Plant height: to 18 in.
Flowers: ¼ in. wide
Full sun
Average to dry soil
Pin-Clover
p. 327

Lopezia hirsuta

Plant height: 1–3 ft.
Flowers: ½ in. long
Full sun
Moist soil
Mosquito Flower
p. 359

Malope trifida

Plant height: 2–3 ft.
Flowers: 2–3 in. wide
Full sun
Average soil
p. 364

Centaurium Erythraea

Plant height: to 20 in.
Flowers: ½ in. wide
Partial shade
Dry, well-drained soil
Centaury
p. 304

Ionopsidium acaule

Plant height: to 3 in.
Flowers: ¼ in. wide
Sun to partial shade
Average soil
Diamond Flower
p. 346

Cynoglossum officinale

Plant height: to 2 ft.
Flowers: ¼ in. long
Sun to partial shade
Average soil
p. 318

Cymbalaria muralis

Creeper: to 3 ft.
Flowers: ⅓ in. long
Sun to partial shade
Average soil
Kenilworth Ivy
p. 316

Nicotiana alata

Plant height: to 5 ft.
Flowers: 2–4 in. long
Sun to partial shade
Average soil
Flowering Tobacco
p. 375

Matthiola longipetala

Plant height:
to 18 in.
Flowers: ¾ in. wide
Sun to partial shade
Average soil
Evening Stock
p. 366

Nicotiana Tabacum

Plant height: to 6 ft.
Flowers: 2 in. long
Full sun
Average soil
Tobacco
p. 375

Clarkia unguiculata

Plant height: 1½–3 ft.
Flowers: 2½ in. wide
Full sun
Average soil
p. 307

Polygonum orientale
Plant height: to 6 ft.
Clusters: to 3½ in. long
Full sun
Average soil
Kiss-Me-Over-the-
Garden-Gate
p. 391

Orthocarpus purpurascens
Plant height: to 12 in.
Flowers: 1 in. long
Full sun
Average soil
Owl's Clover
p. 380

Salvia Sclarea

Plant height: to 3 ft.
Flowers: 1 in. long
Full sun
Average soil
Clary
p. 400

Digitalis purpurea
'Foxy'

Plant height: to 4 ft.
Flowers: 2–3 in. long
Sun to partial shade
Well-drained soil
Annual Foxglove
p. 322

Digitalis purpurea
'Foxy'

Plant height: to 4 ft.
Flowers: 2–3 in. long
Sun to partial shade
Well-drained soil
Annual Foxglove
p. 322

Pueraria lobata

Creeper: to 60 ft.
Clusters: to 12 in. long
Full sun
Average soil
Kudzu Vine
p. 395

Digitalis purpurea
'Campanulata'

Plant height: to 4 ft.
Flowers: 2–3 in. long
Sun to partial shade
Well-drained soil
Campanulata Foxglove
p. 322

Dolichos Lablab

Creeper: to 30 ft.
Flowers: ¾–1 in. long
Full sun
Average soil
Hyacinth Bean
p. 323

Silybum Marianum

Plant height: to 4 ft.
Flowers: 2½ in. wide
Full sun
Average soil
Holy Thistle
p. 406

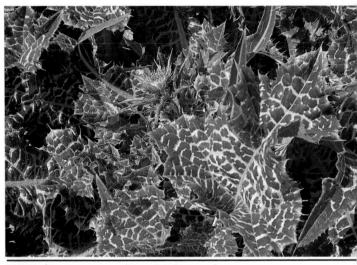

***Xeranthemum
annuum***

Plant height: 2–3 ft.
Flowers: 1½ in. wide
Full sun
Average soil
Everlasting
p. 419

Centaurea americana

Plant height: 4–6 ft.
Flowers: 4–5 in. wide
Full sun
Average soil
Basket-Flower
p. 303

Crepis rubra

Plant height: 8–18 in.
Flowers: 1½ in. wide
Full sun
Average soil
Hawk's Beard
p. 314

Dorotheanthus
bellidiformis

Plant height: to 3 in.
Flowers: 2 in. wide
Full sun
Dry soil
Livingstone Daisy
p. 324

Helipterum roseum

Plant height: to 2 ft.
Flowers: 2 in. wide
Full sun
Average to dry soil
Strawflower
p. 341

Mesembryanthemum
crystallinum

Creeper: to 2 ft.
Flowers:
¾–1¼ in. wide
Full sun
Dry soil
Ice Plant
p. 368

Bellis perennis

Plant height: to 6 in.
Flowers: 1–2 in. wide
Full sun
Moist soil
Double form
English Daisy
p. 290

**Callistephus
chinensis
'Early Charm
Choice'**

Plant height: 9–24 in.
Flowers: 5 in. wide
Full sun
Average to moist soil
China Aster
p. 298

Dahlia hybrid

Plant height: 1–5 ft.
Flowers: 2–4 in. wide
Full sun
Moist soil
Dahlia
p. 318

Dahlia
'Flashlight'

Plant height: 1–5 ft.
Flowers: 2–4 in. wide
Full sun
Moist soil
Dahlia
p. 318

Arctotis
stoechadifolia

Plant height: 2½–4 ft.
Flowers: 3 in. wide
Full sun
Average soil
Blue-eyed African Daisy
p. 285

Senecio elegans

Plant height: to 2 ft.
Flowers: 1 in. wide
Full sun
Average soil
Purple Ragwort
p. 404

**Schizanthus ×
wisetonensis**

Plant height: 1–2 ft.
Flowers: 1½ in. wide
Sun to partial shade
Moist soil
Butterfly Flower
p. 403

Cosmos bipinnatus

Plant height: 4–6 ft.
Flowers: 1–2 in. wide
Sun to partial shade
Average to dry soil
Garden Cosmos
p. 314

Schizanthus pinnatus

Plant height: to 4 ft.
Flowers: 1½ in. wide
Sun to partial shade
Moist soil
Butterfly Flower
p. 403

Nemesia strumosa

Plant height: to 2 ft.
Flowers: 1 in. wide
Full sun
Moist soil
p. 373

Verbena × hybrida
'Pink Bouquet'

Plant height: to 12 in.
Clusters: 2-3 in. wide
Full sun
Average soil
Garden Verbena
p. 416

Verbena × *hybrida*   Plant height: to 12 in.
Clusters: 2–3 in. wide
Full sun
Average soil
Garden Verbena
p. 416

Matthiola incana   Plant height: 1–2½ ft.
'**Annua**'   Flowers: 1 in. wide
Full sun
Average soil
Stock
p. 366

***Pelargonium* ×
*domesticum***

Plant height: to 18 in.
Flowers:
1½–3 in. wide
Sun to partial shade
Average soil
Martha Washington
Geranium
p. 384

***Gomphrena globosa*
'Buddy'**

Plant height: 8–20 in.
Flowers: 1 in. wide
Full sun
Average to dry soil
Globe Amaranth
p. 337

Alcea rosea
'Majorette'

Plant height: 5–9 ft.
Flowers: 3 in. wide
Full sun
Average soil
Double form
Garden Hollyhock
p. 278

Lathyrus odoratus
'Mammoth Mixed'

Creeper: 4–6 ft.
Flowers: 2 in. long
Full sun
Average to moist soil
Sweet Pea
p. 353

Dianthus Armeria

Plant height: to 16 in.
Flowers: ¾ in. long
Full sun
Average to dry soil
Deptford Pink
p. 320

Linaria maroccana
'Fairy Bouquet
Improved'

Plant height: to 18 in.
Flowers: ½ in. long
Full sun
Average soil
Toadflax
p. 357

Diascia Barberae

Plant height: 8–15 in.
Flowers: ½ in. wide
Full sun
Average soil
Twinspur
p. 321

**Antirrhinum majus
'Little Darling'**

Plant height: to 15 in.
Flowers: 1½ in. long
Full sun
Moist soil
Semidwarf form
Common Snapdragon
p. 284

Malcolmia maritima

Plant height: 6–12 in.
Flowers: ¾ in. wide
Sun to partial shade
Average soil
Virginia Stock
p. 363

Silene Armeria

Plant height: to 18 in.
Flowers: ½ in. wide
Full sun
Average soil
Sweet William Catchfly
p. 406

Lychnis Coeli-rosa
'Love'

Plant height:
12–20 in.
Flowers: 1 in. wide
Full sun
Average soil
Rose-of-Heaven
p. 362

Erysimum linifolium
'Variegatum'

Plant height: 6–18 in.
Flowers: ¾ in. long
Full sun
Average to dry soil
Alpine Wallflower
p. 328

Primula malacoides
Plant height: 4–18 in.
Flowers: ½ in. wide
Partial shade
Moist soil
Fairy Primrose
p. 393

Dianthus barbatus
Plant height: 1–2 ft.
Flowers: ⅓ in. wide
Sun to partial shade
Average soil
Sweet William
p. 320

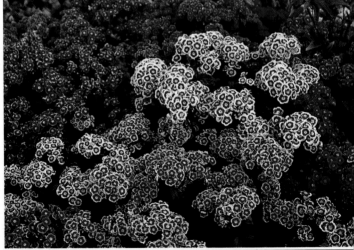

Primula obconica

Plant height: to 12 in.
Flowers: 1 in. wide
Partial shade
Moist soil
German Primrose
p. 393

Iberis umbellata

Plant height: 8–16 in.
Clusters: to 2 in. wide
Full sun
Average soil
Globe Candytuft
p. 345

Lobularia maritima
'Rosie O'Day'

Plant height: to 12 in.
Clusters: to ¾ in. wide
Sun to partial shade
Average soil
Sweet Alyssum
p. 358

Lantana
montevidensis

Creeper: to 3 ft.
Clusters: to 1 in. wide
Full sun
Average soil
Weeping Lantana
p. 353

**Polygonum
capitatum
'Magic Carpet'**

Creeper: to 10 in.
Clusters: to ¾ in. wide
Full sun
Average soil
Knotweed
p. 391

Abronia umbellata

Creeper: to 2 ft.
Clusters: to 2 in. wide
Sun to partial shade
Dry, well-drained soil
Sand Verbena
p. 274

Cleome Hasslerana
Plant height: 4–5 ft.
Clusters: 6–8 in. wide
Sun to partial shade
Dry soil
Spider Flower
p. 308

Scabiosa stellata
Plant height: to 18 in.
Flowers: 1¼ in. wide
Full sun
Average soil
p. 403

Coriandrum sativum

Plant height: to 3 ft.
Clusters: to 2 in. wide
Full sun
Average soil
Coriander
p. 313

Scabiosa atropurpurea

Plant height: 2–3 ft.
Flowers: 2 in. wide
Full sun
Average soil
Sweet Scabious
p. 402

Blue to Purple

Flowers

Trachymene coerulea

Plant height:
1½–2½ ft.
Clusters: 2–3 in. wide
Full sun
Average soil
Blue Laceflower
p. 413

Mimosa pudica

Plant height: to 3 ft.
Flowers: ⅔ in. wide
Full sun
Average soil
Sensitive Plant
p. 368

Gilia capitata

Plant height: to 3 ft.
Clusters: 1 in. wide
Full sun
Well-drained to dry soil
Queen Anne's Thimble
p. 336

Ageratum Houstonianum 'North Sea'

Plant height: to 14 in.
Flowers: ¼ in. wide
Sun to partial shade
Average soil
Common Garden Ageratum
p. 276

Nigella damascena

Plant height:
12–18 in.
Flowers: 1½ in. wide
Full sun
Average soil
Love-in-a-Mist
p. 376

Centaurea Cyanus

Plant height: 1–2 ft.
Flowers: 1½ in. wide
Full sun
Average soil
Bachelor's Button
p. 303

Asperula orientalis

Plant height: to 12 in.
Flowers: ⅜ in. long
Partial shade
Moist soil
Woodruff
_p. 287_

Catananche
caerulea

Plant height: to 2 ft.
Flowers: 2 in. wide
Full sun
Average soil
Cupid's Dart
_p. 301_

Felicia Bergerana
Plant height: 4–8 in.
Flowers: ¾ in. wide
Full sun
Average to dry soil
Kingfisher Daisy
p. 331

Felicia amelloides
Plant height: 1–3 ft.
Flowers: 1 in. wide
Full sun
Average to dry soil
Blue Marguerite
p. 331

Machaeranthera tanacetifolia

Plant height: 1–2 ft.
Flowers: 2 in. wide
Sun to partial shade
Average soil
Tahoka Daisy
p. 363

Brachycome iberidifolia

Plant height: 8–18 in.
Flowers: 1 in. wide
Full sun
Dry soil
Swan River Daisy
p. 293

Senecio × hybridus   *Plant height: 1–3 ft.*
Flowers: 2 in. wide
Sun to partial shade
Moist soil
Cineraria
p. 405

Browallia speciosa
'Blue Bells'   *Plant height: 8–15 in.*
Flowers: 2 in. wide
Sun to partial shade
Moist soil
p. 295

Anagallis Monellii linifolia

Plant height: *to 18 in.*
Flowers: *¾ in. wide*
Full sun
Average soil
Flaxleaf Pimpernel
p. 282

Lobelia Erinus

Plant height: *3–8 in.*
Flowers:
½–¾ in. long
Full sun
Average to moist soil
Edging Lobelia
p. 358

**Nemophila
Menziesii**

*Creeper: to 12 in.
Flowers: 1½ in. wide
Sun to partial shade
Average to dry soil
Baby Blue-Eyes
p. 373*

Browallia viscosa

*Plant height:
12–20 in.
Flowers: ¾ in. wide
Sun to partial shade
Moist soil
p. 295*

Nemophila maculata

Creeper: to 12 in.
Flowers: 1¾ in. wide
Sun to partial shade
Average to dry soil
Five Spot
p. 373

Phacelia campanularia

Plant height: to 8 in.
Flowers: 1 in.
Full sun
Average to dry soil
California Bluebell
p. 387

Viola ×
Wittrockiana

Plant height: to 9 in.
Flowers: 2–5 in. wide
Sun to partial shade
Moist soil
Pansy
p. 418

Viola tricolor

Plant height: to 12 in.
Flowers: ¾ in. long
Sun to partial shade
Average soil
Johnny-Jump-Up
p. 418

Torenia Fournieri

Plant height:
10–12 in.
Flowers: 1 in. long
Partial shade
Moist soil
Wishbone Flower
p. 411

Collinsia grandiflora

Plant height: 8–15 in.
Flowers: ¾ in. long
Partial shade
Dry soil
Blue-Lips
p. 311

Convolvulus tricolor
Plant height: to 12 in.
Flowers: 1½ in. wide
Full sun
Average soil
Dwarf Morning Glory
p. 312

Ipomoea purpurea
Creeper: to 10 ft.
Flowers: 3–5 in. wide
Full sun
Average soil
Common Morning Glory
p. 348

Ipomoea tricolor
'Heavenly Blue'

Creeper: *to 10 ft.*
Flowers: 4–5 in. wide
Full sun
Average soil
Morning Glory
p. 348

Nierembergia
hippomanica
var. *violacea*
'Purple Robe'

Plant height: 6–15 in.
Flowers: 1 in. wide
Sun to partial shade
Moist soil
Cupflower
p. 376

Nicandra
Physalodes

Plant height: 4–8 ft.
Flowers: 1–2 in. wide
Full sun
Average soil
Apple-of-Peru
p. 374

Linum
usitatissimum

Plant height: 3–4 ft.
Flowers: ½ in. wide
Full sun
Average soil
Common Flax
p. 357

Eustoma grandiflorum

Plant height: 2–3 ft.
Flowers: 2 in. wide
Sun to partial shade
Moist soil
Prairie Gentian
p. 330

Lavatera arborea 'Variegata'

Plant height: 4–10 ft.
Flowers: 2 in. wide
Full sun
Average soil
Tree Mallow
p. 354

Cobaea scandens

Creeper: 10–25 ft.
Flowers: 1½ in. wide
Full sun
Average soil
Cup-and-Saucer Vine
p. 309

Campanula
Medium

Plant height: 2–4 ft.
Flowers: 1 in. wide
Sun to partial shade
Average to moist soil
Canterbury Bells
p. 299

Asarina Barclaiana
Creeper: to 10 ft.
Flowers:
1–1¼ in. long
Full sun
Moist soil
p. 286

Echium Lycopsis
Plant height: to 2 ft.
Flowers: ½ in. wide
Full sun
Dry soil
Viper's Bugloss
p. 326

Salvia patens

Plant height: to 3 ft.
Flowers: 2–3 in. long
Full sun
Average soil
Gentian Sage
p. 400

Borago officinalis

Plant height: to 2 ft.
Flowers: ¾ in. wide
Full sun
Average soil
Borage
p. 292

Lupinus texensis
Plant height: to 12 in.
Flowers: ¾ in. long
Full sun
Average soil
Texas Bluebonnet
p. 362

Salvia viridis
Plant height: to 18 in.
Flowers: ½ in. long
Full sun
Average soil
p. 400

Lupinus subcarnosus
Plant height: 8–10 in.
Flowers: ½ in. long
Sun to partial shade
Average soil
Bluebonnet
p. 362

Salvia farinacea
'Victoria'
Plant height: to 3 ft.
Flowers: ½ in. long
Full sun
Average soil
Mealy-Cup Sage
p. 399

Consolida orientalis

Plant height: 1–2 ft.
Flowers: 1¼ in. long
Sun to partial shade
Dry soil
Larkspur
p. 311

Consolida ambigua

Plant height: 1–2 ft.
Flowers: 1¼ in. long
Sun to partial shade
Dry soil
Rocket Larkspur
p. 311

Erysimum linifolium
Plant height: 6–18 in.
Flowers: ¾ in. long
Full sun
Average to dry soil
Alpine Wallflower
p. 328

***Cynoglossum
amabile
'Blanche Burpee'***
Plant height: 1½–2 ft.
Flowers: ⅓ in. long
Full sun
Dry soil
Chinese Forget-Me-Not
p. 318

Heliotropium arborescens 'Marine'

Plant height: 2–4 ft.
Flowers: ¼ in. long
Full sun
Average soil
Common Heliotrope
p. 340

Myosotis sylvatica

Plant height: 6–18 in.
Flowers: ⅓ in. wide
Sun to full shade
Any soil
Forget-Me-Not
p. 372

Anchusa capensis

Plant height: to 18 in.
Flowers: ¼ in. wide
Full sun
Average soil
Cape Forget-Me-Not
p. 282

Oxypetalum caeruleum

Creeper: to 3 ft.
Flowers: ⅛ in. long
Full sun
Average soil
Southern Star
p. 381

Exacum affine

Plant height: 1–2 ft.
Flowers: ½ in. wide
Partial shade
Moist soil
Persian Violet
p. 331

Trachelium caeruleum

Plant height: 1–4 ft.
Clusters: 3–5 in. wide
Sun to partial shade
Average soil
Throatwort
p. 412

White Flowers

Omphalodes linifolia
Plant height: to 12 in.
Flowers: ½ in. wide
Partial shade
Moist soil
Navelwort
p. 379

Lobularia maritima
Plant height: to 12 in.
Clusters: to ¾ in. wide
Sun to partial shade
Average soil
Sweet Alyssum
p. 358

Androsace lactiflora   *Plant height: to 12 in.*
Flowers: ½ in. wide
Full sun
Well-drained soil
p. 283

Satureja hortensis   *Plant height: to 18 in.*
Flowers: ½ in. long
Full sun
Average to dry soil
Summer Savory
p. 401

***Androsace
septentrionalis***

Plant height: to 8 in.
Flowers: ¼ in. wide
Full sun
Well-drained soil
p. 283

Carum Carvi

Plant height: to 2 ft.
Clusters: to 1¼ in. wide
Full sun
Average soil
Caraway
p. 300

Sabatia angularis

Plant height: to 3 ft.
Flowers: 1½ in. wide
Partial shade
Moist soil
Rose Pink
p. 398

Iberis pinnata

Plant height: to 12 in.
Clusters: to 1 in. wide
Full sun
Average soil
p. 345

***Ageratum
Houstonianum***

*Plant height: to 14 in.
Flowers: ¼ in. wide
Sun to partial shade
Average soil
Common Garden
Ageratum
p. 276*

***Osteospermum
'Buttermilk'***

*Plant height: 12–18 in.
Flowers: 2–3 in. wide
Full sun
Well-drained, sandy soil
p. 381*

Mesembryanthemum crystallinum
Creeper: to 2 ft.
Flowers:
¾–1¼ in. wide
Full sun
Dry soil
Ice Plant
p. 368

Helianthus annuus 'Italian White'
Plant height: to 12 ft.
Flowers: 12 in. wide
Sun to partial shade
Average to dry soil
Common Sunflower
p. 339

Actinotus helianthi

Plant height: to 2 ft.
Flowers: 4 in. wide
Bracts: 3 in. wide
Full sun
Dry soil
Flannelflower
p. 276

Dimorphotheca sinuata

Plant height: to 12 in.
Flowers: 1½ in. wide
Full sun
Dry, well-drained soil
p. 323

Dimorphotheca pluvialis

Plant height: to 16 in.
Flowers: 2½ in. wide
Full sun
Dry, well-drained soil
Cape Marigold
p. 323

Chrysanthemum Parthenium 'White Stars'

Plant height: to 3 ft.
Flowers: ¾ in. wide
Sun to partial shade
Average soil
Feverfew
p. 306

Chrysanthemum
Parthenium
'Golden Feather'

Plant height: to 3 ft.
Flowers: ¾ in. wide
Sun to partial shade
Average soil
Feverfew
p. 306

Ammobium alatum
'Chelsea Physic'

Plant height: to 3 ft.
Flowers: 1½ in. wide
Full sun
Average soil
Winged Everlasting
p. 281

Matricaria recutita

Plant height:
to 2½ ft.
Flowers: 1 in. wide
Full sun
Average to dry soil
German Camomile
p. 366

Argemone munita

Plant height: 2–5 ft.
Flowers: 2–5 in. wide
Full sun
Average soil
Prickly Poppy
p. 286

Fragaria vesca
'Alpine'

Plant height: 9–12 in.
Flowers: ½ in. wide
Sun to partial shade
Average soil
Alpine Strawberry
p. 332

Viola Rafinesquii

Plant height: 3–8 in.
Flowers: ½ in. wide
Full sun
Average soil
Field Pansy
p. 417

Oenothera deltoides
Plant height: 2–10 in.
Flowers: 3 in. wide
Sun to partial shade
Average to dry soil
Desert Evening Primrose
p. 378

Viola cornuta
'White Perfection'
Plant height: to 8 in.
Flowers: 1½ in. wide
Full sun
Moist soil
Horned Violet
p. 417

Catharanthus roseus
'Albus'

Plant height: to 2 ft.
Flowers: 1½ in. wide
Full sun
Average soil
Madagascar Periwinkle
p. 302

Datura inoxia

Plant height: to 3 ft.
Flowers: 8 in. long
Full sun
Average to moist soil
Angel's Trumpet
p. 319

Ipomoea alba
Creeper: to 10 ft.
Flowers: 5–6 in. wide
Full sun
Average to moist soil
Moon-Flower
p. 347

Hibiscus Moscheutos
Plant height: 3–8 ft.
Flowers: 4–7 in. wide
Full sun
Average to moist soil
Rose Mallow
p. 341

Martynia annua
Creeper: to 6 ft.
Flowers: 2 in. long
Full sun
Average soil
p. 365

Hyoscyamus niger
Plant height: 1–2 ft.
Flowers: 1¼ in. long
Sun to partial shade
Average soil
Henbane
p. 344

Proboscidea louisianica

Creeper: to 3 ft.
Flowers: 1–2 in. long
Full sun
Average soil
Unicorn-Plant
p. 394

Malva verticillata var. crispa

Plant height: to 6 ft.
Flowers: 1 in. wide
Full sun
Average soil
Curled Mallow
p. 365

Gaura Lindheimeri

Plant height: to 4 ft.
Flowers: ½–1 in. long
Full sun
Average soil
p. 334

Iberis amara

Plant height: to 12 in.
Flowers: ½–1 in. wide
Full sun
Average soil
Rocket Candytuft
p. 345

***Gypsophila elegans*
'Golden Garden
Market'**

*Plant height:
10–18 in.
Flowers: ¼–1 in. wide
Full sun
Average soil
Annual Baby's-Breath
p. 337*

Reseda alba

*Plant height: to 3 ft.
Flowers: ½ in. wide
Sun to partial shade
Average soil
White Mignonette
p. 395*

Nicotiana alata
'Lime Green'

Plant height: to 5 ft.
Flowers: 2–4 in. long`
Sun to partial shade
Average soil
Flowering Tobacco
p. 375

Ipomopsis aggregata

Plant height: to 2 ft.
Flowers: 1 in. wide
Full sun
Average soil
Skyrocket
p. 348

Nicotiana alata
'Niki White'

Plant height: to 5 ft.
Flowers: 2–4 in. long
Sun to partial shade
Average soil
Flowering Tobacco
p. 375

Echinocystis lobata

Creeper: to 20 ft.
Flowers: ¼ in. long
Sun to partial shade
Average soil
Wild Cucumber
p. 325

Grasses, Fruit,

and Foliage

**Lagurus ovatus
var. *nanus***
Plant height: to 12 in.
Full sun
Average soil
Hare's-Tail Grass
p. 351

Pennisetum setaceum
Plant height: 3–4 ft.
Full sun
Average soil
Fountain Grass
p. 384

Pennisetum villosum   *Plant height: to 2 ft.*
Full sun
Average soil
Feathertop
p. 385

Hordeum jubatum   *Plant height: 1–2½ ft.*
Full sun
Any soil
Squirrel-Tail Grass
p. 342

Triticum aestivum

Plant height: to 4 ft.
Full sun
Average soil
Wheat
p. 413

Lamarckia aurea

Plant height: to 18 in.
Full sun
Average soil
Golden Top
p. 352

Panicum miliaceum
'Violaceum'

Plant height: 3–4 ft.
Full sun
Average soil
Millet
p. 382

Polypogon
monspeliensis

Plant height: to 2 ft.
Full sun
Average soil
Rabbit-Foot Grass
p. 392

Setaria italica
Plant height: 3–5 ft.
Full sun
Average soil
Foxtail Millet
p. 405

Phalaris canariensis
Plant height: 1½–2 ft.
Full sun
Average soil
Canary Grass
p. 388

Pennisetum setaceum
'Cupreum'

Plant height: 3–4 ft.
Full sun
Average soil
Fountain Grass
p. 384

Briza maxima

Plant height: 1–2 ft.
Full sun
Average soil
Quaking Oats
p. 294

Panicum miliaceum   Plant height: 3–4 ft.
Full sun
Average soil
Millet
p. 382

Foeniculum vulgare   Plant height: 3–5 ft.
Full sun
Average soil
Common Fennel
p. 332

Agrostis nebulosa
Plant height: to 12 in.
Full sun
Average soil
Cloud Grass
p. 277

Kochia scoparia var. tricophylla 'Childsii'
Plant height: 2–5 ft.
Full sun
Average to dry soil
Summer Cypress
p. 350

Brassica oleracea:
**Acephala Group
'Dynasty Pink'**

*Plant height: to 1 ft.
Full sun
Average to moist soil
Flowering Cabbage
p. 294*

*Centaurea
Cineraria*

*Plant height: 1–3 ft.
Full sun
Average soil
Dusty Miller
p. 303*

Brassica oleracea: **Acephala Group**	*Plant height: to 1 ft.* *Full sun* *Average to moist soil* *Flowering Kale* *p. 294*

Senecio Cineraria **'Silver Dust'**	*Plant height: to 2½ ft.* *Full sun* *Average soil* *Dusty Miller* *p. 404*

Cynara cardunculus — *Plant height: to 6 ft.*
Full sun
Moist soil
Cardoon
p. 317

Euphorbia
marginata
'Summer Icicle'

Plant height: to 3 ft.
Full sun
Average soil
Snow-on-the-Mountain
p. 329

Salvia argentea

Plant height: 2–4 ft.
Full sun
Average soil
Silver Sage
p. 399

Helichrysum petiolatum

Plant height: to 4 ft.
Full sun
Average soil
Licorice Plant
p. 339

Atriplex hortensis
'Rubra'

Plant height: 1–3 ft.
Full sun
Average soil
Garden Orach
p. 288

Perilla frutescens
'Atropurpurea'

Plant height: to 3 ft.
Full sun
Average to dry soil
Beefsteak Plant
p. 386

Ocimum Basilicum
'Dark Opal'

Plant height: 1–2 ft.
Full sun
Average soil
Basil
p. 377

Perilla frutescens
'Crispa'

Plant height: to 3 ft.
Full sun
Average to dry soil
Beefsteak Plant
p. 386

Coleus × hybridus
Plant height: to 3 ft.
Sun to partial shade
Average to moist soil
Garden Coleus
p. 310

Euphorbia cyathophora
Plant height: to 3 ft.
Full sun
Average to dry soil
Annual Poinsettia
p. 329

Coleus* × *hybridus

Plant height: to 3 ft.
Sun to partial shade
Average to moist soil
Garden Coleus
p. 310

Beta vulgaris
'Ruby Chard'

Plant height: 12–14 in.
Full sun
Moist soil
Rhubarb Beet
p. 292

Alternanthera ficoidea

Plant height: 6–12 in.
Full sun
Average soil
Joseph's-Coat
p. 279

Iresine Herbstii 'Jepson'

Plant height: to 6 ft.
Full sun
Average soil
Bloodleaf
p. 349

Amaranthus tricolor
'Illumination'

Plant height: 1–4 ft.
Full sun
Average soil
Joseph's-Coat
p. 280

Hibiscus Acetosella
'Red Shield'

Plant height: to 5 ft.
Full sun
Average to moist soil
p. 341

Capsicum annuum
'Red Missile'

Plant height: *to 10 in.*
Fruit: *to 1½ in. long*
Full sun
Fertile, moist soil
Ornamental Pepper
p. 299

Solanum Melongena
'Golden Eggplant'

Plant height: *to 2 ft.*
Fruit: *3–5 in. wide*
Full sun
Fertile, moist soil
p. 407

Capsicum annuum
'Holiday Cheer'

Plant height: to 8 in.
Fruit: to 1 in. wide
Full sun
Fertile, moist soil
Ornamental Pepper
p. 299

Momordica
Charantia

Creeper: to 10 ft.
Fruit: 4–8 in. long
Full sun
Moist soil
Balsam Pear
p. 371

Benincasa hispida
Creeper: to 10 ft.
Fruit: to 16 in. long·
Full sun
Moist soil
Wax Gourd
p. 291

Lagenaria siceraria
Creeper: to 30 ft.
Fruit: 3–36 in. long
Full sun
Average soil
White-flowered Gourd
p. 350

Cucurbita ficifolia
Creeper: 10–12 ft.
Fruit: to 12 in. long
Full sun
Moist soil
Malabar Gourd
p. 315

Luffa acutangula
Creeper: to 15 ft.
Fruit: to 12 in. long
Full sun
Average soil
Angled Luffa
p. 360

Luffa aegyptiaca

Creeper: to 15 ft.
Fruit: 12–18 in. long
Full sun
Average soil
Sponge Gourd
p. 360

Euphorbia Lathyris

Plant height: to 3 ft.
Fruit: to ⅓ in. wide
Full sun
Average soil
Caper Spurge
p. 329

Cardiospermum Halicacabum

Creeper: to 12 ft.
Fruit: to 1 in. long
Full sun
Average soil
Balloon Vine
p. 300

Dolichos Lablab

Creeper: to 30 ft.
Fruit: to 2½ in. long
Full sun
Average soil
Hyacinth Bean
p. 323

Humulus japonicus
Creeper: 10–20 ft.
Full sun
Average soil
Japanese Hops
p. 343

Origanum
Majorana
Plant height: to 2 ft.
Full sun
Average soil
Sweet Marjoram
p. 379

Coix Lacryma-Jobi

Plant height: 3–6 ft.
Full sun
Average soil
Job's Tears
p. 309

Moluccella laevis

Plant height: 2–3 ft.
Full sun
Moist soil
Bells-of-Ireland
p. 371

Yellow Flowers

Platystemon
californicus

Plant height: 6–12 in.
Flowers: 1 in. wide
Full sun
Moist soil
Creamcups
p. 390

Saxifraga
Cymbalaria

Plant height: to 2 in.
Flowers: ¼ in. wide
Sun to partial shade
Average soil
p. 402

**Limnanthes
Douglasii**

Plant height: 4–12 in.
Flowers: 1 in. wide
Full sun
Moist soil
Meadow Foam
p. 355

Mentzelia Lindleyi

Plant height: 1–2 ft.
Flowers:
1½–2½ in. wide
Full sun
Average soil
Blazing Star
p. 367

Glaucium flavum
Plant height: 2–3 ft.
Flowers: 2 in. wide
Full sun
Average soil
Sea Poppy
p. 336

Argemone mexicana
Plant height: to 3 ft.
Flowers:
1½–2½ in. wide
Full sun
Average soil
Mexican Poppy
p. 286

Oenothera missourensis

Plant height: to 15 in.
Flowers: 5 in. wide
Sun to partial shade
Average soil
Missouri Evening Primrose
p. 378

Oenothera primiveris

Plant height: 6–9 in.
Flowers: 2–3 in. wide
Full sun
Average soil
Evening Primrose
p. 378

Erysimum Perofskianum

Plant height: to 2 ft.
Flowers: ½ in. long
Full sun
Average to dry soil
p. 328

Tagetes tenuifolia 'Tangerine Gem'

Plant height: to 12 in.
Flowers: 1 in. wide
Full sun
Average soil
Dwarf Marigold
p. 408

Cheiranthus Cheiri

Plant height:
to 2½ ft.
Flowers: 1 in. wide
Sun to partial shade
Average soil
Wallflower
p. 305

Nemesia strumosa

Plant height: to 2 ft.
Flowers: 1 in. wide
Full sun
Moist soil
p. 373

Mimulus guttatus

Plant height: *to 2 ft.*
Flowers: *1½ in. wide.*
Partial shade
Moist soil
Monkey Flower
p. 369

***Viola* ×
*Wittrockiana***

Plant height: *to 9 in.*
Flowers: *2–5 in. wide*
Sun to partial shade
Moist soil
Pansy
p. 418

Viola ×
Wittrockiana

Plant height: to 9 in.
Flowers: 2–5 in. wide
Sun to partial shade
Moist soil
Pansy
p. 418

Viola cornuta

Plant height: to 8 in.
Flowers: 1½ in. wide
Full sun
Moist soil
Horned Violet
p. 417

Eschscholzia californica

Plant height: 8–12 in.
Flowers: 3–4 in. wide
Full sun
Average to dry soil
California Poppy
p. 328

Portulaca oleracea

Creeper: to 18 in.
Flowers: ⅜ in. wide
Full sun
Average to dry soil
Garden form
Purslane
p. 392

**Hunnemannia
fumariifolia**

Plant height: 1–2 ft.
Flowers: 2–3 in. wide
Full sun
Average to dry soil
Mexican Tulip Poppy
p. 344

**Tropaeolum
peregrinum**

Creeper: to 8 ft.
Flowers: 1 in. wide
Sun to partial shade
Average to moist soil
Canary-Bird Flower
p. 414

Arachis hypogaea

Creeper: 12–18 in.
Flowers: ¾ in. long
Full sun
Average soil
Peanut
p. 285

*Calceolaria
integrifolia*

Plant height: 2–5 ft.
Flowers: ⅓ in. long
Sun to partial shade
Average to moist soil
p. 297

Calceolaria mexicana

Plant height: to 18 in.
Flowers: ½ in. long
Sun to partial shade
Average to moist soil
p. 297

Calceolaria crenatiflora

Plant height: 1-2 ft.
Flowers:
¾-2½ in. long
Partial shade
Moist soil
Pocketbook Plant
p. 296

Lonas annua

Plant height: to 12 in.
Flowers: ⅓ in. wide
Full sun
Average soil
African Daisy
p. 359

Anethum graveolens

Plant height: to 2½ ft.
Clusters: 6–8 in. wide
Full sun
Average soil
Common Dill
p. 283

**Chrysanthemum
Parthenium**

Plant height: to 3 ft.
Flowers: ¾ in. wide
Sun to partial shade
Average soil
Feverfew
p. 306

Pimpinella Anisum

Plant height: to 2 ft.
Clusters: to 2 in. wide
Full sun
Average soil
Anise
p. 390

Reseda lutea

Plant height: to 30 in.
Flowers: ¼ in. wide
Sun to partial shade
Average soil
Wild Mignonette
p. 395

Barbarea verna

Plant height: 12–18 in.
Flowers: 1/6 in. wide
Full sun
Average soil
Early Winter Cress
p. 289

Reseda odorata

Plant height: to 12 in.
Flowers: ⅓ in. wide
Sun to partial shade
Average soil
Common Mignonette
p. 396

Barbarea vulgaris

Plant height: 2–3 ft.
Flowers: 1/6 in. wide
Full sun
Average soil
Winter Cress
p. 289

Oenothera erythrosepala

Plant height: 2–8 ft.
Flowers: 3½ in. wide
Sun to partial shade
Average soil
Evening Primrose
p. 378

Cerinthe major

Plant height: to 20 in.
Flowers: ¾ in. long
Full sun
Average soil
Honeywort
p. 305

Oenothera biennis

Plant height: 3–6 ft.
Flowers: 1–2 in. wide
Sun to partial shade
Average soil
Evening Primrose
p. 378

Datura Metel

Plant height: to 5 ft.
Flowers: 4 in. wide
Full sun
Moist soil
Horn-of-Plenty
p. 319

Cassia fasciculata
Plant height: to 18 in.
Flowers: ¾ in. long˙
Full sun
Average to dry soil
Partridge Pea
p. 301

Hibiscus Moscheutos
Plant height: 3–8 ft.
Flowers: 4–7 in. wide
Full sun
Average to moist soil
Rose Mallow
p. 341

Oenothera laciniata

Plant height: 6–24 in.
Flowers: 2½ in. wide
Sun to partial shade
Average soil
Evening Primrose
p. 378

Abelmoschus esculentus

Plant height: 2–6 ft.
Flowers: 2–3 in. wide
Full sun
Average soil
Okra
p. 274

Hibiscus Trionum

Plant height: 1½–4 ft.
Flowers:
1–1½ in. wide
Full sun
Average soil
Flower-of-an-Hour
p. 342

Dahlia
hybrid

Plant height: 1–5 ft.
Flowers: 2–4 in. wide
Full sun
Moist soil
Dahlia
p. 318

Thunbergia alata

Creeper: to 6 ft.
Flowers: 1–2 in. wide
Sun to partial shade
Moist soil
Black-eyed Susan Vine
p. 410

**Sanvitalia
procumbens**

Creeper: to 6 in.
Flowers: 1 in. wide
Full sun
Average soil
Creeping Zinnia
p. 400

Rudbeckia hirta
'Gloriosa Daisy'
'Marmalade'

Plant height: 2–3 ft.
Flowers: 6 in. wide
Sun to partial shade
Average to dry soil
Gloriosa Daisy
p. 397

Xanthisma texana

Plant height: 2–4 ft.
Flowers: 2½ in. wide
Full sun
Average to dry soil
Sleepy Daisy
p. 418

Rudbeckia hirta
Plant height: to 3 ft.
Flowers: 2–3 in. wide
Sun to partial shade
Average to dry soil
Black-eyed Susan
p. 397

Chrysanthemum coronarium
Plant height: to 4 ft.
Flowers: 1½ in. wide
Sun to partial shade
Average soil
Crown Daisy
p. 306

Gazania rigens

Plant height: to 16 in.
Flowers: 1½ in. wide
Full sun.
Dry, well-drained soil
Treasure Flower
p. 334

Gaillardia pulchella

Plant height: 1–2 ft.
Flowers: 2–3 in. wide
Full sun
Average to dry soil
Blanket Flower
p. 333

Gazania rigens

Plant height: to 16 in.
Flowers: 1½ in. wide
Full sun
Dry, well-drained soil
Treasure Flower
p. 334

Venidium fastuosum

Plant height: 2–3 ft.
Flowers: 4–6 in. wide
Full sun
Average to dry soil
Cape Daisy
p. 415

Ursinia anthemoides
'Sunshine Blend'

Plant height: to 18 in.
Flowers: 2½ in. wide.
Full sun
Average soil
p. 415

Coreopsis tinctoria

Plant height: 2–3 ft.
Flowers: 1¼ in. wide
Full sun
Average soil
Double form
Golden Coreopsis
p. 313

Coreopsis tinctoria

Plant height: 2–3 ft.
Flowers: 1¼ in. wide
Full sun
Average soil
Golden Coreopsis
p. 313

Thelesperma Burridgeanum

Plant height: 12–18 in.
Flowers: 1½ in. wide
Full sun
Average soil
p. 409

Tolpis barbata

Plant height: 8–12 in.
Flowers: 1¼ in. wide
Full sun
Average soil
Yellow Hawkweed
p. 411

Dyssodia tenuiloba

Plant height: 8–12 in.
Flowers: 1 in. wide
Full sun
Dry soil
Dahlberg Daisy
p. 324

Zinnia angustifolia
'Classic'

Plant height: 12–16 in.
Flowers: 1½ in. wide
Full sun
Average soil
Zinnia
p. 420

Layia platyglossa

Plant height: 1–2 ft.
Flowers: 2 in. wide
Full sun
Average soil
Tidy-Tips
p. 355

Helianthus annuus   Plant height: to 12 ft.
Flowers: 12 in. wide
Sun to partial shade
Average to dry soil
Common Sunflower
p. 339

Helianthus annuus   Plant height: to 2 ft.
'Teddy Bear'   Flowers: 12 in. wide
Sun to partial shade
Average to dry soil
Dwarf form
Common Sunflower
p. 339

Baileya
multiradiata

Plant height: to 20 in.
Flowers: 2 in. wide
Full sun
Average soil
Desert Marigold
p. 289

Tagetes erecta

Plant height: 1½–3 ft.
Flowers: 2–6 in. wide
Full sun
Average soil
African Marigold
p. 408

Red to Orange

Flowers

Tagetes erecta

Plant height: 1½–3 ft.
Flowers: 2–6 in. wide
Full sun
Average soil
African Marigold
p. 408

Tagetes patula
'Tiger Eyes'

Plant height: to 18 in.
Flowers: 2–3 in. wide
Full sun
Average soil
Crested form
French Marigold
p. 408

Zinnia elegans

Plant height: to 3 ft.
Flowers: 4 in. wide
Full sun
Average soil
Common Zinnia
p. 420

Tagetes patula
'Queen Sophia'

Plant height: to 18 in.
Flowers: 2–3 in. wide
Full sun
Average soil
Double form
French Marigold
p. 408

Calendula
officinalis
'Orange Coronet'

Plant height:
12–18 in.
Flowers: 1–3 in. wide
Full sun
Average soil
Pot Marigold
p. 297

Cosmos sulphureus
'Bright Lights'

Plant height: 2–6 ft.
Flowers: 3 in. wide
Sun to partial shade
Average to dry soil
Yellow Cosmos
p. 314

**Tithonia
rotundifolia**

Plant height: 4–6 ft.
Flowers: 3 in. wide
Full sun
Average soil
Mexican Sunflower
p. 410

**Tagetes patula
'Cinnabar'**

Plant height: to 18 in.
Flowers: 2–3 in. wide
Full sun
Average soil
French Marigold
p. 408

Zinnia Haageana
'Chippendale Daisy'

Plant height: to 2 ft.
Flowers: 2½ in. wide
Full sun
Average soil
Mexican Zinnia
p. 420

Chrysanthemum
carinatum
'Merry Mixture'

Plant height: 2–3 ft.
Flowers: 2½ in. wide
Sun to partial shade
Average soil
Tricolor Chrysanthemum
p. 306

Gaillardia pulchella

Plant height: 1–2 ft.
Flowers: 2–3 in. wide
Full sun
Average to dry soil
Blanket Flower
p. 333

Chrysanthemum carinatum

Plant height: 2–3 ft.
Flowers: 2½ in. wide
Sun to partial shade
Average soil
Tricolor Chrysanthemum
p. 306

Helianthus annuus
hybrid

Plant height: to 12 ft.
Flowers: 12 in. wide
Sun to partial shade
Average to dry soil
Common Sunflower
p. 339

Gaillardia pulchella
'Gaiety'

Plant height: 1–2 ft.
Flowers: 2–3 in. wide
Full sun
Average to dry soil
Double form
Blanket Flower
p. 333

Rudbeckia hirta
'Gloriosa Daisy'

Plant height: 2–3 ft.
Flowers: 6 in. wide
Sun to partial shade
Average to dry soil
Gloriosa Daisy
p. 397

Zinnia Haageana
'Old Mexico'

Plant height: to 2 ft.
Flowers: 2½ in. wide
Full sun
Average soil
Mexican Zinnia
p. 420

Gerbera Jamesonii
'Happipot'

Plant height: to 18 in.
Flowers: 4 in. wide
Full sun
Average soil
Transvaal Daisy
p. 335

Zinnia elegans
'Peter Pan Mix'

Plant height: to 3 ft.
Flowers: 4 in. wide
Full sun
Average soil
Common Zinnia
p. 420

Dorotheanthus
bellidiformis
'El Cerrito'

Plant height: to 3 in.
Flowers: 2 in. wide
Full sun
Dry soil
Livingstone Daisy
p. 324

Osteospermum
hyoseroides

Plant height: to 2 ft.
Flowers: 2 in. wide
Full sun
Average to dry soil
p. 381

***Helichrysum bracteatum* 'Bikini'**

Plant height: to 1 ft.
Flowers: 1–2 in. wide
Full sun
Average to dry soil
Strawflower
p. 339

Bellis perennis

Plant height: to 6 in.
Flowers: 1–2 in. wide
Full sun
Moist soil
Semidouble form
English Daisy
p. 290

Bellis perennis   Plant height: to 6 in.
                       Flowers: 1–2 in. wide
                       Full sun
                       Moist soil
                       Double form
                       English Daisy
                       p. 290

Senecio × hybridus   Plant height: 1–3 ft.
                          Flowers: 2 in. wide
                          Sun to partial shade
                          Moist soil
                          Cineraria
                          p. 405

246

Verbena × hybrida
'Springtime'

Plant height: to 12 in.
Clusters: 2–3 in. wide
Full sun
Average soil
Garden Verbena
p. 416

Phlox Drummondii

Plant height: to 18 in.
Flowers:
1–1½ in. wide
Full sun
Average soil
Annual Phlox
p. 389

Primula × polyantha

Plant height: to 12 in.
Flowers:
1½–2 in. wide
Partial shade
Moist soil
Polyanthus
p. 394

Petunia × hybrida 'Flash Series'

Plant height: 8–18 in.
Flowers: 2–4 in. wide
Full sun
Average to moist soil
Common Garden Petunia
p. 387

Viola ×
Wittrockiana
'Clear Crystal Mix'

Plant height: *to 9 in.*
Flowers: *2–5 in. wide*
Sun to partial shade
Moist soil
Pansy
p. 418

Salpiglossis sinuata

Plant height: *to 3 ft.*
Flowers: *2 in. wide*
Full sun
Average soil
Painted-Tongue
p. 398

Mimulus ×
hybridus

Plant height:
12–14 in.
Flowers: 2 in. wide
Partial shade
Moist soil
Monkey Flower
p. 369

Tropaeolum majus

Creeper: to 12 ft.
Flowers: 2½ in. wide
Sun to partial shade
Average to dry soil
Nasturtium
p. 414

Begonia ×
semperflorens-
cultorum

Plant height: 8–12 in.
Flowers: 1 in. wide
Sun to shade
Moist soil
Wax Begonia
p. 290

Anagallis arvensis

Creeper: 12–18 in.
Flowers: ¼ in. wide
Full sun
Average soil
Scarlet Pimpernel
p. 282

Impatiens
'New Guinea'

Plant height: 1–2 ft.
Flowers:
2–2½ in. wide
Sun to partial shade
Moist soil
p. 346

Impatiens
Wallerana

Plant height: 1–2 ft.
Flowers: 1–2 in. wide
Sun to partial shade
Moist soil
Busy Lizzy
p. 346

Dianthus chinensis
'Telestar Mix'

Plant height:
12–18 in.
Flowers: 1–2 in. wide
Full sun
Average soil
China Pink
p. 321

Papaver nudicaule

Plant height: to 12 in.
Flowers: 1–3 in. wide
Full sun
Average to dry soil
Iceland Poppy
p. 382

Portulaca grandiflora

Creeper: to 10 in.
Flowers: 1 in. wide
Full sun
Average to dry soil
Rose Moss
p. 392

Glaucium corniculatum

Plant height: to 18 in.
Flowers: 2 in. wide
Full sun
Average soil
Horned Poppy
p. 336

Papaver somniferum
Plant height: 3–4 ft.
Flowers: 3–4 in. wide
Full sun
Average to dry soil
Opium Poppy
p. 383

Alcea rosea
Plant height: 5–9 ft.
Flowers: 3 in. wide
Full sun
Average soil
Garden Hollyhock
p. 278

Papaver Rhoeas

Plant height: to 3 ft.
Flowers: 2 in. wide
Full sun
Average to dry soil
Corn Poppy
p. 383

Impatiens Balsamina

Plant height: 2–2½ ft.
Flowers: 1–2 in. wide
Sun to partial shade
Moist soil
Garden Balsam
p. 346

Alonsoa
Warscewiczii

Plant height: 1–3 ft.
Flowers:
⅝–¾ in. wide
Full sun
Average soil
Mask Flower
p. 279

Penstemon
gloxinioides
'Scarlet and White'

Plant height: 2–3 ft.
Flowers: 2 in. wide
Sun to partial shade
Well-drained soil
Penstemon
p. 385

Asclepias curassavica

Plant height: 2–4 ft.
Flowers: ¼ in. long
Full sun
Moist soil
Blood Flower
p. 287

Pelargonium × hortorum

Plant height: 1–3 ft.
Flowers:
2–2½ in. wide
Sun to partial shade
Average soil
Zonal Geranium
p. 384

Lantana Camara
'Radiation'

Plant height: to 4 ft.
Clusters: 1–2 in. wide
Full sun
Average soil
Yellow Sage
p. 352

Verbena peruviana

Creeper: 1–2 ft.
Clusters: 1–2 in. wide
Full sun
Average soil
p. 416

Lantana Camara

Plant height: to 4 ft.
Clusters: 1–2 in. wide
Full sun
Average soil
Yellow Sage
p. 352

Verbena × hybrida
'Showtime Blaze'

Plant height: to 12 in.
Clusters: 2–3 in. wide
Full sun
Average soil
Garden Verbena
p. 416

Pelargonium peltatum

Creeper: to 3 ft.
Flowers:
2–2½ in. wide
Sun to partial shade
Average soil
Ivy Geranium
p. 384

Abutilon hybridum

Plant height: 1–3 ft.
Flowers:
1½–2½ in. wide
Sun to partial shade
Average to moist soil
Flowering Maple
p. 275

Hedysarum coronarium

Plant height: 2–4 ft.
Flowers: ¾ in. long
Full sun
Well-drained soil
French Honeysuckle
p. 338

Eccremocarpus scaber

Creeper: to 10 ft.
Flowers: 1 in. long
Full sun
Moist soil
Glory Flower
p. 325

Phaseolus coccineus

Creeper: to 8 ft.
Flowers: 1 in. long
Full sun
Moist soil
Scarlet Runner
p. 389

Ipomoea × multifida

Creeper: to 10 ft.
Flowers: 2 in. long
Full sun
Average soil
Cardinal Climber
p. 347

Ipomoea coccinea
Creeper: to 10 ft.
Flowers: 1½ in. long
Full sun
Average soil
Star Ipomoea
p. 347

Ipomoea Quamoclit
Creeper: to 20 ft.
Flowers: 1½ in. long
Full sun
Average soil
Cypress Vine
p. 348

Cuphea ignea
'Hidcote'

Plant height: 8–15 in.
Flowers: 1 in. long
Sun to partial shade
Average soil
Firecracker Plant
p. 316

Salvia splendens
'Red Hussar'

Plant height: to 3 ft.
Flowers: 1½ in. long
Full sun
Average soil
Scarlet Sage
p. 400

Nicotiana alata
'Niki Red'

Plant height: to 5 ft.
Flowers: 2–4 in. long
Sun to partial shade
Average soil
Flowering Tobacco
p. 375

Ipomopsis rubra

Plant height: 2–3 ft.
Flowers: 2 in. long
Full sun
Average soil
Standing Cypress
p. 349

Limonium sinuatum
Plant height:
12–30 in.
Flowers: ⅜ in. wide
Full sun
Well-drained, sandy
soil
Statice
p. 356

Ricinus communis
'Gibsonii'
Plant height: 4–15 ft.
Flowers: ½ in. wide
Full sun
Moist soil
Castor Bean
p. 396

Antirrhinum majus   Plant height: to 3 ft.
                      Flowers: 1½ in. long
                      Full sun
                      Moist soil
                      Common Snapdragon
                      p. 284

Ricinus communis   Plant height: 4–15 ft.
                     Flowers: ½ in. wide
                     Full sun
                     Moist soil
                     Castor Bean
                     p. 396

***Amaranthus
caudatus***

Plant height: 3–5 ft.
Clusters: to 18 in. long
Full sun
Average soil
Love-Lies-Bleeding
p. 280

Celosia cristata
'Golden Torch'

Plant height: 1–2 ft.
Clusters: 6–12 in. long
Full sun
Average soil
Plumed Celosia
p. 303

Amaranthus
hybridus
var. *erythrostachys*

Plant height: 3–4 ft.
Clusters: to 6 in. long
Full sun
Average soil
Prince's Feather
p. 280

Celosia cristata
'Century Mixed'

Plant height: 1–2 ft.
Clusters: 6–12 in. long
Full sun
Average soil
Plumed Celosia
p. 303

Celosia cristata
'Jewel Box'

Plant height: 1–2 ft.
Clusters: 6–12 in. wide
Full sun
Average soil
Crested Celosia
p. 303

Emilia javanica

Plant height: 1–2 ft.
Flowers: ½ in. wide
Full sun
Average to dry soil
Tassel Flower
p. 327

Celosia cristata

Plant height: 1–2 ft.
Clusters: 6–12 in. wide
Full sun
Average soil
Crested Celosia
p. 303

Cirsium japonicum

Plant height: to 2½ ft.
Flowers: 1–2 in. wide
Sun to partial shade
Average soil
Plumed Thistle
p. 307

Abelmoschus
Mallow family
Malvaceae

Ab-el-mos'kus. A group of 6 or more species, native in s. Asia. They are related to *Hibiscus*.

Description
Leaves large, palmately lobed or divided. Calyx thin, split along one side, united at the base to the base of the petals and the staminal column.

How to Grow
Plant seeds outdoors as soon as the ground is warm. In summer the plants need a great deal of water. They prefer warm weather.

esculentus p. 219
Okra; Gumbo. A garden vegetable annual grown for its immature pods. 2–6 ft. (60–180 cm) high; leaves to 1 ft. (30 cm) wide. Flowers solitary in leaf axils, 2–3 in. (5.0–7.5 cm) wide, yellow, with a red eye. Pods ribbed and beaked, 4–12 in. (10–30 cm) long. Old World tropics. Fruit matures in summer. Tender annual.

Abronia
Four O'Clock family
Nyctaginaceae

A-bro'ni-a. Sand Verbena. About 30 species of annual and perennial plants mostly from w. North America.

Description
Stems erect or prostrate, leaves opposite, stalked, all usually sticky-hairy. Flowers tubular, in a loose, stalked head, below which are 5 or more colored bracts. Calyx petal-like.

How to Grow
The species described below needs a long, cool growing season. Start indoors or in a coldframe, and plant after the last frost. Removing the seed husks before planting will speed germination. Used for borders or rock gardens.

umbellata p. 117
Sand Verbena. A vinelike herb 6–24 in. (15–60 cm) long. Flowers ½ in. (13 mm)

long, pink, usually with 10–15 in an
umbel-like cluster, 2 in. (5 cm) across.
Pacific Coast. Cultivar 'Grandiflora'
has larger flowers; 'Rosea' has pale rose
flowers. Tender perennial grown as a tender
annual.

Abutilon
Mallow family
Malvaceae

A-bu'ti-lon. Flowering Maple; Chinese
Lantern. About 150 species of tropical shrubs
(rarely herbs) of the mallow family, a few of
which are grown as bedding plants.

Description
Leaves alternate, often veined and resembling
a maple leaf; some varieties are variegated.
Flowers showy, solitary, and borne in leaf
axils, usually drooping and often
trumpet-shaped.

How to Grow
Abutilon makes a good show of color. Start
seeds indoors in midwinter at 70–75° F (21–
24° C) and set in the garden after last frost.
Propagate by taking tip cuttings before fall
frost or in late spring. Needs afternoon
shade. A good pot plant or houseplant.
Prefers warm weather.

hybridum p. 260
Flowering Maple; Chinese Lantern. 1–3 ft.
(30–90 cm) high. Flowers 1½–2½ in.
(4–6 cm) wide, red, pinkish, purple,
yellow, or white, bell- or trumpet-shaped.
Many showy named forms. Tender perennial
grown as a tender annual.

Actinotus
Carrot family
Umbelliferae

Ak-ti-no'tus. A group of about 15 herbs,
native to Australia and New Zealand.

Description
Leaves alternate, twice- or thrice-compound,
hairy or woolly. Flowers very small and
numerous, in dense umbels that are
surrounded by raylike bracts.

How to Grow
Difficult to grow. Direct seed in sandy soil in spring after last frost. Scatter seeds thinly in a shallow furrow and cover with sand to 3 times the diameter of the seed. Germination occurs in 7 days. Prefers warm weather.

helianthi p. 156
Flannelflower. A white-woolly annual, to 2 ft. (60 cm) high. Flowerheads white, to 4 in. (10 cm) across, with 10–18 raylike bracts, 3 in. (7.5 cm) across. Australia. Perennial grown as a tender annual.

Ageratum
Daisy family
Compositae

A-jur-a'tum. A group of nearly 30 species of chiefly tropical American annual herbs, one of which is perhaps the most popular of all edging plants.

Description
Leaves opposite, generally oval, the margins with rounded teeth. Flowers blue, pink, or white in some horticultural forms, in compact, clustered heads, without rays.

How to Grow
Ageratum is rarely direct seeded in the garden because the small seedlings can be swamped by weeds. Start seeds indoors at 70–75° F (21–24° C) and set in the garden after frost danger. Prefers full sun but where summers are long and hot, place in light shade. In moderate shade the plants will stretch. They prefer warm weather.

Houstonianum pp. 123, 154
Common Garden Ageratum; Flossflower. Usually 14 in. (35 cm) high. Flowerheads just over ¼ in. (6 mm) in diameter, blue, the outside somewhat sticky. Central and South America. There are many cultivars. 'Album' has white flowers; 'North Sea' is deep blue and blooms until late fall. Pink-flowered and dwarf varieties available. Also often sold as *A. mexicanum*. Tender annual.

Agrostemma
Pink family
Caryophyllaceae

A-gro-stem′ma. A small genus containing 3 species of annual herbs, native to the Mediterranean region. The seeds are poisonous, and the plants grow as weeds in grain fields.

Description
Leaves opposite and entire. Flowers solitary, with 5 petals.

How to Grow
Sow seeds outdoors as soon as the soil can be worked, and space 12 in. (30 cm) apart. For earlier bloom, start indoors. Prefers cool weather.

Githago *p. 84*
Corn Cockle. 1–3 ft. (30–90 cm) high. Flowers magenta-purple, solitary, 1 in. (2.5 cm) wide; petals traced with dotted line. E. Mediterranean. The cultivar 'Milas' has rosy-purple flowers, to 3 in. (7.5 cm) wide. Half-hardy annual.

Agrostis
Grass family
Gramineae

A-gros′tis. Bent Grass. A large genus of widely distributed annual and perennial grasses, a few of which are much used in hay and lawn seed.

Description
Leaves narrow. Flowers in small spikelets that are borne in open, loose panicles.

How to Grow
Easy to grow in ordinary garden soil in full sun. A good choice for borders and for large containers; transplant it in large clumps. Prefers warm weather.

nebulosa *p. 179*
Cloud Grass. To 12 in. (30 cm) high, with very short and narrow leaves. Grown only for its wide cluster of tiny spikelets, which are on very slender stalks and persistent enough to be used for dry bouquets. Spain. Also sold as *A. capillaris*. Hardy annual.

Alcea
Mallow family
Malvaceae

Al-see′a. Hollyhock. A genus of about 60 species of tall, leafy-stemmed biennial or perennial herbs, all from the temperate regions of the Old World.

Description
They have usually hairy alternate leaves and a terminal, spirelike cluster of showy flowers, the 5 petals usually notched, originally red or white, but variously colored in the horticultural forms. Below the calyx is a series of 6–9 bracts.

How to Grow
Several varieties will bloom reliably the first year from seeds started indoors. Many overwinter and give a second year (and sometimes succeeding years) of bloom. Where summers are long, direct seed in groups of 5 seeds, then thin to the 3 best seedlings. Prefers warm weather.

rosea pp. 109, 254
Garden Hollyhock. 5–9 ft. (1.5–2.7 m) high, the stem leafy, spirelike, and hairy. Flowers essentially stalkless, 3 in. (7.5 cm) wide, in stiff, terminal clusters, typically single, and red or white, but the horticultural forms of many colors and often double. China. There are many cultivars. 'Majorette', a dwarf form, comes in many colors. Also sold as *Althaea rosea*. Biennial grown as a hardy annual.

Alonsoa
Snapdragon family
Scrophulariaceae

A-lon-zo′a. Ten species of tropical American herbs grown as annuals outdoors or as greenhouse plants for their attractive, red, winter-blooming flowers.

Description
Leaves opposite or in threes. Flowers in terminal finger-shaped clusters, the corolla very irregular, 2-lipped, and turned upside down by twisting of its individual stalklets.

How to Grow
Plants grow best in cool, northern gardens and in cool places such as Calif. and the

Northwest. However, they are sensitive to frost. Start seeds indoors and set out after frost danger. Space plants 6–12 in. (15–30 cm) apart.

Warscewiczii p. 256
Mask Flower. 1–3 ft. (30–90 cm) high. Flowers red, ⅝–¾ in. (16–19 mm) wide, the cluster loose. Peru. Cultivar 'Compacta' has scarlet flowers. Also sold as *A. grandiflora* or *A. Mutissii.* Tender perennial grown as a tender annual.

Alternanthera
Amaranth family
Amaranthaceae

Al-ter-nan'ther-ra, A genus of some 20 low-growing foliage plants, often sold under the name *Telanthera* or *Achyranthas.* They are perennial plants, mostly Brazilian, not well understood botanically.

Description
They have opposite, narrow, small leaves, often colored, and minute flowers in dense clusters in the leaf axils. The flowers, however, are rarely produced because foliage is usually cut low and used as ground cover.

How to Grow
They need a warm, sunny place and not too rich a soil. Must be propagated by cuttings or by division in the fall, and carried through the winter in the greenhouse. Plant outdoors 4–5 in. (10.0–12.5 cm) apart. Keep 4–6 in. (10–15 cm) high by shearing whenever necessary. Prefers warm weather.

ficoidea p. 188
Joseph's-Coat; Copperleaf. To 20 in. (50 cm) high, but generally shorter in cultivated varieties. Leaves elliptic, egg-shaped or inverted egg-shaped, with a short apical spine, ⅓–2½ in. (1–6 cm) long, green, or variously variegated with yellow, pink, orange, purple, or red. Flowerheads inconspicuous, whitish or yellowish, in leaf axils. Mexico to Argentina. Tender perennial grown as a tender annual.

Amaranthus
Amaranth family
Amaranthaceae

Am-a-ran'thus. The amaranths are coarse, often weedy, mostly annual herbs. They are widely distributed.

Description
Leaves alternate, often colored in the horticultural forms, without marginal teeth. Flowers very small, without petals, but often conspicuous because congested in a chaffy, often brightly colored cluster.

How to Grow
Seeds require very warm soil to sprout. Direct seed where summers are long and warm. Farther north, start seeds indoors in peat pots at 75° F (24° C). Seeds will germinate in 10–14 days; transfer to raised beds in full sun. Heavy clay soil helps reduce the incidence of root rot. Once it flowers, *Amaranthus* transplants poorly. The species below prefer warm weather.

caudatus p. 268
Love-Lies-Bleeding; Kiss-Me-Over-the-Garden-Gate; Tassel-Flower. Erect but spreading, 3–5 ft. (90–150 cm) high. Flower-spikes long and slender, often in branched clusters, drooping, all deep red. Tropical. Varieties have blood-red foliage, and green, yellow, or red spikes. Also sold as *A. dussi, A. elegantissima, A. margaritae,* and *A. superbus.* Tassels last for weeks. Tender annual.

hybridus var. erythrostachys p. 269
Prince's Feather. A showy plant, 3–4 ft. (90–120 cm) high, the foliage often reddish. Flowers minute, clusters dense, much-branched and chaffy, red or brownish red. Tropical. Tender annual.

tricolor p. 189
Joseph's-Coat; Fountain Plant; Tampala. 1–4 ft. (30–120 cm) high, except in the dwarf forms. Flowers minute, in stalkless, headlike clusters in the leaf axils, or sometimes spikelike and interrupted. Leaves sometimes blotched and colored. Tropical. Var. *Salicifolius* has narrow leaves; 'Splendens' has deep red flowers; 'Illumination' has scarlet, orange, yellow, green, and bronze leaves. Also sold as *A. melancholicus.* Tender annual.

Ammobium
Daisy family
Compositae

Am-moe'bi-um. A small genus of Australian herbs, valued as an everlasting because its white blossoms do not fade with age.

Description
Leaves white, felty, alternate or basal. Flowers yellow, in chaffy heads that are solitary at the ends of the small branches and surrounded by silvery white bracts. No ray flowers.

How to Grow
Easily grown in ordinary garden soil. Start seeds indoors and set out when night temperatures are above 50° F (10° C). Before flowers are mature, cut and hang with heads down in a shady, cool place; when dry, they will hold their color almost indefinitely. This species prefers warm weather.

alatum p. 158
Winged Everlasting. Bushy, to 3 ft. (1 m) high, the branches prominently winged. Heads 1½ in. (4 cm) wide, the bracts petal-like and silvery white. Australia. Cultivar 'Grandiflora' has larger heads. Will self-sow in sandy soil. Tender perennial grown as a tender annual.

Anagallis
Primrose family
Primulaceae

A-na-gal'lis. The pimpernels are rather weedy, mostly prostrate herbs comprising perhaps 40 widely distributed species, only 2 of which are of garden interest.

Description
Leaves opposite or in whorls, without marginal teeth. Flowers small, mostly solitary in leaf axils, short-stalked, the corolla bell-shaped, its 5 lobes somewhat spreading.

How to Grow
Start seeds indoors and transplant to the garden 2–3 weeks before the spring frost-free date. Mulch lightly with straw for protection against cold winds and snap frosts. Space plants 1 ft. (30 cm) apart. Both cool- and warm-weather species.

arvensis p. 250
Scarlet Pimpernel; Poor-Man's-Weatherglass.
Prostrate to 18 in. (45 cm) long. Flowers
scarlet or white, ¼ in. (6 mm) wide.
Flowers close at night and on cloudy days.
Europe. Form *caerulea* has blue flowers.
Prefers cool weather. Blooms in spring and
summer. Hardy annual.

Monelli linifolia p. 129
Flaxleaf Pimpernel. 8–18 in. (20–45 cm)
high. Flowers blue, purple, or red, ¾ in.
(19 mm) wide. Mediterranean. Prefers warm
regions. Blooms in summer. Tender
perennial grown as a tender annual.

Anchusa
Borage family
Boraginaceae

An-koo′sa. Alkanet; Bugloss. A genus of
perhaps 40 species of Old World herbs, a
few grown for their showy flowers.

Description
The plants are all more or less hairy, and
have alternate leaves and leafy, usually one-
sided, flower clusters not unlike (in some
species) those of forget-me-not. Flowers
small, trumpet-shaped, but somewhat closed
at the throat.

How to Grow
Where winters are mild, direct seed in the
fall for bloom the following spring or early
summer. Elsewhere, start seeds indoors and
set out when danger of frost is past. Direct
seeding where seasons are short may result
in large plants that will not flower and may
winterkill. Cut back after first bloom to
promote second bloom. Prefers cool weather.

capensis p. 146
Cape Forget-Me-Not; Bugloss. Usually less
than 18 in. (45 cm) high. Flower buds red,
the expanded flower blue, ¼ in. (6 mm)
wide. S. Africa. Cultivar 'Blue Bird' has
blue flowers; 'Pink Bird' has pink flowers;
A. c. alba has white flowers. Tender
biennial grown as a tender annual.

Androsace
Primrose family
Primulaceae

An-dros′a-see. Rock Jasmine. A large genus
of herbs, many grown in rock gardens.

Description
They are low, often tufted, plants, nearly all
with small basal leaves, often in rosettes.
Flowers resemble a miniature primrose, but
the corolla constricted at the throat.

How to Grow
These plants need well-drained soil that is
never allowed to dry out completely. They
prefer cool weather.

lactiflora p. 151
Erect and usually to 1 ft. (30 cm) high.
Flowers white, ½ in. (13 mm) wide, in
rather large clusters. Siberia (U.S.S.R.).
Blooms spring to early summer. Perennial
grown as a hardy annual.

septentrionalis p. 152
To 8 in. (20 cm) high. Flowers white or
pink, ¼ in. (6 mm) wide, in umbels.
Europe. Blooms in late spring. Perennial
grown as a hardy annual.

Anethum
Carrot family
Umbelliferae

A-ne′thum. Common Dill. The fruits and
leaves are used for seasoning. Native to the
Old World.

Description
Leaves are pinnately divided. Flowers small
and borne in umbels.

How to Grow
Easily grown from seed. Sow in a sunny,
open place with average soil. Prefers cool
weather.

graveolens p. 212
Common Dill. To 2½ ft. (75 cm) high.
Flowers less than ¼ in. (6 mm) wide,
yellowish, the petals soon falling, arranged in
a large umbel. Fruit aromatic, flattened. Sw.
Asia. Half-hardy annual.

Antirrhinum
Snapdragon family
Scrophulariaceae

An-tir·ry′num. About 40 species of hardy,
herbaceous perennials or annuals, natives of
the northern hemisphere.

Description
Erect or spreading, sometimes covered with
short, sticky hairs. Leaves alternate, lance-
shaped or ovalish, with heart-shaped base,
sometimes bluntly lobed. Flowers solitary or
in long terminal racemes, the individual
flower growing from the axil of a small,
leafy bract, white, yellow, pink, red, or
purple. Calyx of 5 sepals. Corolla tubular,
pouched, forming a mouth, the upper lip
2-lobed, the lower lip 3-lobed, the lips
turning outward. 5 stamens: 4 fertile, 1
sterile, growing inside the corolla tube.

How to Grow
Start seeds indoors. Move seedlings outside
when planting bed can be worked. Plant
6–12 in. (15–30 cm) apart in full sun. In
long-season areas a fine crop of late fall snaps
can be grown from seeds sown in a shaded
nursery bed in Aug. or Sept. Prefers cool
weather.

majus pp. 111, 267
Common Snapdragon; Toad's-Mouth. To 3
ft. (90 cm) high. Flowers reddish-purple,
red, white, yellow, orange, or pink, to 1½
in. (4 cm) long, in long terminal racemes.
Mediterranean region. Choose a rust-resistant
variety. Will survive a slight frost. 'Little
Darling', a semidwarf form, has pink
flowers. Perennial grown as a half-hardy
annual.

Arachis
Bean family
Leguminosae

A′ra-kis. A genus of about a dozen species in
South America, of which the peanut is of
wide economic importance.

Description
Leaves alternate, compound; leaflets oblong,
without marginal teeth. Flowers yellow.

How to Grow
Although *Arachis* rarely sets fruit in the
North, its flowers are lovely. Sow seeds
outdoors after danger of frost is past. It
needs full sun and warm weather.

hypogaea p. 210
Peanut. 12–18 in. (30–45 cm) high. Flowers
of 2 kinds: one showy, yellow, pealike, and
sterile; the other, also yellow, but fertile and
on recurved stalks that touch the ground
and penetrate it, carrying the fertilized ovary
beneath the surface, where it ripens as a
peanut. Unlike other fruits of the pea family,
this one does not split. Seeds oily and
nutritious. Tender annual.

Arctotis
Daisy family
Compositae

Ark-toe′tis. A genus of South African,
white-woolly herbs, some widely grown.

Description
They have alternate leaves, usually toothed
or deeply cut, and handsome, long-stalked,
blue, yellow, or orange heads with both ray
and disk flowers.

How to Grow
Start seeds indoors. When night temperatures
rise to 50° F (10° C), move outdoors. Space
6–12 in. (15–30 cm) apart. These plants
prefer a long, cool growing season and
average soil with good drainage.

stoechadifolia p. 103
Blue-eyed African Daisy. Stout, 2½–4 ft.
(75–120 cm) high. Flowerheads 3 in.
(7.5 cm) across; disk flowers violet, ray
flowers creamy above, red beneath. Many
cultivars, in a variety of colors. South Africa.
Tender annual.

Argemone
Poppy family
Papaveraceae

Are-jem′o-nee. The prickly poppies are
tropical American herbs of perhaps 30
species, one very widely grown.

Description
Stout with yellow juice, the cut leaves more or less toothed and spiny-margined. Flowers large, with 2 or 3 sepals and 4–6 rather showy petals.

How to Grow
Start seeds indoors in peat pots. When frost is past, move outdoors. Or plant seeds outdoors when soil is warm. Space 2–3 ft. (60–90 cm) apart. Add lime to soil and make sure drainage is good. Argemones do not transplant well. They prefer warm weather.

mexicana p. 202
Mexican Poppy. To 3 ft. (90 cm) high. Flowers 1½–2½ in. (4–6 cm) across, yellow, scented. West Indies. Oil is obtained from the seeds. Half-hardy annual.

munita p. 159
Prickly Poppy. 2–5 ft. (0.6–1.5 m) high. Flowers white, 2–5 in. (5.0–12.5 cm) wide. Calif. and n. Baja, Mexico, to N. Mex. Half-hardy annual.

Asarina
Snapdragon family
Scrophulariaceae

A-sa-ri′na. A small genus of tender, usually climbing, herbs native to North America and Europe.

Description
Leaves mostly triangular and flowers showy, 2-lipped, borne in leaf axils. They are closely related to *Antirrhinum* but differ in the climbing habit and the symmetrical shape of the capsule.

How to Grow
Seeds are not widely available so propagate by cuttings. These plants need fertile, moist soil and prefer warm weather.

Barclaiana p. 139
A vine to 10 ft. (3 m) long. Flowers trumpet-shaped, first pink, then velvety-purple, to 1¼ in. (3 cm) long, the sticky sepals long-tapering. Mexico. Also sold as *Maurandya Barclaiana*. Tender perennial grown as a tender annual.

Asclepias
Milkweed family
Asclepiadaceae

As-klee′pi-as. Milkweed. Milky-juiced, rather
showy, but sometimes weedy, perennial
herbs, including about 200 species, chiefly
from the New World, but a few African.
The cultivated species are mostly North
American.

Description
Leaves opposite or in whorls, rarely alternate;
without marginal teeth. Flowers regular,
often showy, usually in close, roundish
umbels, but sometimes in few-flowered
clusters in leaf axils. Corolla with 5 deep
lobes.

How to Grow
Easy to grow in warm climates. Start seeds
indoors, and move to sunny site with moist,
fertile soil after last frost. *A. curassavica*
flowers about 5 months after it is sown.

curassavica p. 257
Blood Flower. 2–4 ft. (60–120 cm) high,
the stem smooth or nearly so. Flowers ¼ in.
(6 mm) long, brilliant orange-red, in
clusters. Tropical America. Tender
perennial grown as a tender annual.

Asperula
Madder family
Rubiaceae

As-per′u-la. A large genus of Old World
herbs, some cultivated for ornament.

Description
Leaves in whorls of 6 or more. Flowers
small, more or less funnel-shaped, and very
numerous in forking cymes.

How to Grow
Sow seeds in a partially shaded, moist site,
such as a stream bank. Prefers warm
weather.

orientalis p. 125
Woodruff. To 1 ft. (30 cm) high. Flowers
lavender-blue, fragrant, ⅜ in. (9 mm) long,
borne in terminal clusters beneath which are
found leafy bracts. Eurasia. Also sold
as *A. azurea* var. *Setosa*. Hardy annual.

Atriplex
Goosefoot family
Chenopodiaceae

At'ri-plex. A large genus of herbs and salt-tolerant shrubs of wide distribution. One is a secondary garden vegetable, several are troublesome weeds, and a number are cultivated in gardens in arid areas.

Description
Leaves mostly alternate, or rarely opposite, often mealy or whitish. Flowers inconspicuous, mostly unisexual, in simple or branched clusters.

How to Grow
Sow seeds after frost. When seedlings are 2 in. (5 cm) high, thin to 6 in. (15 cm) apart. The leaves can be used like spinach, and should be picked while young. Prefers warm weather.

hortensis p. 184
Garden Orach; Sea Purslane; Mountain Spinach; French Spinach. Stout, 1–3 ft. (30–90 cm) high. Leaves somewhat triangular or arrow-shaped, or heart-shaped; short-stalked, 4–5 in. (10.0–12.5 cm) long, varying from yellow-green to pale red. Asia. Cultivar 'Cupreatorosea' has coppery-red foliage; 'Rosea' has light red, veined foliage; 'Rubra' has blood-red to purplish foliage. Half-hardy annual.

Baileya
Daisy family
Compositae

Bay-lay'a. A small genus of 3 or 4 species of herbs, native to dry desert areas, with only one of gardening interest.

Description
Leaves alternate, at base and on lower stem. Flowerheads solitary, their disk and ray flowers yellow. Ray flowers become papery and can be used for dried arrangements.

How to Grow
In mild-winter areas, work up soil and sow seeds thickly in small patches in early fall.

Cover lightly with sand and firm down. Where winters are severe, sow seeds in spring. In a favorable location, plants will spread from seeds that drop around mother plants. Prefers cool weather.

multiradiata p. 231
Desert Marigold. To 20 in. (50 cm) high. Flowerheads yellow, to 2 in. (5 cm) wide, made up of 20–50 ray flowers. W. North America. Blooms spring to fall. Perennial grown as a half-hardy annual.

Barbarea
Mustard family
Cruciferae

Bar-ba-ree'a. The winter cresses are weedy herbs, used as substitutes for watercress.

Description
Leaves divided or compound. Small yellow flowers in terminal racemes.

How to Grow
Sow seeds outdoors after danger of frost. The species below prefer cool weather.

verna p. 214
Early Winter Cress; Belle Isle Cress; Scurvy-Grass. 12–18 in. (30–45 cm) high. Flowers 1/6 in. (4 mm) wide. Europe. Sometimes cultivated for salad. Blooms in early spring. Biennial grown as a hardy annual.

vulgaris p. 215
Winter Cress; Bitter Winter Cress. 24–36 in. (60–90 cm) high. Similar to *B. verna* but blooms in late spring. Common weeds in U.S. Biennial grown as a hardy annual.

Begonia
Begonia family
Begoniaceae

Bee-go'ni-a. An immense genus of tropical herbs with soft or succulent stems.

Description
Leaves alternate, often brightly colored or with colored veins. Flowers red, pink, yellow, or white, slightly irregular, the male and female separate.

How to Grow
Sow seeds indoors 4–6 months before last
frost. Press gently into a fine potting
medium. Keep moist and provide light.
Germinate at 70–80° F (21.0–26.5° C), and
keep above 50° F (10° C) at night. When
large enough to handle, transfer seedlings to
individual pots. Then plant outdoors after
frost danger is past. Where summer sun is
intense, provide shade from the afternoon
sun. If planted in moderate to deep shade,
begonia plants will elongate and set fewer
flowers. For houseplants, dig up before first
frost. Prefers warm weather.

× *semperflorens-cultorum* pp. 80, 250
Wax Begonia. A group of hybrids and
cultivars. Usually 8–12 in. (20–30 cm) high.
Leaves bronzy-green or green. Flowers white,
pink, or red, 1 in. (2.5 cm) wide, blooming
continuously outdoors in summer. Many
varieties, with single or double blossoms,
some with large flowers, others have many
more clusters of small flowers. South
America. Tender perennial grown as a tender
annual.

Bellis
Daisy family
Compositae

Bel'lis. A genus of 5 European herbs, one
cultivated for centuries as the true daisy.

Description
Leaves mostly basal, forming a tuft.
Flowerheads solitary, on naked stalks, their
ray flowers typically white or pink, the center
of disk flowers yellow.

How to Grow
Where winters are mild, direct seed in late
summer for winter and spring bloom; if
weather is cool, bloom will continue into
summer. Elsewhere, for a good show of late
spring color, start seeds indoors in midwinter
at 55–65° F (13.0–18.5° C). Transplant to
the garden as soon as soil can be worked.
Protect seedlings with a light mulch of straw
until frost danger is past. Prefers cool
weather.

perennis pp. 101, 244, 245
English Daisy. To 6 in. (15 cm) high.
Flowerheads with white, pink, or red rays,

1–2 in. (2.5–5.0 cm) wide. Eurasia. There are double and semidouble forms available. Blooms in spring or early summer. Perennial but treated in warm areas as a hardy biennial; in severe-winter areas, as a tender annual or biennial.

Benincasa
Cucumber family
Cucurbitaceae

Ben-in-kay′sa. A pumpkinlike and tendril-bearing Asiatic vine. Known here for its ornamental fruit; in China it is the source of the Chinese preserving melon.

Description
Fleshy and creeping vine. Leaves alternate, large, and angled. Flowers solitary, yellow, large, the stamens and pistils never in the same flower. Fruit large, melonlike, but without a hard rind.

How to Grow
Start seeds early indoors in individual peat pots. Transplant to a sunny site after frost. Provide a tall strong trellis or arbor to support heavy vines and fruit. Prefers warm weather.

hispida p. 192
Wax Gourd; White Gourd. A trailing vine, to 10 ft. (3 m) long or more, the stem brown-hairy. Flowers 3–4 in. (7.5–10.0 cm) wide, yellow, corolla veiny. Fruit round-oblong, hairy, to 16 in. (40.5 cm) long. Tropical Asia. Fruit matures late summer to fall. Tender annual.

Beta
Goosefoot family
Chenopodiaceae

Bee′ta. About 12 species of Old World herbs, and including the Garden Beet and Ornamental Chard.

Description
Flowers greenish, in spikes or panicles, without petals, and extremely simple. Leaves simple and oblongish, in a basal rosette or alternate on the stem; often red-stalked. Fruit an aggregate of 2 or more flowers joined

together at the base and forming a dry, corky cluster, called a seed ball.

How to Grow
Wash seed balls in detergent, rinse well, and soak for 2 or 3 hours. For continuous foliage, sow the seed balls in the garden in late spring and again in late summer. Space seeds 2–3 in. (5.0–7.5 cm) apart in rows 24 in. (60 cm) apart and cover with ¼ in. (6 mm) of sand. Thin plants to 6 in. (15 cm) apart. Plants do best in cooler areas.

vulgaris '**Ruby Chard**' *p. 187*
Rhubarb Beet; Chard. 12–14 in. (30–35 cm) high, with large, puckered, purplish leaves and red or purple stems. Leaves edible. Eurasia. Biennial grown as a half-hardy annual.

Borago
Borage family
Boraginaceae

Bore-ray′go. A small genus of European herbs, much liked by bees; also planted in herb gardens.

Description
They usually have stiff-hairy foliage. Leaves alternate. Flowers blue, wheel-shaped, in a loose, leafy cluster.

How to Grow
Easy to grow from seeds sown outdoors 2–3 weeks before the frost-free date and at 30-day intervals thereafter for a continuous supply of blossoms. Space plants 12–18 in. (30–45 cm) apart. Grow in full sun except where the midsummer sun is intense. Borage plants are often placed in the vegetable garden to draw bees to pollinate the vine crops. They prefer warm weather.

officinalis *p. 140*
Borage; Talewort. To 2 ft. (60 cm) high. Flowers ¾ in. (19 mm) wide, blue or purple, the stamens protruding as much as ¼ in. (6 mm). S. Europe and n. Africa. Borage has a cucumberlike fragrance. Its young leaves may be used in salads, and young blossoms for garnish. Hardy annual.

Brachycome
Daisy family
Compositae

Bra-kick′o-me. A large genus of mostly
Australian herbs, one, the Swan River Daisy,
a very popular annual.

Description
Alternate, small leaves are divided, feather-
fashion, into narrow segments. Flowerheads
solitary on the ends of long stalks, the
rays white, blue, or rose.

How to Grow
Where summers are short, start seeds indoors
6 weeks before the last frost. In the garden,
plant 6 in. (15 cm) apart. Where winters are
mild, sow outside in early spring in a sunny,
well-drained site. Prefers cool weather. Use
small, twiggy branches to support flowers.

iberidifolia p. 127
Swan River Daisy. 8–18 in. (20–45 cm)
high. Flowerheads 1 in. (2.5 cm) wide, the
rays blue, white, or rose. An excellent edging
plant and an attractive, low covering for bare
places. Half-hardy annual.

Brassica
Mustard family
Cruciferae

Brass′i-ka. An important genus of temperate
Old World annual or biennial herbs,
containing all the vegetables of the cabbage
tribe, including mustard, kale, rape, and
turnip. Some are pernicious weeds.

Description
They have mostly smooth, often bluish-
green, water-shedding leaves. Flowers yellow
or white, with 4 petals, and in terminal
racemes.

How to Grow
Although Flowering Kale and Flowering
Cabbage are often sold as spring bedding
plants, they do best when started in late
summer to mature in the fall. Sow seeds in
the garden, and protect seedlings from
cabbage worms and aphids. If grown in
spring, start indoors 8–10 weeks before
frost-free date and set out as soon as the soil

can be worked. Harden off the transplants thoroughly. Plants prefer cool weather.

oleracea: Acephala Group *pp. 180, 181*

Flowering Kale; Flowering Cabbage. A form with a stem topped with a cluster of leaves, not in a dense cabbagelike head. Two kinds are important in cool-weather gardens for their richly colored purple-, cream-, pink-, white-, and rose-variegated leaves. Plants are quite resistant to frost. Flowering Kale has frilly leaves and an open growth habit. It is relatively heat-resistant and can be grown through the summer. Flowering Cabbage forms lower growing, flattened plants with broad heads. Both kinds are excellent for formal borders in the fall or can be grown in pots around the patio. Nw. Europe. There are many cultivars available, including 'Dynasty Pink' with pink-variegated leaves. Biennial grown as a hardy annual.

Briza
Grass family
Gramineae

Bry'za. A group of slender grasses, usually called quaking grass.

Description
Leaf blades flat, the spikelets suggesting small, flattened hops, often nodding on threadlike stalks.

How to Grow
In early spring work up the soil and lay down a 2–3 ft. (60–90 cm) square of clear plastic. Secure the edges with soil. Cut a 6-in. (15-cm) cross in center, and plant seeds where they can grow through the slits. Later, cover plastic with dried grass clippings to shade out weeds. Prefers cool weather.

maxima p. 177
Quaking Oats. 1–2 ft. (30–60 cm) high. Spikelets ½ in. (13 mm) long, reddish-brown or tan touched with green, turning pale or metallic, borne on slender, drooping pedicels. S. Europe. Good for dried bouquets. Also sold as *B. major.* Hardy annual.

Browallia
Potato family
Solanaceae

Brow-wall′i-a. A genus of mostly tropical
American herbs, several widely grown,
mostly blue-flowered.

Description
Leaves simple, mostly alternate. Flowers
solitary or in somewhat 1-sided racemes.
Calyx tubular, usually with 5 teeth. Corolla
tubular, the 5-lobed limb more or less
irregular.

How to Grow
Plants need a relatively warm growing season
and plenty of moisture. They may not bloom
until fall where summer is short, but plants
may be brought indoors for winter color.
Start seeds indoors; they require light and
65° F (18.5° C) to germinate.

speciosa p. 128
Smooth-branching, 8–12 in. (20–30 cm), or
rarely 15 in. (38 cm), high. Flowers, 2 in.
(5 cm) wide, with the tube 1 in. (2.5 cm)
long, purplish, violet, blue, and white. South
America. The cultivar 'Major' has dark blue
flowers; 'Blue Bells' has violet-blue flowers.
Tender annual.

viscosa p. 130
Sticky-hairy, 12–20 in. (30–50 cm) high.
Flowers ¾ in. (19 mm) wide, violet-blue,
with a white "eye." South America. Cultivars
include 'Alba', which has white flowers, and
'Compacta', a low-growing form. Tender
annual.

Calandrinia
Portulaca family
Portulacaceae

Kal-an-drin′i-a. A large genus of fleshy herbs,
found in w. North America and w. South
America. Commonly called rock purslane in
Calif.

Description
Leaves alternate or basal. Flowers short-lived,
in bracted racemes. Petals 3–7, rose-pink or
red. Sepals 2, and persistent.

How to Grow
They grow best in Calif., the Northwest, and other cool or high-altitude gardens. Plants need a dry, sunny site. They can be direct seeded in late spring or transplanted from seeds sown indoors in early spring. Seeds germinate at 55–60° F (13.0–15.5° C). Plants prefer cool weather.

umbellata p. 84
Rock Purslane. To 6 in. (15 cm) high. Flowers red or crimson-magenta, ¾ in. (19 mm) wide, borne in racemes or panicles. Peru. A good choice for rock gardens. Tender perennial grown as a half-hardy annual.

Calceolaria
Snapdragon family
Scrophulariaceae

Kal-see-o-lay´ri-a. A very large genus of tropical American herbs or shrubby plants, called slipperworts.

Description
Leaves opposite or in whorls, simple or pinnately divided; leafstalk often winged. Flowers in irregular, often 1-sided, clusters, generally yellow, but often spotted with orange-brown. Corolla very irregular and 2-lipped, the upper lip small, the lower one large, inflated, and slipperlike. Stamens 2.

How to Grow
Seldom grown outside of coastal Calif. and cool or high-altitude gardens. Plants are not at all resistant to heat. For good spring color, start seeds indoors 12 weeks before last spring frost. Press very small seeds into potting soil; do not bury them. When winter-grown in mild climates, blossoms are large; when spring-sown, blossoms are smaller. The species below prefer cool weather.

crenatiflora p. 211
Pocketbook Plant; Slipperwort. 1–2 ft. (30–60 cm) high. Flowers ¾–2½ in. (2–6 cm) long, yellow, but spotted orange-brown, red, or rose-pink. Chile. Many cultivars available. Difficult to grow. Also sold as *C. hybrida* or *C. herbeohybrida*. Tender perennial grown as a half-hardy annual.

integrifolia p. 210

2–5 ft. (0.6–1.5 m) high, shrubby. Flowers ⅓ in. (8 mm) long, yellowish to red-brown, with spots. Chile. Many varieties without spots. Taller plants need support. Also sold as *C. rugosa*. Tender perennial grown as a half-hardy annual.

mexicana p. 211

To 1½ ft. (45 cm) high. Flowers lemon-yellow, ½ in. (13 mm) long. Mexico; Central America. Tender annual.

Calendula
Daisy family
Compositae

Ka-len′dew-la. A genus of 15 species of herbs, chiefly from the Mediterranean region.

Description
Leaves undivided, alternate, simple, and faintly toothed. Flowerheads large, the rays yellow, orange, or cream.

How to Grow
Calendulas grown to flower in spring are tall with small blossoms, while winter-grown plants are small with immense blossoms. For spring bloom, start seeds very early indoors and set out as soon as soil can be worked. For fall or winter bloom in warm regions, direct seed and transplant 12 in. (30 cm) apart. Prefers cool weather.

officinalis p. 236

Pot Marigold. 12–18 in. (30–45 cm) high. Flowerheads solitary, stalked, 1–3 in. (2.5–7.5 cm) wide, the day-blooming and night-closing rays flattish and orange, yellow, or cream. S. Europe. Many cultivars are available. Plants prey to slugs. Long-lasting flowers good for cutting. Blooms spring to frost. Hardy annual.

Callistephus
Daisy family
Compositae

Kal-lis′tee-fuss. A single, very variable Asiatic herb, known as the China, or Garden, Aster. Not closely related to the true genus *Aster*. Good for cutting.

Description
Leaves broadly oval, deeply and irregularly toothed. Flowerheads solitary, at the ends of relatively long stalks.

How to Grow
Sow seeds directly in garden after danger of frost is past. For earlier flowers, start seeds indoors, and move to garden when the nights are warm. To avoid damage from aster yellow disease, adjust planting dates: Start seeds early indoors and transplant good-sized plants at the frost-free date. Or direct-seed asters in late summer under a screen cover to keep out leafhoppers and aphids. Thin to 12 in. (30 cm) apart. Remove the screen in early fall and spray weekly to protect asters until cool weather reduces the insect problem. The species below prefers warm weather.

chinensis p. 102
China Aster. 9–24 in. (22.5–60.0 cm) high. Ray flowers to 5 in. (12.5 cm) wide, showy, single or double blossoms, of nearly every color, but predominately blue or violet. China. Among the many cultivars, 'Early Charm Choice' blooms very early. Dwarf varieties make good edging plants. Susceptible to wilt; should never be planted in same place twice. Tender annual.

Campanula
Bellflower family
Campanulaceae

Kam-pan'you-la. The bellflowers comprise 300 known species, over 2 dozen of which are cultivated for their handsome bloom.

Description
Basal leaves often unlike the stem leaves, the latter alternate. Flowers typically bell-shaped, showy, mostly blue or white, the calyx persistent on the egg-shaped pod that opens by a terminal pore in some, by valves in others.

How to Grow
Can be manipulated to bloom as a hardy annual or, in mild-winter climates, it can be direct seeded in fall for bloom the following late spring. Protect with a mulch of evergreen branches until the danger of hard frost is past. Prefers cool weather.

Medium p. 138
Canterbury Bells. 2–4 ft. (60–120 cm) high.
Flowers violet-blue, solitary or in loose
racemes, 1 in. (2.5 cm) wide and 2 in.
(5 cm) long. S. Europe. A wide variety of
forms are available. Blooms 6 months after
germination. Biennial grown as a hardy
annual.

Capsicum
Potato family
Solanaceae

Kap'si-kum. A genus of tropical woody
plants yielding Red (but not black) Peppers,
Tabasco, and Cayenne Peppers, as well as the
milder peppers commonly grown as
vegetables. Most are from tropical America.

Description
Leaves alternate, simple, without marginal
teeth. Flowers white or greenish white,
usually stalked and solitary or in 2- to
3-flowered clusters, generally wheel-shaped
and 5-lobed. Fruit typically podlike with a
thickish rind. Most are hot; all are edible.

How to Grow
Start seeds indoors 8–10 weeks before the
frost-free date. Set plants in the garden 2–3
weeks after the frost-free date. They benefit
from enriched soil and prefer warm weather.

annuum pp. 190, 191
Ornamental Pepper. To 30 in. (75 cm) high.
Flowers generally borne singly in leaf axils,
to ½ in. (13 mm) across. Fruit upright,
slender to cone-shaped, and yellow, orange,
red to purple, or nearly black. Many new
varieties are heat-resistant and humidity
tolerant. 'Red Missile' is 10 in. (25 cm)
high; its oblong fruit, 1½ in. (4 cm) long.
'Holiday Cheer' grows to 8 in. (20 cm); its
round fruit, 1 in. (2.5 cm) wide. Tender
annual.

Cardiospermum
Soapberry family
Sapindaceae

Kar-dee-o-sper'mum. A genus of perhaps 12
species of chiefly tropical herbaceous vines,

one cultivated, mostly in warm regions, for ornament.

Description
Leaves alternate, twice-compound, the ultimate leaflets coarsely toothed. Flowers small but numerous, unisexual, in clusters that bear tendrils. Sepals and petals each 4. Fruit a papery, inflated, and veiny capsule, 3-valved, and with black seeds with a white, heart-shaped spot, hence the common name of heart-seed for these vines.

How to Grow
Start the seeds indoors 6 weeks before last frost, and move outdoors 2–3 weeks after last frost. Prefers warm weather.

Halicacabum p. 195
Balloon Vine. To 12 ft. (3.5 m) long. Flowers white, ¼ in. (6 mm) wide, the clusters scarcely longer than the leaves. Pods 3-angled, 1 in. (2.5 cm) long, the seeds pea-size. Tropical regions; naturalized in the se. U.S. Tender perennial grown as a tender annual.

Carum
Carrot family
Umbelliferae

Kair'um. A genus of about 30 species of Old World temperate zone herbs.

Description
Leaves mostly basal, much compounded into tiny segments. Flowers minute, white, in small umbels that are grouped in larger umbels. Fruit dry and seedlike.

How to Grow
To reap a good harvest of the edible seeds, start caraway early in the season as soon as the danger of frost is past. Prefers cool weather.

Carvi p. 152
Caraway. 1–2 ft. (30–60 cm) high. Leaves so finely divided that the ultimate segments are threadlike. Flowers white, in clusters, to 1¼ in. (3 cm) wide. Fruit strongly ribbed. Eurasia. Biennial grown as a hardy annual.

Cassia
Pea family
Leguminosae

Cash'i-a. An immense genus of perhaps 500 species of herbs, shrubs, and mostly tropical trees, with a few herbs grown in the temperate zone.

Description
They have compound leaves, the leaflets arranged feather-fashion and without an odd one at the end. Flowers very nearly regular, but one of the clawed petals often a little larger than the other 4.

How to Grow
The species listed below is easy to grow from seed in average to dry soil. It does best in full sun. Prefers warm weather.

fasciculata p. 218
Partridge Pea. To 18 in. (45 cm) high. Flowers yellow, ¾ in. (19 mm) long, in clusters. E. and cen. U. S. Hardy annual.

Catananche
Daisy family
Compositae

Kat-a-nann'ke. Of the 5 known species of this genus, only the Cupid's Dart is grown in the garden for its showy blue heads.

Description
Leaves mostly basal and narrow. Flowers in long-stalked heads, the rays flat and toothed.

How to Grow
This hardy, deep-rooted perennial will bloom the first year in short-season areas if seeds are started indoors in the very early spring. Transplant to the garden as soon as soil can be worked. Where winters are mild, direct-seed from late summer through fall. Thin to 18 in. (45 cm) apart. Also, propagate by division. Prefers warm weather.

caerulea p. 125
Cupid's Dart; Blue Succory. To 2 ft. (60 cm) high. Flowerheads nearly 2 in. (5 cm) wide, the rays blue, white, or blue and white, and solitary on long stems. Violet and bicolored cultivars available. An excellent

dried flower. S. Europe. Perennial treated as a
hardy annual.

Catharanthus
Dogbane family
Apocynaceae

Kath-ar-an'thus. A genus of 5 species of
annual or perennial herbs native to the
tropics of the Old World.

Description
Leaves opposite, entire. Flowers borne singly
or 2–3 together, the corolla tubular, the
lobes spreading to form a flat, platelike apex.

How to Grow
Sow seeds indoors and germinate at 70–
80° F (21.0–26.5° C). Plant out once
danger of frost is past. Prefers warm weather.

roseus pp. 81, 162
Madagascar Periwinkle. Erect, growing to
2 ft. (60 cm). Flowers showy, 1½ in.
(4 cm) across, pink or white, often with
reddish eye. Madagascar. Heat and humidity
resistant. Tender perennial grown as a tender
annual.

Celosia
Amaranth family
Amaranthaceae

Sell-o'si-a. A large genus of tropical herbs or
shrubs, grown for their often fantastic or
grotesque flower clusters. Native to warm
areas of U.S. and Africa.

Description
Leaves alternate, lobed, or simple. Flowers
minute and chaffy, crowded into dense spikes
that are much enlarged, flattened, crested, or
otherwise modified, and often brilliantly
colored.

How to Grow
Sow seeds in early summer in garden soil
enriched with organic matter. Indoors start
in peat pots to minimize transplant shock.
Celosias in full flower may refuse to develop
and wither away when transplanted. They
prefer warm weather.

cristata *pp. 268, 269, 270, 271*
Plumed Celosia; Crested Celosia; Cockscomb.
1–2 ft. (30–60 cm) high. Flower clusters
very diverse in size, shape, and color. One
common type has a crested or rolled cluster,
6–12 in. (15–30 cm) wide, much like a
cockscomb; or congested and monstrous.
Another popular type is open and feathery,
6–12 in. (15–30 cm) high. Some others are
very broad and fanlike and others spirelike.
A good dried flower. Sometimes sold as *C.
plumosa*. Tender annual.

Centaurea
Daisy family
Compositae

Sen-tor′ree-a. A genus of chiefly Eurasian
herbs comprising over 400 species.

Description
Leaves basal or alternate on stems, entire to
divided, not spiny. Flowerheads contain
tubular flowers; along the edge, they are
often expanded and raylike. Below the head
is a series of overlapping bracts.

How to Grow
The daisy-type *Centaurea* should be direct
seeded in early spring where growing seasons
are short, and in late summer through fall
where winters are mild. The foliage types
should be started very early indoors. Set out
when plants are large. *C. americana* and *C.
Cyanus* prefer cool weather, while *C.
Cineraria* needs a warm growing season.

americana *p. 99*
Basket-Flower. 4–6 ft. (1.2–1.8 m) high.
Heads 4–5 in. (10.0–12.5 cm) wide, rose to
pink, the marginal flowers raylike, hence the
head set as though in a shallow basket.
Fringed bracts below the head. Cen. U.S. to
Mexico. Hardy annual.

Cineraria *p. 180*
Dusty Miller. 1–3 ft. (30–90 cm) high,
grown for its prominently white-felty foliage.
Leaves to 1 ft. (30 cm) long, parted into
blunt but narrow lobes. S. Italy. Half-
hardy annual.

Cyanus *p. 124*
Bachelor's Button; Cornflower; Bluebottle;

Ragged Sailor; Blue Bonnets. Sprawling annual, 1–2 ft. (30–60 cm) high. Heads 1½ in. (4 cm) wide, typically pale blue, or purple, pink, or white in horticultural forms. S. Europe. Double-flowered forms in nearly all colors. Hardy annual.

Centaurium
Gentian family
Gentianaceae

Sen-tor′ree-um. A genus made up of about 30 herbs, most of them annual or biennial, widely distributed, mostly throughout the northern hemisphere.

Description
Leaves opposite, simple. Flowers pale pink to rose or red, in clusters.

How to Grow
Sow seeds in the garden where plants are to remain in very early spring; in mild-winter areas start in early fall. The longest show of color is obtained in cool summer gardens, but flowers perform well over much of the country. Young plants are quite hardy to frost.

Erythraea p. 90
Centaury. To 20 in. (50 cm) high. Flowers pale pink to pink-purple, ½ in. (13 mm) wide, in clusters. Eurasia. Biennial treated as a hardy annual.

Cerinthe
Borage family
Boraginaceae

Sir-rin′the. A small group of Eurasian herbs, one an annual flower garden plant cultivated for its showy bloom.

Description
Leaves alternate, often red or white-spotted. Flowers in 1-sided clusters, yellow, borne among numerous purple bracts. Corolla nearly regular, tubular.

How to Grow
Start seeds early indoors. Transplant to sunny borders (or, in hot climates, to partially shaded sites) after danger of frost is past.

Where summers are cool, direct seed in late spring and thin to 12 in. (30 cm) apart. Prefers cool weather.

major p. 216
Honeywort. To 20 in. (50 cm) high. Flowers to ¾ in. (19 mm) long, yellow, tipped with purple, protruding beyond the colored bracts. Greece. Hardy annual.

Cheiranthus
Mustard family
Cruciferae

Ky-ran'thus. Perhaps a dozen perennial herbs, scattered from Madeira to the Himalayas, one the widely cultivated Wallflower.

Description
Leaves narrow with few marginal teeth. Flowers with 4-clawed petals, yellow or orange-brown, fragrant.

How to Grow
Can be grown as biennials in mild-winter areas from direct seeding in early fall, but they need cold to trigger flowering. To grow as hardy annuals for spring bloom, start seeds indoors in midwinter. Shift seedlings to 4-in. (10-cm) pots, set in cold frame, and cover on very cold nights. After danger of hard frost, plant in well-drained soil. Prefers cool weather.

Cheiri p. 205
Wallflower. To 2½ ft. (75 cm) high, covered with minute, forked hairs. Flowers yellow, orange, red, purple, or red-brown, 1 in. (2.5 cm) wide, in terminal spikes or racemes. S. Europe. Biennial or tender perennial grown as a half-hardy annual.

Chrysanthemum
Daisy family
Compositae

Kris-san'thee-mum. An important genus of usually erect herbs, comprising about 100 species, nearly all from the temperate or subtropical regions of the Old World. Some have been cultivated for over 3000 years in China and Japan.

Description
Leaves alternate, often more or less divided, and strong-smelling. Generally much branched. Flowers daisylike, in all colors except blue and purple and in heads that are usually showy and immense, but sometimes small and buttonlike.

How to Grow
Sow seeds in full sun to partial shade in well-drained soil as soon as the ground can be worked in the spring and again after midsummer. Thin to 18 in. (45 cm) apart. Most species prefer a cool growing season and low humidity.

carinatum pp. 238, 239
Tricolor Chrysanthemum. 2–3 ft. (60–90 cm) high, not much branched. Flowerheads 2½ in. (6 cm) wide, white, red, purple, or yellow, with a contrasting ring at base of rays. Many cultivars. Morocco. Hardy annual.

coronarium p. 223
Crown Daisy. To 4 ft. (120 cm) high. Flowerheads numerous, 1½ in. (4 cm) wide, sometimes double, yellow to yellowish white. S. Europe. Hardy annual.

Parthenium pp. 157, 158, 213
Feverfew. 2–3 ft. (60–90 cm) high. Flowerheads many, to ¾ in. (19 mm) wide, buttonlike, disk flowers yellow, rays white, short, or lacking altogether. Se. Europe to the Caucasus. Many cultivars. Sometimes offered as *Matricaria capensis*. Does best in warm weather. Tender perennial but blooms during the first year, so often grown as a half-hardy annual.

Cirsium
Daisy family
Compositae

Sir'si-um. Of 200 known species of thistles, most are weeds.

Description
Prickly herbs with alternate or basal leaves that are nearly always cut or lobed and spiny-margined. Flowers tiny, tubular, often handsome, crowded in a dense, usually spiny-bracted head.

How to Grow
Easy to grow in any garden soil. Sow seeds
in early spring in full sun to partial shade.
Prefers cool weather.

japonicum p. 271
Plumed Thistle. To 2½ ft. (75 cm) high.
Flowers 1–2 in. (2.5–5.0 cm) wide, in
solitary heads, rose-red, tubular, with bristles.
Japan. Biennial grown as a hardy annual.

Clarkia
Evening primrose family
Onagraceae

Clark′i-a. Very showy herbs, mostly from the
w. U.S., some popular in the flower garden.

Description
Leaves alternate, narrow, sometimes with
very small marginal teeth. Flowers solitary or
in small clusters. Petals 4, clawed, the upper
part widely spread and sometimes 3-toothed.

How to Grow
Where winters are mild, sow seeds late
summer through fall; elsewhere, as soon as
soil can be worked in the spring. Do not
thin too much, because crowding encourages
blooming. These plants prefer cool weather.

amoena p. 86
Farewell-to-Spring. 1–3 ft. (30–90 cm) high.
Flowers 1–2 in. (2.5–5.0 cm) wide, the petals
satiny, lilac-crimson or reddish pink. British
Columbia to Calif. Many cultivars, some
white, some double-flowered, and one
crimson-blotched. Also sold as *Godetia
amoena*. Hardy annual.

purpurea p. 85
To 3 ft. (90 cm) high. Flowers red, purple,
or pink, 2 in. (5 cm) wide, with a dark eye
at center. Oreg. and Calif. Variously colored
cultivars. Hardy annual.

unguiculata p. 93
Stems erect, reddish, 1½–3 ft. (45–90 cm)
high. Flowers purple, rose-colored, or
whitish, 2½ in. (6 cm) wide, petals
triangular to rhombic, buds deflexed. Calif.
Hardy annual.

Cleome
Caper family
Capparaceae

Klee-o'me. 200 known species, chiefly
tropical, only one of garden importance.

Description
Usually strong-smelling herbs. Leaves
compound, with 3–7 leaflets arranged finger-
fashion. Flowers solitary or in clusters, with
4 long-clawed petals, long stamens, and
stalked ovary.

How to Grow
Where summers are long and warm, sow
seeds in early spring; seeds will sprout when
the soil warms. Elsewhere, start seeds indoors
8–10 weeks before the last spring frost and
set out in the garden 2–3 weeks before the
last frost. Needs plenty of space, so thin out
seedlings. Prefers warm weather.

Hasslerana p. 118
Spider Flower. 4–5 ft. (1.2–1.5 m) high,
bushy. Flowers 2–3 in. (5.0–7.5 cm) long
and wide, rose-purple, pink, or white, the
stamens 2–3 in. (5.0–7.5 cm) long. Tropical
America. Also sold as *C. pungens.* Half-
hardy annual.

Cobaea
Phlox family
Polemoniaceae

Ko-bee'a. Tendril-climbing, tropical
American woody vines, the species below
quick growing and showy.

Description
Leaves alternate, compound, the leaflets
arranged feather-fashion, the terminal one
replaced by a branched tendril. Flowers
solitary, on long stalks from the leaf axils.
Corolla bell-shaped or cylindric, its limb
5-lobed.

How to Grow
Start seeds indoors 8 weeks before last frost.
Set out when danger of frost is past. Provide
tall, strong supports to prevent wind
damage. Where summers are cool, plant
facing the west or south; where summers are
warm, plant in an area with afternoon shade.
Prefers warm weather.

scandens *p. 138*
Cup-and-Saucer Vine; Mexican Ivy. 10–25 ft. (3.0–7.5 m) long. Flowers violet, greenish purple, or white, 2 in. (5 cm) long, 1½ in. (4 cm) wide, the calyx inflated and leaflike, the protruding stamens curved. Mexico. Sold under a variety of names, including Cathedral Bells. There is a white-flowered form. Tender perennial grown as a tender annual.

Coix
Grass family
Graminae

Ko'icks. A small genus of Indo-Malayan grasses, the species below grown here for ornament; but in its native region, its beadlike seeds are used to make rosaries.

Description
Stem jointed. Leaves flat. Flower cluster terminal, the male clusters at the end, the female below, the latter containing a white beadlike structure and the edible kernel.

How to Grow
Start seeds indoors and set outdoors when danger of frost is past. The plants are more curious than ornamental, and are sometimes grown 5 or 6 per large container so they do not disturb the landscape effect. They prefer cool weather.

Lacryma-Jobi *p. 197*
Job's Tears. 3–6 ft. (0.9–1.8 m) high. Leaves 1–2 ft. (30–60 cm) long, ¾–1½ in. (2–4 cm) wide, sword-shaped, with a prominent midrib. Beads ¾ in. (19 mm) wide, very striking, white to bluish gray, sometimes mottled, hard and shiny. Tropical Asia. May not bear fruit outside of warm climates. A variety has yellow-striped leaves. Half-hardy annual.

Coleus
Mint family
Labiatae

Ko'lee-us. About 150 species of foliage plants of the Old World tropics. In the Midwest, called the Foliage Plant.

Description
Mostly succulent herbs, with stems square,
leaves opposite and toothed. Flowers in
clusters of 6 or more, with a short 2-lipped
calyx, lower lip with 4 teeth; corolla
2-lipped, the upper short with 2–4 lobes, the
lower boat-shaped. Stamens 4.

How to Grow
Start seeds indoors 10 weeks before last
spring frost, providing 70–75° F (21–24° C)
bottom heat, but raising this to 80° F
(26.5° C) if germination does not occur in
10 days. Do not cover the seeds with soil.
Cover pots with plastic wrap. After last frost,
plant in moderately shady site outdoors.
Keep moist. Pinch off flowers to promote
bushy plants. Where summers are humid,
Coleus will grow in full sun, but the foliage
will be less vividly colored and will droop in
the afternoon. This species prefers warm
weather.

× *hybridus* pp. 186, 187
Garden Coleus. To 3 ft. (90 cm) high.
Grown for its showy, variously colored
leaves, which may be scalloped or fringed.
Stem cuttings make attractive winter
houseplants. Hundreds of cultivars. Also sold
as *C. blumei.* Tender perennial grown as a
tender annual.

Collinsia
Snapdragon family
Scrophulariaceae

Kol-lin'si-a. 25 species of attractive herbs,
most natives of w. North America.

Description
Leaves opposite or in whorls of 3–5. Flowers
solitary or in small clusters in leaf axils, the
corolla irregular and 2-lipped, the calyx
bell-shaped.

How to Grow
Easy to grow. Sow seeds in spring, after
warm weather has arrived. Plants prefer dry
soil, partial shade, and cool nights. Not heat-
resistant. This species prefers cool weather.

grandiflora p. 133
Blue-Lips. 8–15 in. (20–38 cm) high.
Flowers ¾ in. (19 mm) long, upper lip
purple or white, lower lip blue or violet.
British Columbia to Calif. Half-hardy
annual.

Consolida
Buttercup family
Ranunculaceae

Con-sol'id-da. About 40 species of annuals
from s. and e. Europe to cen. Asia, 2 fairly
commonly cultivated. They are related to
Delphinium, from which they differ in having
the 2 upper petals united into 1, and the 2
lower petals lacking.

Description
Leaves narrow and divided. Flowers in showy
spikes, with sepals and petals similar in
shape, but one bearing a long spur.

How to Grow
Since seedlings are so frost-hardy, sow seeds
in raised beds with heavy soil, in fall in areas
with mild winters, and in very early spring
elsewhere. When plants are 12–18 in.
(30–45 cm) high, provide mulch of dried
grass clippings to keep roots cool. Difficult
to transplant unless started in peat pots.
Especially tall varieties need supports. The
species below prefer cool weather.

ambigua p. 143
Rocket Larkspur. 1–2 ft. (30–60 cm) high,
with erect branches. Flowers 1¼ in. (3 cm)
long, violet, rose, pink, blue, or white. S.
Europe. Blooms in late spring to summer.
Many cultivars are available, some to 5 ft.
(1.5 cm) high. All make excellent bedding
plants for the back of the garden or against a
fence. They are popular cut flowers. Also
sold as *Delphinium Ajacis.* Hardy annual.

orientalis p. 143
Larkspur. Similar to *C. ambigua,* but with
branches more horizontal. N. Africa, s.
Europe. Also sold as *Delphinium consolida.*
Hardy annual.

Convolvulus
Morning glory family
Convolvulaceae

Kon-voll'view-lus. About 200 widely
distributed species, including a few garden
plants and some pernicious weeds.

Description
Trailing or twining plants with alternate
leaves. Flowers chiefly day-bloomers but
sometimes close by noon, solitary or a few in
the leaf axils, often long-stalked. Corolla bell-
or funnel-shaped, usually showy.

How to Grow
Where summers are long and warm, sow
seeds outdoors after danger of frost is past.
Elsewhere, start indoors 6 weeks before last
frost. Prick the hard seed coats or wash seeds
in a detergent to remove surface oils, rinse,
and soak overnight in lukewarm water. The
species below prefers warm weather.

tricolor p. 134
Dwarf Morning Glory. To 1 ft. (30 cm)
high. Stems more or less erect, branching,
and forming a mound. Flowers 1½ in. (4 cm)
wide, blue to purple, with yellow throat and
white margins. S. Europe. Good in baskets.
Tender annual.

Coreopsis
Daisy family
Compositae

Ko-ree-op'sis. Comprising about 100 species,
perhaps a dozen grown for their showy
bloom.

Description
Leaves generally opposite, often lobed or
dissected, but entire in some. Flowerheads
solitary or in branched clusters, composed of
central disk flowers and showy ray flowers.
Usually about 8 rays in the single varieties,
more in the double forms.

How to Grow
Sow seeds outdoors in early spring. In warm
areas, sow again late summer through fall for
winter and spring flowers. Plants need good
drainage and full sun. Do not thin; bloom
best when crowded. Plants prefer warm
weather.

tinctoria pp. 226, 227
Golden Coreopsis. 2–3 ft. (60–90 cm) high.
Flowerheads long-stalked, to 1¼ in. (3 cm)
across, the disk flowers dark red or purple,
the ray flowers yellow with brown base, or
entirely yellow, brown, or purple-red. Cen.
U.S. There are forms with double flowers, as
well as dwarf varieties. Heat-resistant. Hardy
annual.

Coriandrum
Carrot family
Umbelliferae

Kor-ee-an′drum. Two species of herbs native
to s. Europe and Asia Minor. The species
below is cultivated for its fragrant seeds and
foliage, used as a seasoning.

Description
Compound leaves and small white flowers in
compound umbels.

How to Grow
Easy to grow from seeds. Start indoors in
spring or sow outdoors after the danger of
frost is past. Needs full sun and average soil.
Prefers cool weather.

sativum p. 119
Coriander. To 3 ft. (90 cm) high. Flowers
small, ⅛ in. (3.2 mm) wide, white, rose, or
lavender, in compound umbels, the outer
flowers in each umbel sometimes enlarged
and raylike. S. Europe. Hardy annual.

Cosmos
Daisy family
Compositae

Kos′mus. Tropical American garden plants.
Of the 25 known species, 2 are especially
popular and derived from *C. bipinnatus*.

Description
Leaves opposite, in the species given below,
much cut into fine segments. Flowers in
heads, the latter solitary and long-stalked, or
in loose, open clusters. Ray flowers showy, of
many colors, rays often notched, disk flowers
yellow or red. Both of the species below
make excellent cut flowers.

How to Grow
Either sow the seeds outdoors after the last
frost or start indoors 6 weeks earlier. These
species are easy to transplant. The taller
forms may require staking. Both prefer warm
weather.

bipinnatus p. 105
Garden Cosmos. 4–6 ft. (1.2–1.8 m) high.
Flowerheads 1–2 in. (2.5–5.0 cm) wide
(wider in some horticultural forms); the rays
white, pink, or crimson, the disk flowers
yellow. Mexico. Many cultivars are available.
Tender annual.

sulphureus p. 236
Yellow Cosmos. 2–6 ft. (0.6–1.8 m) high.
Flowerheads solitary, to 3 in. (7.5 cm)
across, long-stalked, both ray and disk
flowers orange-yellow, yellow, or reddish
orange. Mexico. Some cultivars have double
flowers; others bloom early in the season.
Dwarf varieties are also available. Very heat-
resistant. Tender annual.

Crepis
Daisy family
Compositae

Kreep′is. About 200 species of annual to
perennial herbs, with milky juice, many
rosette-forming, native in the northern
hemisphere. Related to *Hieracium,* the
hawkweeds.

Description
Flowerheads without ray flowers, pink,
yellow, or white.

How to Grow
Sow seeds outdoors in fall in mild climates,
in early spring elsewhere. Prefers well-drained
soil and cool weather. Needs no thinning.

rubra p. 99
Hawk's Beard. 8–18 in. (20–45 cm) high.
Flowers 1½ in. (4 cm) wide, in small,
solitary, long-stalked heads, red or pink.
Italy. The cultivar 'Alba' has white flowers.
Hardy annual.

Cucurbita
Cucumber family
Cucurbitaceae

Kew-kur'bi-ta. Mostly annual, trailing or
climbing vines, comprising perhaps 20
species, and chiefly tropical. Includes Squash,
Pumpkin, and many ornamental gourds.

Description
Mostly rough-hairy vines with forked tendrils
and large leaves, often lobed. Flowers yellow,
large, usually more or less bell-shaped, but
lobed halfway down the tube. Fruit a large
berry, smooth-skinned or deeply furrowed,
with wide range of forms.

How to Grow
When danger of frost is past, plant seeds
outdoors, 1 ft. (30 cm) apart. Seedlings do
not transplant well, but in colder regions
start seeds indoors in peat pots. Apply
bottom heat. To prevent fruit from rotting
on the ground, provide supports. Prefers
warm weather.

ficifolia p. 193
Malabar Gourd. A running or climbing vine,
10–12 ft. (3–3.5 m) long, grown for
ornament, its fruit inedible. Leaves nearly
round or kidney-shaped, 7–10 in. (18–25 cm)
wide, margins wavy or lobed, more or
less weakly prickle-toothed. Flowers 5–6 in.
(12.5–15 cm) wide, with large spreading
lobes, the tube funnel-shaped. Fruit roundish
or oblong, 6–12 in. (15–30 cm) long,
smooth, green with white stripes, the seeds
black. E. Asia. Tender perennial grown as a
tender annual.

Cuphea
Loosestrife family
Lythraceae

Kew'fee-a. A large group of over 200 species
of tropical American herbs or shrubs.

Description
Leaves opposite or crowded. Flowers
irregular, the calyx tubular and corolla-like,
often longer than the 6 unequal petals,
sometimes swollen and pouchlike, or curved
at the base. In the species below there are no
petals. Stamens generally 11.

How to Grow
Start seeds indoors 8–10 weeks before last
spring frost. Seeds germinate at 75° F (24° C).
Prick out small seedlings and transplant to
individual pots. Wait until the soil is warm
before setting out in the garden. Prefers
warm weather.

ignea p. 264
Firecracker Plant; Cigar-Flower. 8–15 in.
(29–38 cm) high. Flowers 1 in. (2.5 cm)
long, solitary, slender-stalked, and chiefly in
leaf axils. Calyx tube spurred at base, red
with darker ring near the tip and an
ash-white mouth; no petals. Mexico.
Cultivars available. Blooms 4 months after
germination. Tolerates heat and humidity.
Tender perennial grown as a tender annual.

Cymbalaria
Snapdragon family
Scrophulariaceae

Sim-ba-lay'ri-a. A genus of 10 species of
generally prostrate, Old World herbs.

Description
Herbaceous stems and alternate or opposite
leaves, sometimes lobed and veined finger-
fashion. Flowers solitary in leaf axils,
irregular, and spurred, usually small; throat
nearly closed. Stamens 4.

How to Grow
The species below is easy to grow from seeds
sown in the garden after the danger of frost
is past. It is widely planted for hanging
baskets, window boxes, and small indoor
trellises. Often escapes in the South,
becoming a lawn weed. Reseeds itself.
Prefers warm weather.

muralis p. 91
Kenilworth Ivy; Coliseum Ivy. A creeping
vine, to 3 ft. (90 cm) long, easily rooting at
the joints. Flowers ⅓ in. (8 mm) long,
lilac-blue, white, or pink, upper part of the
corolla yellowish inside. Europe. Sometimes
naturalized in e. North America. Many
cultivars are available, some with larger
flowers. Also called *Linaria Cymbalaria*.
Tender perennial, but acts like a tender
annual in the North.

Cynara
Sunflower family
Compositae

Sin′a-ra. About a dozen coarse, thistle-like herbs, mostly from the Mediterranean region.

Description
Leaves large, more or less lobed, cut, or both, sometimes spiny. Flowers tubular, disk-shaped, no rays, in large, dense heads, one terminating most of the larger branches. Cluster of bracts in many series below and surrounding each head, spiny-tipped and purple in the Cardoon.

How to Grow
Plants need a long, cool growing season to develop to full size. Start seeds indoors in very early spring to get good-sized plants for setting out in garden. Transplant twice to successively larger pots. If hardened off, the young plants will withstand a few degrees of frost. They need rich soil and plenty of moisture.

cardunculus *p. 182*
Cardoon. To 6 ft. (1.8 m) high. Root and thickened leafstalks edible. Leaves large, very deeply cut, grayish green above, but white-felty beneath, densely spiny. Flowerheads purple, to 3 in. (7.5 cm) wide, with spiny-tipped bracts. S. Europe. Most dramatic from late summer through fall. Perennial except where winters are severe but usually treated as a half-hardy annual.

Cynoglossum
Borage family
Boraginaceae

Sin-o-gloss′um. A genus of 90 species of widely distributed herbs, most of them weedy.

Description
Leaves alternate, undivided, often rough. Flowers small, often in arching, one-sided racemes. Corolla funnel-shaped, with 5 rounded lobes.

How to Grow
Where winters are mild, sow seeds in the garden in fall; elsewhere, in early spring.

Thin plants to stand 1 ft. (30 cm) apart.
The species below prefer cool weather.

amabile *p. 144*
Chinese Forget-Me-Not. 18–24 in. (45–60 cm)
high. Flowers ⅓ in. (8 mm) long, in a
relatively showy cluster, usually blue, but
may be pink or white. E. Asia. Biennial, but
blooms from seed the first year; usually
grown as a hardy annual.

officinale *p. 91*
To 2 ft. (60 cm) high. Flowers ¼ in. (6 mm
long, purple to pinkish purple. Europe.
Biennial grown as a hardy annual.

Dahlia
Daisy family
Compositae

Dahl'ya, also day'li-ya. A small but very
important genus of tuberous-rooted herbs,
the source of all the garden dahlias, most
from the uplands of Mexico and Guatemala.

Description
Tuberous roots. Leaves opposite, often
compound or twice-compound, the leaflets or
segments toothed or cut. Flowers very varied
due to breeding, ranging from small ball-
shaped pompons to large multipetaled
blossoms with curled, quill-like petals. Wild
types always have both ray and disk flowers.

How to Grow
While moderately heat-resistant, dahlias
grown from seeds for first-year bloom will
burn out in midsummer except in northern
and cool western gardens. Sow seeds indoors
6–8 weeks before last frost. Set out in moist,
fertile soil when danger of frost is over. Tall
plants may need staking. Tubers will mature
at base of main stem at end of first season.
Save plants you like by digging up tuber
cluster, shaking off soil, and storing during
winter in a cool, moist place. Separate tubers
carefully before planting. These flowers prefer
warm weather.

hybrids *pp. 102, 103, 220*
Although dahlias are officially classed in 14
groups based on flower shape, for gardening
purposes they can be separated into 2 types:
those of medium to tall height with
long-stemmed blossoms used for cutting, and

the dwarf types used for bedding. 1–5 ft.
(0.3–1.5 m) high, depending on the cultivar.
Flowers yellow, red, pink, purple, white,
orange, scarlet, or bicolored, usually 2–4 in.
(5–10 cm) wide, but sometimes to 12 in.
(30 cm). Dwarf varieties available, with
green or bronze leaves. Abundant blooms
from early summer to frost. Parent species
are possibly *D. coccinea* and *D. pinnata*.
Tender perennial treated as a tender annual.

Datura
Potato family
Solanaceae

Dah-toor′ra. A genus of 12–15 species,
ranging from annual weeds to tropical trees,
all with foliage that is malodorous when
crushed.

Description
Leaves alternate, often coarsely but remotely
toothed. Flowers usually trumpet-shaped,
solitary, mostly from the leaf axils. Calyx
with a long tube splitting lengthwise or
across. Corolla with a spreading limb.

How to Grow
Daturas are slow to develop and bloom. For
autumn flowers, start seeds indoors in
midwinter. Germinate at 65–70° F (18.5–
21.0° C). Transplant outdoors in full sun
2–3 weeks after danger of frost is past.
Although they will grow in ordinary soil,
they do best in enriched, moist soil. Will
overwinter where only light frost occurs.
The species below prefer warm weather.

inoxia p. 162
Angel's Trumpet. To 3 ft. (90 cm) high,
spreading, gray-hairy. Flowers white to pink
or lavender, to 8 in. (20 cm) long, tubular.
Sw. U.S. and Mexico. Commonly offered as
D. meteloides. Tender perennial grown as a
tender annual.

Metel p. 217
Horn-of-Plenty; Trumpet Flower; Angel's
Trumpet. To 5 ft. (1.5 m) high. Flowers
7 in. (17.5 cm) long, 4 in. (10 cm) wide,
calyx purple and tubular, corolla white,
violet, or yellow. India. There are
double-flowered varieties, and some have
variously colored flowers, such as the cultivar
'Huberana' with blue, yellow, and red

blossoms. Seeds are poisonous. Tender
annual.

Dianthus
Pink family
Caryophyllaceae

Dy-an'thus. About 300 species of mostly
Eurasian herbs, some important as garden
plants.

Description
Leaves opposite and usually narrow. Joints
swollen. Flowers terminal, usually grouped in
small, often dense, cymes or panicles, but
sometimes solitary. Calyx veiny, with 5
teeth, and often with 2 or more bracts
beneath it. Petals 5 (much doubled in some
horticultural forms), fringed or toothed in
some species, always with a longish basal
shank. Stamens 10.

How to Grow
The species listed below are easy to grow in
any ordinary, well-drained garden soil. Most
prefer full sun. In mild climates, sow seeds
outdoors in the fall. Elsewhere, to get first-
year bloom, start seeds indoors about 8
weeks before last frost. Transplant when
danger of frost is past. Exposure to cold will
help ensure same-season bloom. Plants prefer
cool weather.

Armeria p. 110
Deptford Pink. To 16 in. (40.5 cm) high.
Flowers to ¾ in. (19 mm) long, clustered in
heads, rose-colored with minute white spots,
petals toothed and bearded, bracts resembling
leaves. Cen. and s. Europe to n. Iran.
Naturalized in e. North America. Tolerates
dry soil. Biennial grown as a hardy annual.

barbatus p. 114
Sweet William. 1–2 ft. (30–60 cm) high.
Flowers fragrant, ⅓ in. (8 mm) wide, in
dense heads, red, rose-purple, white, or
varicolored, and in a few forms double-
flowered. Many cultivars, including
'Nanus', a dwarf variety, and 'Auriculiflorus',
with lobed petals. Eurasia and sometimes an
escape in e. U.S. Tolerates light shade.
Mostly a biennial or short-lived perennial,
but many hardy annual types are available.

chinensis p. 252

China Pink; Indian Pink. 12–18 in. (30–45 cm) high, with stems erect and stiffish. Flowers faintly fragrant, red, white, or lilac, solitary or loosely clustered, 1–2 in. (2.5–5.0 cm) wide. Eurasia. Sometimes sold as *D. sinensis* or *D. Seguieri*. Where summers are hot, provide afternoon shade. Biennial or short-lived perennial grown as a half-hardy annual.

Diascia
Snapdragon family
Scrophulariaceae

Dy-ass'see-a. Fifty species of small South African annuals or perennials.

Description
Leaves ovate and mostly opposite. Flowers purplish or reddish, 2-lipped, with 2 spurs.

How to Grow
Start seeds indoors 6–8 weeks before last frost. Move to garden when danger of frost is past. Grow in full sun. Prefers cool, dry climate; not heat-resistant. Thin to stand 6 in. (15 cm) apart. After the first flowers have faded, cut the plants back to 2 in. (5 cm) to encourage new growth and flowers.

Barberae p. 111

Twinspur. 8–15 in. (20–38 cm) high. Flowers irregular, rose-pink with yellow throat dotted with green, ½ in. (13 mm) wide. The plant is showy because of the terminal raceme, which is often 6 in. (15 cm) long. Half-hardy annual.

Digitalis
Snapdragon family
Scrophulariaceae

Di-ji-tay'lis. Of the 19 known species, all Eurasian, only a few are in cultivation; of these, the species below is by far the most important; its leaves yield an important heart remedy.

Description
Erect herbs with alternate leaves, or the lower ones sometimes crowded. Flowers in long, terminal, often 1-sided racemes, very

showy, usually purple, yellow, or white. Corolla more or less bell-shaped at the base, the tube a little inflated, the top slightly 2-lipped. Stamens 4.

How to Grow
Does best in relatively cool, moist climates, especially in coastal New England, Wash., and Oreg. Sow seeds outdoors in late summer through fall where winters are mild. Elsewhere, start seeds indoors 8–10 weeks before the last frost. Harden off seedlings and set out 2–3 weeks before last frost; early transplanting lets good vegetative frame develop before warm weather forces blooming. Grow in full sun, 18 in. (45 cm) apart. Needs afternoon shade in hot climates.

purpurea pp. 95, 96, 97
Annual Foxglove. To 4 ft. (120 cm) high. Flowers 2–3 in. (5.0–7.5 cm) long, hanging, purple but spotted, borne in a 1-sided raceme 1–2 ft. (30–60 cm) long. W. Europe. The finest of the foxgloves; planted in several forms, ranging from white to yellow and from pink to magenta. Some forms to 5 ft. (1.5 m) high. The variety 'Foxy' has been bred for first-year bloom; 'Campanulata' is crowned by a very large bell-shaped blossom, 2 in. (5 cm) or wider; it may not bloom reliably the first year. Biennial or short-lived perennial grown as a hardy annual.

Dimorphotheca
Daisy family
Compositae

Dy-more-fo-thee′ka. The Cape marigolds comprise about 7 species of annual or perennial South African herbs.

Description
Leaves alternate or basal, few-toothed. Flowerheads showy, solitary, and long-stalked. Rays long and strap-shaped, chiefly yellow, orange, or white, the disk flowers yellow, blue, or orange.

How to Grow
Plants need a cool growing season and dry, well-drained soil to produce large blossoms. In areas with mild winters, sow seeds in late summer for fall to winter bloom and again

in late spring. Elsewhere, start seeds indoors 4–6 weeks before last frost. Transplant to site with full sun after danger of frost is past.

pluvialis p. 157
Cape Marigold. To 16 in. (40.5 cm) high. Flowerheads to 2½ in. (6 cm) across, showy, the rays white but purplish below. Some double forms. Tender annual.

sinuata p. 156
To 1 ft. (30 cm) high. Flowerheads to 1½ in. (4 cm) across, showy, the rays yellow to creamy white, sometimes deep violet at base. Tender annual.

Dolichos
Bean family
Leguminosae

Do′li-kos. A large genus of tropical, mostly herbaceous, vines, important in the tropics as food forage plants, but used here only as ornamentals.

Description
Leaves compound, with 3 leaflets. Flowers pealike, showy, often solitary or a few clustered in the leaf axils.

How to Grow
After danger of frost is past, sow seeds in groups of 5; thin to the 3 strongest seedlings. Or start indoors in peat pots 6 weeks before last frost; they resent being transplanted. Provide a fence or latticework for support. Vines are most successful in southern regions and at low, warm elevations in Calif. Prefers warm weather.

Lablab pp. 97, 195
Hyacinth Bean; Bonavist. Vine growing to 30 ft. (9 m) long, but usually about 15 ft. (4.5 m). Leaflets broadly oval, the side ones lopsided, 3–6 in. (7.5–15.0 cm) long. Flowers pinkish purple or white, ¾–1 in. (2.0–2.5 cm) long. Pod flat, 1–2½ in. (2.5–6.0 cm) long, papery, and beaked, the seeds black or white. Old World tropics. Cultivar 'Giganteus' is quite large. Tender perennial grown as a half-hardy annual.

Dorotheanthus
Carpetweed family
Aizoaceae

Dor-o-thee-an'thus. A small genus of succulent herbs native to South Africa and formerly included in *Mesembryanthemum.*

Description
Leaves opposite or alternate, forming rosettes. Flowers solitary, petals few to many, calyx 5-lobed.

How to Grow
Sow seeds outdoors in full sun after danger of frost is past. Tolerates poor, dry soil. Prefers warm weather.

bellidiformis *pp. 100, 243*
Livingstone Daisy. Stems spreading, to 3 in. (7.5 cm) high. Flowers to 2 in. (5 cm) wide, the petals rounded and rose or white. South Africa. Cultivars have pink, red, or orange flowers. Useful as an easy-to-grow ground cover. Tender annual.

Dyssodia
Daisy family
Compositae

Diss-o'di-a. A genus of about 32 strong-scented herbs, native in sw. U.S. and Mexico.

Description
Leaves alternate or opposite, simple or divided. Flowerheads usually with rays, solitary at end of stalk or in slender, 1-sided clusters.

How to Grow
Sow seeds indoors 6–8 weeks before last frost and transplant outdoors when danger of frost is past. If grown in full sun and dry soil, they will produce flowers 4 months after planting. These plants prefer cool weather.

tenuiloba *p. 228*
Dahlberg Daisy. 8–12 in. (20–30 cm) high. Flowerheads 1 in. (2.5 cm) across, with yellow disk flowers and yellow-orange ray flowers. S.-cen. Tex., Mexico. Also called *Thymophylla tenuiloba.* Hardy annual.

Eccremocarpus
Trumpet-creeper family
Bignoniaceae

Ek-krem′o-kar-pus. A small genus of Andean vines, one species of which is grown in warm regions for its showy flowers.

Description
Leaves opposite, twice compound. Flowers showy, in terminal racemes, corolla tubular.

How to Grow
Plants do best in full sun and moist, well-drained soil. In cool climates, choose a site with reflected heat. Start seeds indoors 4–6 weeks before last frost. Transplant to garden 2–3 weeks after danger of frost is past. Use stout strings to support the vines. These plants prefer warm weather.

scaber p. 261
Glory Flower. A stem-climbing, tendril-bearing vine, 8–10 ft. (2.4–3.0 m) long. Flowers orange-red, corolla 1 in. (2.5 cm) long, the limb 2-lipped and slightly irregular. Chile. Cultivar 'Aureus' has golden-yellow flowers, 'Carmineus' is red. Tender perennial grown as a tender annual.

Echinocystis
Cucumber family
Cucurbitaceae

Ee-ky-no-sis′tis. Herbaceous vines, comprising about 25 species from North or South America, only one of garden interest.

Description
Leaves palmately divided with 3–7 lobes. Male flowers in panicles, corolla with 6 lobes. Female flowers solitary or paired in small axils.

How to Grow
Start seeds indoors 4–6 weeks before last frost and transfer to the garden when danger of frost is past. Prefers warm weather.

lobata p. 169
Wild Cucumber; Prickly Cucumber. Stems slender, angled, to 20 ft. (6 m) long. Flowers small, whitish, ¼ in. (6 mm) long. New Brunswick to Saskatchewan, south to Fla. and Tex. This vine grows rapidly and is

often planted to conceal unsightly areas in the yard. Half-hardy annual.

Echium
Borage family
Boraginaceae

Ek'i-um. A genus of over 35 species of Eurasian herbs or shrubby plants, a few grown for ornament.

Description
Rough foliage, with alternate, simple leaves. Flowers showy, blue, in forked or unforked, 1-sided spikes. Corolla funnel- or trumpet-shaped, its limb somewhat oblique. Stamens 5, nearly always protruding.

How to Grow
Sow seeds of this cool-weather wildflower in dry, sandy soil (pH 6.5–7.0) in fall where winters are mild, in early spring elsewhere. Or start indoors 6–8 weeks before last frost. No need to thin.

Lycopsis p. 139
Viper's Bugloss. To 2 ft. (60 cm) high. Flowers ½ in. (13 mm) wide, blue, lavender, purple, rose, or white; corolla of 5 unequal, spreading or erect lobes. S. Europe. Biennial grown as a hardy annual.

Emilia
Daisy family
Compositae

E-mil'i-a. Twenty species of herbs from the Old World tropics, at least 2 of which are pantropical weeds. Related to *Senecio*.

Description
Leaves alternate. Flowerheads small, solitary, or clustered, disk-shaped. Involucre cylindrical or cupped.

How to Grow
Where winters are mild, sow seeds in fall. Elsewhere, sow 2–3 weeks before last frost. Since transplanting is tricky, if you start seeds early indoors, plant in peat pots. Germinate at 60–65° F (15.5–18.5° C). The species below prefers cool weather.

javanica *p. 270*
Tassel Flower. 1–2 ft. (30–60 cm) high.
Flowerheads showy, loosely clustered, ½ in.
(13 mm) in diameter, red or scarlet. Tropics.
'Lutea', a popular cultivar, has yellow
flowers. Good as a cut flower. Hardy annual.

Erodium
Geranium family
Geraniaceae

Ee-ro'di-um. Nearly 60 species of widely
distributed herbs, a few grown for ornament,
some weedy, a few planted for forage in dry
regions, and 2 important as bee plants in
Calif. Commonly called stork's-bill or
heron's-bill.

Description
Leaves generally divided or compound,
feather-fashion. Flowers in auxillary umbels;
sepals and petals 5 each.

How to Grow
Easy to grow in average to dry soil. Sow
seeds in spring after the danger of frost is
past. Prefers cool weather.

cicutarium *p. 88*
Pin-Clover; Alfilaria; Filaree. To 18 in. (45 cm)
high, erect or sprawling. Flowers ¼ in.
(6 mm) wide, purplish or pink, bracts
united. S. Europe, but naturalized in the
U.S. Best known of the heron's-bills, widely
cultivated for forage, and for bees in Calif.; a
serious weed in western states. Hardy annual.

Erysimum
Mustard family
Cruciferae

E-riss'i-mum. A large genus of north
temperate zone herbs, closely related to the
Wallflower (*Cheiranthus*), differing only in
technical characters. Commonly called
blister-cresses.

Description
Somewhat resembling stocks, with yellow,
lilac, or blue flowers, usually in terminal
racemes that lengthen considerably as the
long, 4-sided, usually beaked pods ripen.

How to Grow

Easy to grow in average to dry soil in full sun. The plants are almost like weeds in their ability to withstand unfavorable conditions. They flower profusely, except in excessive heat, and prefer cool weather.

linifolium pp. 113, 144

Alpine Wallflower. 6–18 in. (15–45 cm) high, somewhat prostrate. Flowers ¾ in. (19 mm) long, lilac, mauve, or yellow. Spain. Often sold as *Cheiranthus linifolius.* Adapted only to cool climates. Start seeds very early indoors; transplant outdoors as soon as soil can be worked. Perennial treated as a hardy annual.

Perofskianum p. 204

To 2 ft. (60 cm) high. Flowers ½ in. (13 mm) long, in crowded racemes, yellow or orange, petals and sepals 4 each. Afghanistan and Pakistan. Often sold as *Cheiranthus allionii.* Withstands moderate heat if humidity is not excessive. Sow seeds in fall where winters are mild. Elsewhere, sow as early as soil can be worked in spring. Hardy annual.

Eschscholzia
Poppy family
Papaveraceae

Esh-sholt'zi-a. Very popular garden flowers from w. North America.

Description

Leaves alternate, usually smooth, and finely divided. Flowers solitary, yellow to orange, petals 4. Fruit a slender capsule.

How to Grow

Where winters are mild, sow seeds in fall. Elsewhere, sow in spring as soon as soil can be worked. Little is gained by starting seeds indoors, but if you do so, start them early and under glass. Prefers cool weather.

californica p. 208

California Poppy. 8–12 in. (20–30 cm) high. Flowers long-stalked, solitary, very showy, 3–4 in. (7.5–10.0 cm) wide, orange-yellow, opening in sunshine, each of the 4 petals with a deep-orange spot at the base. Calif. Many cultivars in different colors and some with semidouble blooms. Perennial grown as a hardy annual.

Euphorbia
Spurge family
Euphorbiaceae

You-for'bi-a. Probably over 1600 species of
great variety, ranging from weeds and
tropical, cactuslike succulents to popular
garden annuals. The species below are grown
for their foliage.

Description
Leaves alternate, opposite, or whorled,
sometimes toothed. Flowers have no petals
or sepals but often have showy, highly
colored bracts.

How to Grow
Plants need soil temperatures of 70–75° F
(21–24° C) to germinate. Sow seeds at the
frost-free date; thin to 2 ft. (60 cm) apart.
Where summers are short, start seeds indoors
6 weeks before last frost. The species below
prefer warm weather.

cyathophora p. 186
Annual Poinsettia; Mexican Fire Plant;
Painted Leaf. To 3 ft. (90 cm) high. Leaves
linear, egg-shaped, inverted egg-shaped, or
fiddle-shaped. Upper leaves and bracts
becoming red, or with a patch of red at the
base. Flowers small and yellow-green.
Mexico, widespread in the e. U.S. Usually
grown under misapplied name *E. heterophylla,*
a nearly identical species with bracts green or
purple-spotted, never red. Half-hardy annual.

Lathyris p. 194
Caper Spurge; Mole Plant. Single erect stem
to 3 ft. (90 cm) high. Leaves in 4 ranks,
linear-oblong to oblong lance-shaped, 2–6 in.
(5–15 cm) long. Flowers small, yellow-green,
in loose, leafy-bracted clusters at top of stem.
Fruit with 4 glands, ⅓ in. (8 mm) wide.
Europe. Reputed to repel moles. Biennial
grown as a hardy annual.

marginata p. 182
Snow-on-the-Mountain; Ghostweed. To 3 ft.
(90 cm) high. Lower leaves green, the upper
white-margined. Bracts of the flower cluster
white and very showy. Flowers small and
greenish white. S. Dak. to Tex. Sometimes
sold as *E. variegata.* Its milky juice can be a
skin irritant. Half-hardy annual.

Eustoma
Gentian family
Gentianaceae

You-sto′ma. A small genus of North
American prairie herbs, the species below
cultivated in the garden.

Description
Leaves opposite, ovalish, sometimes
stem-clasping. Flowers solitary or in clusters,
corolla with 5–6 lobes.

How to Grow
Blooms reliably the first year if seeds are
started very early indoors and transplanted
outdoors after last frost. Grow in full sun to
partial shade. Heat-resistant if planted in
moist, well-drained soil. Prefers warm
weather.

grandiflorum *p. 137*
Prairie Gentian; Bluebell. 2–3 ft. (60–90 cm)
high. Flowers pale purple, with dark purple
blotches at the base, usually in a branched
panicle, the corolla nearly bell-shaped,
flaring, 2 in. (5 cm) long and wide. Nebr.
to Colo., south to Tex. and Mexico.
Spectacular cut flower. Also called *Lisianthus
Russellianus.* Cultivars have pink, white, or
lavender flowers; dwarf varieties available.
Biennial grown as a half-hardy annual.

Exacum
Gentian family
Gentianaceae

Ecks′a-kum. A genus of 20 species of herbs
or subshrubs from the Old World tropics,
the species below grown for ornament.

Description
Leaves opposite, mostly stalkless or very
short-stalked, without marginal teeth.
Flowers mildly fragrant, in forked cymes, the
calyx 4- to 5-parted. Corolla more or less
twisted, its lobes usually 5 and blunt or
pointed. Stamens 4–5, attached to the throat
of the corolla.

How to Grow
Seeds need light and temperatures of 60–
65° F (15.5–18.5° C) to germinate. Start
indoors 8 weeks before last frost and set out
2 weeks after last frost. Grow in moist, well-

drained soil. Good as a pot plant in light to moderate shade. Prefers warm weather.

affine p. 147
Persian Violet. 1–2 ft. (30–60 cm) high. Flowers bluish to mauve, ½ in. (13 mm) wide, the corolla lobes pointed. South Yemen. Cultivar 'Atrocaeruleum' has dark lavender flowers. Biennial grown as a tender annual.

Felicia
Daisy family
Compositae

Fe-liss´i-a. A large genus of chiefly South African subshrubs (rarely annuals).

Description
Leaves alternate or opposite, or sometimes in rosettes. Flowerheads showy, usually blue, and radiating.

How to Grow
The species below need cool weather and well-drained, average to dry soil; best suited to West Coast and cool northern gardens. Start seeds indoors in spring. Set out in full sun after danger of frost is past.

amelloides p. 126
Blue Marguerite; Blue Daisy. Bushy shrub, 1–3 ft. (30–90 cm) high. Flowerheads solitary, daisylike, 1 in. (2.5 cm) wide, the numerous rays blue to purple, the small disk flowers yellow. Also sold as *Agathea coelestis*. South Africa. Half-hardy annual.

Bergerana p. 126
Kingfisher Daisy. 4–8 in. (10–20 cm) high. Flowerheads bright blue, solitary, ¾ in. (19 mm) wide. Good for window boxes. South Africa. Half-hardy annual.

Foeniculum
Carrot family
Umbelliferae

Fee-nick´you-lum. Three species of Old World herbs.

Description
Leaves twice-compound, leaflets arranged

feather-fashion. Flowers small, yellow, in
compound umbels.

How to Grow
Sow seeds outdoors in spring or start indoors
4–6 weeks before last frost. Easy to grow in
full sun and ordinary soil. Prefers cool
weather.

vulgare *p. 178*
Common Fennel. Stems 3–5 ft. (0.9–1.5 m)
high, bluish green. Ultimate leaflets
numerous, threadlike. Flowers yellow, small,
15–25 in an umbel. The var. *azoricum*
(Florence, or Sweet, Fennel) has an enlarged
leaf base and, when blanched, is used as
food; widely grown in Calif. The var. *dulce*
(Carosella) is grown for its tender young
edible stems. 'Redform' has plumelike bronze
foliage. Perennial or biennial grown as a
hardy annual.

Fragaria
Rose family
Rosaceae

Fra-gay′ri-a. Strawberry. About 12 species of
stemless plants (except for the long runners)
chiefly found in the north temperate zone.

Description
Leaves compound, the leaflets 3. Flowers
generally white, rarely reddish, in few-
flowered clusters atop a slender stalk. Calyx
5-toothed, the lobes spreading and forming
the hull of the strawberry. Petals 5, mostly
broad and rounded. Stamens many. The
"fruit" is an enlarged, juicy, fleshy receptacle,
upon which are embedded the true fruits,
incorrectly called the "seeds."

How to Grow
Strawberries for ornament should be started
early from seeds sown indoors in late winter;
seeds are tiny and slow to germinate. Shift
seedlings to progressively larger pots. Harden
off and set out after danger of hard frost is
past. These plants prefer cool weather.

vesca *p. 160*
Alpine Strawberry. 9–12 in. (22.5–30.0 cm)
high. Leaves thin and light green. Flower
cluster forking. Flowers ½ in. (13 mm)
wide, white, standing above the foliage. Fruit
small, the hull widely spreading. Europe and

possibly North America. Blooms in the spring. Grown as a border plant. Perennial treated as a hardy annual.

Gaillardia
Daisy family
Compositae

Gay-lar'di-a. Fourteen species of showy North American herbs, some very popular flower garden plants from the w. U.S.

Description
Leafy, erect, branching herbs with alternate or basal leaves that are more or less dotted. Flowerheads extremely handsome, the rays 3-toothed or almost fringed, yellow, orange, orange-red, or white, the head appearing fringed. Disk flowers purple.

How to Grow
Sow seeds outdoors in fall where winters are mild, in early spring elsewhere. Where summers are short, start seeds indoors 6 weeks before last frost. Set out small seedlings when large enough to handle. Grows quickly and blooms precociously. Prefers warm weather.

pulchella pp. 224, 239, 240
Blanket Flower; Indian Blanket. A very showy, popular garden flower, 1–2 ft. (30–60 cm) high. Flowerheads 2–3 in. (5.0–7.5 cm) wide, the rays red with yellow tips, or all red or all yellow. Va. to Fla., west to Colo. and N. Mex. Blooms late spring and summer. Many cultivars, including newer, nearly ball-shaped varieties with blossoms in a wide range of colors and bicolors; dwarf and double forms are available. Hardy annual.

Gaura
Evening primrose family
Onagraceae

Gau'ra. About 20 species of rather coarse, chiefly perennial North and South American herbs, the one below grown for ornament.

Description
Stout herbs with alternate leaves. Flowers white or pink, in terminal spikes or racemes. Calyx tubular, its 4 lobes separate and bent

backward. Petals slightly unequal, separate, the base narrowed into a claw.

How to Grow
The species below is easy to grow in ordinary garden soil. Start indoors 4–6 weeks before last spring frost; transplant outdoors when danger of frost is past. Provide a mulch in cooler climates. Prefers warm weather.

Lindheimeri p. 166
To 4 ft. (120 cm) high. Flowers white aging to rose, petals ½–1 in. (1.3–2.5 cm) long, in open panicles. La. to Tex. and Mexico. Perennial grown as a half-hardy annual.

Gazania
Daisy family
Compositae

Ga-zay′ni-a. Showy South African herbs comprising about 16 species, a few long cultivated for their pretty flowerheads.

Description
Leaves alternate and basal. Flowerheads solitary, long-stalked, closing at night or in cloudy weather. Rays yellow, golden, or white, often with a dark spot at the base, the head thus with a dark eye. Good ground cover or edging plants.

How to Grow
Best adapted to dry desert gardens, where they will endure for months. In hot, humid climates, plants perish soon after first bloom unless given excellent drainage. Start seeds indoors 6–8 weeks before last frost; set out in sunny, dry, well-drained soil after danger of frost is past. Or propagate by basal cuttings taken in late summer. The species below prefers warm weather.

rigens pp. 224, 225
Treasure Flower. To 16 in. (40.5 cm) high, trailing, and branched. Flowerheads 1½ in. (4 cm) wide, the rays orange, yellow, gold, cream, pink, or bronze-red, with a black spot near base. Var. *leucolaena* has unspotted, yellow flowers. Newer varieties include multicolored blossoms, as well as dwarf kinds with large flowers. Flowers close at night. Also sold as *G. splendens.* Tender perennial grown as a tender annual.

Gerbera
Daisy family
Compositae

Ger'ber-ra. A genus of perhaps 70 species of South African or Asiatic, mostly stemless, herbs.

Description
From a basal rosette of leaves arise stout stalks bearing a single daisylike flower.

How to Grow
These plants grow slowly. For first-year bloom, start seeds indoors in late fall or midwinter at 70–75° F (21–24° C). Give light; do not cover with soil. Shift to progressively larger pots, and set out in sunny site when danger of frost is past. Needs cool nights to bloom. Where summers are hot, give afternoon shade and ample moisture. Will overwinter in mild climates if the soil is well drained. Prefers warm weather.

Jamesonii p. 242
Transvaal Daisy; Barberton Daisy. To 1½ ft. (45 cm) high. Flowerheads solitary, 4 in. (10 cm) wide, the rays orange or orange-red in the typical form, but white, yellow, pink, salmon, or violet in cultivars. Transvaal. Perennial grown as a half-hardy annual.

Gilia
Phlox family
Polemoniaceae

Gil'li-a. A genus of nearly 30 species of herbs, most from the w. U.S., a few rather showy garden flowers.

Description
Leaves alternate or opposite, usually without marginal teeth, sometimes dissected or divided. Flowers varied, mostly in clusters. Corolla more or less bell- or funnel-shaped, the stamens attached to the tube of the corolla.

How to Grow
In mild winter climates, sow in the fall, elsewhere in early spring. Plant close together in well-drained to dry soil. The species below prefers cool weather.

capitata p. 123
Queen Anne's Thimble. To 3 ft. (90 cm) high. Flowers light blue or white, in stalked, headlike clusters that are 1 in. (2.5 cm) wide. Wash. to Calif. Hardy annual.

Glaucium
Poppy family
Papaveraceae

Glaw'si-um. Stout herbs native in regions from the Mediterranean to Afghanistan and related to *Argemone* and *Papaver*.

Description
Leaves pinnately lobed, forming a basal rosette. The flowers are solitary, yellow or red, with 2 sepals and 4 petals.

How to Grow
Sow seeds outdoors in fall where winters are mild, or as soon as the ground can be worked elsewhere. The species below prefer cool weather.

corniculatum p. 253
Horned Poppy. To 18 in. (45 cm) high. Flowering stalk usually shorter than the leaves. Flowers 2 in. (5 cm) wide, orange to red, with a black spot at the base of the petals. Europe and sw. Asia. Does not transplant well. Also sold as *G. grandiflorum*. Hardy annual.

flavum p. 202
Sea Poppy; Horned Poppy. Branching, 2–3 ft. (60–90 cm) high. Flowers solitary, long-stalked, orange-yellow, to 2 in. (5 cm) wide. Stamens numerous. Mediterranean region; naturalized in e. North America. Biennial grown as a hardy annual.

Gomphrena
Amaranth family
Amaranthaceae

Gom-free'na. A genus of about 100 tropical herbs related to *Alternanthera* and *Iresine*.

Description
Leaves opposite, oblong or elliptical, with

minutely hairy margins. Flowers in dense, chaffy heads.

How to Grow
Truly resistant to heat and humidity. Start seeds indoors 6–8 weeks before last frost and set out as soon as danger of frost is past. To harvest for drying, cut blossoms before they begin to elongate. Prefers warm weather.

globosa p. 108
Globe Amaranth. 8–20 in. (20–50 cm) high, superficially resembling a clover. Flowers 1 in. (2.5 cm) wide, in long-stalked, cloverlike heads of red, pink, white, or orange, without petals. Old World tropics. Many cultivars. The fine blooms are excellent for drying. Tender annual.

Gypsophila
Pink family
Caryophyllaceae

Jip-sof'fill-a. A genus of 125 handsome, small-flowered herbs, chiefly Eurasian, known generally as baby's-breath for the profusion of mostly small flowers.

Description
Leaves small, bluish green, opposite. Joints slightly swollen. Flowers numerous, usually in profuse branched panicles. Calyx 5-toothed. Petals 5, sometimes toothed, usually with a minute claw. Stamens 10.

How to Grow
Sow seeds in fall where winters are mild, early spring elsewhere. For a steady supply of blossoms for cutting, start replacement crops every 30 days except during the hottest part of the summer. Plant in full sun. Where the summer sun is intense, give afternoon shade. Blooms best with some lime added to soil and if somewhat crowded, so do not thin too much. Prefers cool weather.

elegans p. 167
Annual Baby's-Breath. Upright, forking, 10–18 in. (25–45 cm) high. Flowers small, ¼–1 in. (0.6–2.5 cm) wide, long-stalked, white or pinkish, petals slightly notched. Caucasus to n. Iran. Many cultivars, including 'Carminea', with carmine-rose flowers; 'Grandiflora Alba', with larger, white flowers; 'Purpurea', with purple flowers; and

'Rosea', with rose-pink flowers. Hardy
annual.

Hedysarum
Pea family
Leguminosae

Hed-i-sar′rum. A large genus of chiefly Old
World herbs, perhaps a dozen of its 150
species found in North America.

Description
Herbs or subshrubs with compound leaves,
the leaflets arranged feather-fashion with an
odd one at the tip. Flowers small, pealike,
mostly in showy racemes.

How to Grow
Easy to grow in well-drained soil. Start seeds
indoors 6–8 weeks before last spring frost.
Prefers cool weather.

coronarium p. 261
French Honeysuckle; Sulla Clover. Bushy,
2–4 ft. (60–120 cm) high. Flowers to ¾ in.
(19 mm) long, red, fragrant, densely
crowded in spikes or racemes from leaf axils.
Europe. Blooms first year. A white-flowered
variety is also offered. Perennial grown as a
hardy annual.

Helianthus
Daisy family
Compositae

He-li-an′thus. Rather coarse, hardy herbs
comprising about 150 species, found mostly
in North America. They are very diverse in
size and character, since they readily
hybridize in their natural surroundings.

Description
Varied rootstocks, some thick, woody, and
compact; some thick, woody, and spreading;
others tuberous. Leaves alternate, sometimes
opposite above, the margins usually coarsely
toothed. Flowers in terminal heads, 3–12 in.
(7.5–30.0 cm) across.

How to Grow
Sow seeds outdoors when danger of frost is
past ½ in. (13 mm) deep in average to dry
soil. Thin to stand 18 in. (45 cm) apart.

These aggressive sunflowers inhibit all nearby plant growth. They prefer warm weather.

annuus pp. 155, 230, 240

Common Sunflower. To 12 ft. (3.5 m) high. Flowers in heads to 1 ft. (30 cm) or more across, white, many shades of yellow, orange, chestnut, maroon, or bicolored, the disk flowers purplish brown. Minn. to Wash. and Calif. Small-flowered dwarf forms and double-flowered varieties. Hardy annual.

Helichrysum
Daisy family
Compositae

Hell-i-kry′zum. A well-known group of everlastings comprising over 300 species from the Old World.

Description
Herbs or shrubs with chiefly alternate leaves without marginal teeth. Flowerheads wholly of disk flowers, the parts chaffy, mostly yellow, and maintaining their color long after drying. The bracts of the involucre beneath the heads are colored and almost petal-like.

How to Grow
Start plants indoors 6–8 weeks before last frost. Or, where summers are long, sow seeds outdoors after last frost. In sandy soil, plants will self-seed.The species below prefer warm weather.

bracteatum p. 244

Strawflower; Everlasting. 2–3 ft. (60–90 cm) high. Bracts of involucre red, yellow, orange, or white. Disk flowers yellow, red, salmon, purple, white, rose, or orange, 1–2 in. (2.5–5.0 cm) wide. Australia. Good cut or dried flower. Varieties include 'Monstrosum', with larger heads, and several dwarf forms, to 1 ft. (30 cm) high, including the 'Bikini' cultivars. Half-hardy annual.

petiolatum p. 183

Licorice Plant. To 4 ft. (120 cm) high. Woody at base, stems woolly, slender shoots vinelike, leaves to 1½ in. (4 cm) long, ovalish, woolly. Flowerheads (lacking in some cultivars) in branching clusters to 2 in. (5 cm) across, disk flowers yellow, bracts of involucre cream-white. South Africa. Chiefly

a foliage plant. Also sold as *H. lanatum* or
Gnaphalium lanatum. Half-hardy annual.

Heliotropium
Borage family
Boraginaceae

He-li-o-tro′pi-um. Over 200 species of mainly
tropical or subtropical herbs, some woody,
one a widely cultivated garden plant grown
for its fragrant flowers.

Description
Leaves mostly alternate, usually hairy.
Flowers small, borne in forking, usually
1-sided cymes. Calyx tubular, as long as the
corolla in some species. Corolla tubular,
stamens not protruding from it.

How to Grow
Start seeds indoors 10–12 weeks before last
frost; germinate at 70–75° F (21–24° C). Set
in the garden 2–3 weeks after danger of frost
is past. Plant in full sun; where summers are
hot, afternoon shade is needed. Will grow in
average soil, but does best in rich soil.
Prefers warm weather.

arborescens p. 145
Common Heliotrope; Cherry Pie. 2–4 ft.
(60–120 cm) high. Flowers small, purple,
violet, or white, to ¼ in. (6 mm) long,
strongly vanilla-scented. Peru. Also sold as
H. peruvianum. Tender perennial grown as a
tender annual.

Helipterum
Daisy family
Compositae

Hell-lip′ter-rum. An important group of
more than 60 species of garden everlastings
from South Africa and Australia, widely
grown for dried bouquets.

Description
Leaves alternate, often white-felty, without
marginal teeth. Flowerheads wholly of disk
flowers, generally yellow, chaffy, and
maintaining their color for long periods.
Bracts of the involucre below the flowerhead
are green or petal-like and white, yellow, or
rose-pink.

How to Grow
Sow seeds in late spring, but where summers
are short, start indoors 6–8 weeks before last
frost. Transplant outdoors when the soil is
warm. Grows best in full sun and sandy soil.
Prefers warm weather.

roseum p. 100
Strawflower. To 2 ft. (60 cm) high.
Flowerheads usually solitary, to 2 in. (5 cm)
wide, bracts of involucre white or rose-
colored. Australia. Also sold as *Acroclinium
roseum.* Not heat-resistant. Tender annual.

Hibiscus
Mallow family
Malvaceae

Hy-bis′kus. An important genus of over 250
species of herbs, shrubs, and trees, with
many popular garden annuals.

Description
Leaves alternate, with veins arranged finger-
fashion, sometimes lobed or parted. Flowers
usually large, generally bell-shaped, with 5
petals and sepals, or sometimes the sepals
united to form a 5-toothed calyx. Stamens
united in a tubular structure that surrounds
the style. Often a series of bracts beneath
the calyx.

How to Grow
Start seeds indoors at 70–75° F (21–24° C)
8–10 weeks before last frost. After danger of
frost is past, set in the garden in average to
moist but not soggy soil. The species below
prefer warm weather.

Acetosella p. 189
To 5 ft. (1.5 m) high. Leaves variable, lobed
or unlobed, green and red or all red. Flowers
solitary, yellow or purple-red, 2½ in. (6 cm)
wide, in angle between leaf and stem. E.
Africa. Blooms 10 months after germination.
Cultivar 'Red Shield' has red leaves. Grown
for hedges, bedding, or as a pot plant.
Half-hardy annual.

Moscheutos pp. 163, 218
Rose Mallow; Swamp Mallow; Sea
Hollyhock. 3–8 ft. (0.9–2.4 m) high. Flowers
4–7 in. (10.0–17.5 cm) wide, creamy white
or pink, with no eye; wilting within an hour
when picked. Brackish marshes, Mass. to Va.;

rarely, in fresh marshes westward to Ill. Many cultivars, including new dwarf forms with huge flowers. Nick seeds before sowing and place in soil that is rich in organic matter. Perennial grown as a half-hardy annual.

Trionum p. 220
Flower-of-an-Hour. 1½–4 ft. (45–120 cm) high. Flowers solitary, pale yellow or yellowish white, with a dark eye, 1–1½ in. (2.5–4 cm) wide, in angle between leaf and stem. Old World tropics, naturalized elsewhere. Sometimes self-sows. Half-hardy annual.

Hordeum
Grass family
Gramineae

Hor'dee-um. About 25 species of grasses widely distributed in temperate regions, including Barley.

Description
Leaves flat, grasslike, terminal. Flower clusters more or less cylindrical. Spikes mostly dense, with conspicuous awns, the individual spikelets 1-flowered, 3 of the spikelets at each node of the jointed stalk. Due to the infertility of some spikes, the resulting cluster may be 2-rowed or 4-rowed.

How to Grow
In early spring work up the soil and lay down a 2–3 ft. (60–90 cm) square of clear plastic secure the edges with soil. Cut 6-in. (15-cm) crosses, and plant seeds where they can grow through the slits. Cover plastic with dried grass clippings to shade out weeds. Plants prefer warm weather.

jubatum p. 173
Squirrel-Tail Grass; Squirrel-Tail Barley. 12–30 in. (30–75 cm) high, mostly unbranched. Spikes 4 in. (10 cm) long, light green to silvery to golden tan, awns slender and to 3 in. (7.5 cm) long. North and South America; Siberia. Can be a troublesome weed if not controlled. Perennial treated as a hardy annual.

Humulus
Hemp family
Cannabinaceae

Hew'mew-lus. Three species of rough-
stemmed vines, called hops, natives of the
north temperate zone.

Description
Leaves opposite, more or less lobed. Male
and female flowers green, on separate plants.
Male flowers in catkinlike racemes, with a
5-parted calyx, no petals, 5 stamens. Female
flowers in pairs beneath large bracts, which
at maturity form a conelike body that
contains lupulin, used in beer-making.

How to Grow
Sow seeds outdoors after danger of frost is
past. Or start indoors 6 weeks before last
frost and transplant when soil is warm. Place
in average, well-drained soil in full sun.
These rampant vines need sturdy, tall
supports and adequate water. They prefer
warm weather.

japonicus p. 196
Japanese Hops. Stem-climbing vine, 10–20 ft.
(3–6 m) long. Leaves rough, deeply 5- to
7-lobed, the lobes coarsely toothed, the stalk
as long as the blade. Male flowers small,
light green, in long, hanging clusters to 10
in. (25 cm) long. E. Asia. Cultivars include
'Variegatus', with white-streaked foliage, and
'Lutescens', with golden leaves. Also sold as
H. scandens. Perennial grown as a half-hardy
annual.

Hunnemannia
Poppy family
Papaveraceae

Hun-nee-man-i'a. A single species related to
Eschscholzia, but with 2 separate sepals.

Description
Leaves bluish green and dissected into blunt,
narrow segments. Flowers showy, with 4
petals and 2 sepals.

How to Grow
Where winters are mild, sow seeds in fall.
Elsewhere, sow in spring as soon as soil can
be worked. Choose well-drained, average to
dry soil in full sun. Little is gained by

starting seeds indoors, but if you do so, start them early and under glass. Plants prefer warm weather.

fumariifolia p. 209
Mexican Tulip Poppy; Gold Cup. 12–24 in. (30–60 cm) high. Flowers 2–3 in. (5.0–7.5 cm) wide, yellow; stamens many, orange, showy. Mexico. Perennial grown as a half-hardy annual.

Hyoscyamus
Potato family
Solanaceae

Hy-o-sy′a-mus. Very poisonous or medicinal herbs from the Mediterranean region.

Description
Leaves coarsely toothed. Corolla funnel-shaped, whitish or yellowish.

How to Grow
Easy to grow. Sow seeds outdoors after danger of frost is past. Somewhat weedy. Prefers cool weather.

niger p. 164
Henbane; Black Henbane; Stinking Nightshade. Bad-smelling, poisonous herb, 1–2 ft. (30–60 cm) high. Flowers funnel-shaped, to 1¼ in. (3 cm) long, greenish yellow to creamy, purple-veined, nearly stalkless in leaf axils, or the upper ones in a small leafy cluster. Eurasia. Naturalized in e. North America. Hardy annual.

Iberis
Mustard family
Cruciferae

Eye-beer′is. About 30 species of garden plants, mostly from the Mediterranean region.

Description
Leaves divided or undivided, alternate. Flowers in flat-topped or finger-shaped clusters, the 4 petals separate. Sometimes the outer flowers of a cluster are sterile.

How to Grow
Sow seeds outdoors in late summer in areas with mild winters, or in very early spring

where winters are severe. Place in full sun and thin to 1 ft. (30 cm) apart. Blooms about 6 weeks after germination and keeps on blooming until frost. The species below prefer cool weather.

amara p. 166
Rocket Candytuft. More or less erect, to 1 ft. (30 cm) high. Flowers ½–1 in. (1.3–2.5 cm) wide, fragrant, white, in clusters that gradually elongate. Europe. Often a winter crop along the Gulf Coast and at lower elevations in Calif. In warm climates, provide midday shade. Many forms available, some dwarf. Hardy annual.

pinnata p. 153
To 1 ft. (30 cm) high. Flowers white to lilac, fragrant, in dense, convex clusters, to 1 in. (2.5 cm) wide; petals small and irregular. S. Europe. Hardy annual.

umbellata p. 115
Globe Candytuft; Annual Candytuft. More or less erect, 8–16 in. (20.0–40.5 cm) high. Flowers small, in dense umbels 2 in. (5 cm) across, pink, red, lilac, or violet, not fragrant. Europe. Widely adapted for late spring bloom. Hardy annual.

Impatiens
Balsam family
Balsaminaceae

Im-pay'shens. Nearly 500 species of tender, succulent plants, widely distributed in Asia, tropical Africa, and North America.

Description
Simple leaves, alternate, opposite, or whorled. Flowers irregular, spurred, solitary or clustered in leaf axils.

How to Grow
Start *I. Balsamina* and *I. Wallerana* from seeds sown indoors 6–8 weeks before last frost at 70–75° F (21–24° C). Do not cover seeds with soil; they need light to sprout. Stretch clear plastic over the seed flat. Transplant seedlings to the garden or to containers 2 weeks after danger of frost is past. Both also propagated by cuttings. 'New Guinea' can only be started from cuttings or nursery-grown seedlings. All 3 species prefer warm weather.

Balsamina p. 255

Garden Balsam; Lady's Slipper. 24–30 in.
(60–75 cm) tall, stiff, and erect. Flowers
1–2 in. (2.5–5.0 cm) wide, some very double
or "camellia-flowered," in salmon-pink, old
rose, scarlet, yellow, purple, or white.
Subtropical India and China. Does well in
sunny or lightly shaded gardens. Tender
annual.

'New Guinea' *pp. 81, 251*

Very showy, 1–2 ft. (30–60 cm) high. Leaves
variegated. Flowers extra-large, red to pinkish
purple, 2–2½ in. (5–6 cm) wide. New
Guinea. Some varieties require full sun.
Tender annual.

Wallerana pp. 80, 251

Busy Lizzy; Patient Lucy; Patience Plant;
Sultana. Brittle, 1–2 ft. (30–60 cm) high.
Flowers solitary or 2–3 on a short, slender
stalk, 1–2 in. (2.5–5.0 cm) wide. Bright
scarlet in original form, but hybrids are red,
pink, orange, salmon, purple, white, or
variegated. Tanzania to Mozambique. Where
summers are hot, this species needs light to
moderate shade. Good houseplant. Tender
perennial grown as a tender annual.

Ionopsidium
Mustard family
Cruciferae

Eye-on-op-sid′i-um. A few species of annual
herbs, related to *Aethionema* and *Iberis*.

Description
Leaves basal, in rosettes, nearly round.
Inflorescence leafy at the base; 4 sepals and 4
petals.

How to Grow
Sow seeds outdoors in fall where winters are
severe, early spring elsewhere. Will grow in
full sun to partial shade. Prefers cool
weather; not heat-resistant. Do not thin.

acaule p. 90

Diamond Flower. Creeping plant, to 3 in.
(7.5 cm) high. Flowers solitary, ¼ in.
(6 mm) wide, purple, pinkish violet, or
white, on slender threadlike stalks 3–4 in.
(7.5–10.0 cm) long. Portugal. Hardy annual.

Ipomoea
Morning glory family
Convolvulaceae

Ip-po-mee′a. Mostly twining vines, many of
the 500 species of tropical origin and a few
of garden importance, including the
Common Morning Glory.

Description
Leaves alternate, generally stalked, simple, or
compound, with several leaflets. Flowers
large and showy, usually solitary or a few in
leaf axils. Calyx lobed or parted. Corolla
chiefly funnel-shaped (rarely, bell-shaped),
more or less 5-pointed or 5-angled at the top.
Stigma club-shaped or 2-lobed.

How to Grow
Sow seeds in any garden soil. To hasten
germination, notch these very hard seeds or
soak them in tepid water for 8 hours. Or
spread seeds on or just under wet sand in a
closed bell jar or empty aquarium kept at
about 80° F (26.5° C) with an electric bulb.
These plants prefer warm weather.

alba p. 163
Moon-Flower. Milky-juiced vine, 8–10 ft.
(2.4–3.0 m) long, with somewhat prickly
stems. Flowers white, sometimes green-
banded, fragrant, 5–6 in. (12.5–15.0 cm)
wide. Opens at night. Tropical America and
in s. Fla. Tender perennial grown as a tender
annual.

coccinea p. 263
Star Ipomoea. To 10 ft. (3 m) long. Flowers
1½ in. (4 cm) long, corolla scarlet with
yellow throat. Tropical America; naturalized
in the southern states. Also sold as *Quamoclit
coccinea.* Tender annual.

× *multifida* p. 262
Cardinal Climber. 8–10 ft. (2.4–3.0 m) long.
Flowers to 2 in. (5 cm) long, corolla
crimson or scarlet, with a white to cream-
colored eye. Hybrid derived from *I. coccinea*
and *I. Quamoclit.* Tender annual.

Nil p. 83
Morning Glory. To 10 ft. (3 m) long.
Flowers 4 in. (10 cm) wide, purple, blue,
red, or pink, often double, corolla fluted or
fringed. Tropical America. Also sold as *I.
imperialis,* the Imperial Japanese Morning

Glory, with flowers that are large, bright-colored, and variously striped or margined. Roots can be dug up in fall and stored. Tender perennial grown as a tender annual.

purpurea p. 134
Common Morning Glory. To 10 ft. (3 m) long. Flowers nearly 3–5 in. (7.5–12.5 cm) long, purple, pink, or blue, the tube paler. Tropical America. Cultivar 'Alba' has white flowers; 'Huberi' has silver-white leaf markings; 'Violacea' has double violet-purple flowers. Hardy annual.

Quamoclit p. 263
Cypress-Vine. To 20 ft. (6 m) long. Flowers scarlet, funnel-shaped, 5-lobed, to 1½ in. (4 cm) long. Tropical America, naturalized in the South and planted in Calif. Also sold as *Quamoclit pennata.* Tender annual.

tricolor p. 135
Morning Glory. To 10 ft. (3 m) long. Flowers purplish-blue, 4–5 in. (10–12.5 cm) long, corolla with white tube and red tip before opening. Cultivars with flowers white, lavender, and various shades of blue. Tropical America. Tender perennial grown as a tender annual.

Ipomopsis
Phlox family
Polemoniaceae

Ip-po-mop'sis. Herbs mostly native in w. North America, with one species in Argentina.

Description
Leaves to 2 in. (5 cm) long, dissected into linear segments, on erect stems. Corolla generally tubular; calyx 5-lobed.

How to Grow
Easy to grow in well-drained soil but will tolerate dryness. Where winters are mild, sow seeds in fall. Elsewhere, plant in spring after danger of hard frost is past. Established plants may naturalize. The species below prefer cool weather.

aggregata p. 168
Skyrocket. To 2 ft. (60 cm) high. Flowers trumpet-shaped, 1 in. (2.5 cm) long, fragrant, fiery red, golden yellow, pink,

whitish, or red with yellow mottling, in a long cluster. W. North America. Also sold as *Gilia aggregata.* Half-hardy biennial grown as a hardy annual.

rubra p. 265
Standing Cypress. Usually 2–3 ft. (60–90 cm) high in garden, but can reach 6 ft. (1.8 m) high. Flowers very showy, tubelike, 2 in. (5 cm) long, scarlet outside, yellow with red dots inside, in a narrow panicle. S. U.S. Biennial grown as a half-hardy annual.

Iresine
Amaranth family
Amaranthaceae

Eye-re-sy'ne. Seventy known species, chiefly tropical, the species below grown for its ornamental foliage and used mostly as a summer-bedding plant.

Description
Leaves opposite, stalked, generally ovalish. Flowers, rarely produced, woolly, chaffy or membranous, small, whitish, crowded in dense spikes that are gathered in branched panicles.

How to Grow
Easy to grow in full sun in average soil. Will tolerate wet soil but cannot survive frost. Propagate by cuttings wintered in the house or greenhouse. Prefers warm weather.

Herbstii p. 188
Bloodleaf. To 6 ft. (1.8 m) high. Leaves 4–5 in. (10.0–12.5 cm) long, generally purplish red or green, yellow-veined, notched at the tip. Flowers small, white, usually nonexistent in the North. Cultivar 'Aureo-Reticulata' has green leaves with yellow veins; 'Jepson' has brownish-purple leaves with red veins. South America. Tender perennial grown as a tender annual.

Kochia
Goosefoot family
Chenopodiaceae

Ko'ki-a. Eighty species, chiefly Eurasian, one widely cultivated and valued for its bushy, brilliantly colored foliage.

Description
Leaves alternate and narrow. Flowers small, solitary or clustered, growing in leaf axils.

How to Grow
The species below is difficult to transplant except in peat pots or as small seedlings. Where summers are long, sow outdoors after danger of frost is past. For short-season gardens, start seeds indoors 8 weeks before last frost. Grow in full sun. Prefers warm weather.

scoparia var. *tricophylla* p. 179
Summer Cypress; Burning Bush; Belvedere; Firebush. 2–5 ft. (0.6–1.5 m) high, bushy, sometimes nearly globe-shaped. Leaves extremely numerous, alternate, often hairy, very narrow, red, green, or yellow, turning purple-red in the fall. Flowers greenish, inconspicuous. S. Europe to Japan. Maintains leaf color all summer. Self-sows in the South and is apt to become weedy. Causes hay fever. Half-hardy annual.

Lagenaria
Cucumber family
Cucurbitaceae

Laj-en-a'ri-a. A small genus of herbaceous vines, native in the tropics of the Old World and South America, related to the melons.

Description
Leaves broadly heart-shaped to ovate, with irregular margins. Flowers solitary, white, male flowers with long pedicle, female flower with ovary below petals.

How to Grow
Where summers are long, sow seeds outdoors. Elsewhere, start seeds indoors 6 weeks before last frost; they sprout in 7–10 days. Harden off and protect seedlings from wind and frost damage. Since vines ramble, plant them where they can be trained up into a tree, over an outbuilding, or over a large, sturdy arbor. Prefers warm weather.

siceraria p. 192
White-flowered Gourd; Calabash Gourd. A musky-scented, quick-growing vine to 30 ft. (9 m) long, grown for its fruit. Sticky-hairy stem and branched tendrils. Leaves green, alternate, broadly oval or kidney-shaped,

6–10 in. (15–25 cm) wide. Flowers rather showy, usually withering by midday, 2–4 in. (5–10 cm) wide, petals 5. Fruit 3–36 in. (7.5–90.0 cm) long, very variable: round or flattish; crooknecked; bottle-, dipper-, dumbbell- or club-shaped. Needs heat and a long growing season to produce fruit. Also called *L. vulgaris* or *L. leucantha.* Tender annual.

Lagurus
Grass family
Gramineae

Lag-you′rus. A single species of annual grass of the Mediterranean region, grown for dried bouquets. Related to *Agrostis.*

Description
An erect grass, its narrow, grasslike leaves softly hairy. The flowering cluster in an oblongish head.

How to Grow
Although this species can be sown outdoors 3 weeks before the last spring frost, seedlings may become lost among weeds. Instead, start seeds indoors, 3–5 seeds per pot, 8 weeks before last frost. Transplant in clumps for best landscape effect. Requires full sun. Prefers warm weather.

ovatus p. 172
Hare's-Tail Grass. To 12 in. (30 cm) high. Flowering cluster off-white, 1¼ in. (3 cm) long, composed of many 1-flowered spikelets, all softly woolly, with slender, protruding awns ½ in. (13 mm) long. Hardy annual.

Lamarckia
Grass family
Gramineae

La-mark′i-a. A single species of annual grass of the Mediterranean region, commonly grown for its handsome spikelets. Related to *Briza* and *Poa.*

Description
A tufted grass, with numerous flat, grasslike leaves. Spikelets crowded in dense, drooping clusters.

How to Grow

Easy to grow when sown outdoors in early spring. To discourage other grasses and weeds, and to keep drooping heads clean for cutting, cut squares of black plastic 2 ft. × 2 ft. (60 cm × 60 cm) and sink edges in prepared soil. Cut 6-in. (15-cm) crosses, and plant seeds where they can grow through slits. You can hide the plastic with dried grass clippings. This species prefers warm weather.

aurea p. 174

Golden Top. To 18 in. (45 cm) high. Leaves soft to the touch, sheaths inflated. Spikelets golden yellow or violet, grouped in a 1-sided cluster 1–3 in. (2.5–7.5 cm) long. Sometimes sold as *Achyrodes*. Hardy annual.

Lantana
Verbena family
Verbenaceae

Lan-ta′na. Tropical or subtropical shrubs, one of the 155 species grown for its profuse bloom.

Description

Very ornamental. Leaves usually opposite. Stem usually hairy, sometimes prickly. Flowers small, borne in dense spikes or heads that may be terminal. Calyx minute. Corolla tubular, 4- to 5-parted, slightly irregular, but not 2-lipped. Stamens 4.

How to Grow

In the North, start seeds indoors in late winter; germination takes 8 weeks. Elsewhere, sow outdoors. Soft wood cuttings root easily. *Lantana* prefers warm weather.

Camara pp. 258, 259

Yellow Sage; Red Sage. To 4 ft. (120 cm) high. Flower clusters 1–2 in. (2.5–5.0 cm) wide, flat-topped. Flowers ⅓ in. (8 mm) wide, yellow at first, then orange or red to lavender, sometimes all colors in a single cluster. Tropical America north to Tex. and Fla. Abundant flowers. Foliage unpleasantly scented. Many cultivars available, including 'Alba', which has white flowers. Perennial grown as a half-hardy annual.

montevidensis p. 116
Weeping Lantana. A vinelike shrub trailing to 3 ft. (90 cm) long. Flowers pink-lilac in clusters 1 in. (2.5 cm) wide. South America. Perennial grown as a half-hardy annual.

Lathyrus
Pea family
Leguminosae

La'thi-russ. An important group of over 100 species chiefly from the north temperate zone, several widely grown for ornament.

Description
Most cultivated species are tendril-bearing, vinelike plants, usually with winged or angled stems. Leaves alternate, compound, the leaflets usually few. Flowers typically pealike, often showy, especially in the cultivated strains of the Sweet Pea. Fruit a flattish pod.

How to Grow
For the species below, sow seeds as soon as the soil can be worked. Only a short show of color can be enjoyed before very hot weather kills the vine. To lengthen the season, apply a mulch of clear plastic over the prepared soil in late winter. Plant seeds through small slits in the plastic, 4–5 seeds every 1 ft. (30 cm); cover with soil ½ in. (13 mm) deep. When plants are ankle high, spread grass clippings over the plastic to shade out weeds. Provide support for the tall types. In areas with mild winters, plant in late fall for spring bloom. Winter bloom only in very protected areas in the West and coastal Fla. Prefers cool weather.

odoratus p. 109
Sweet Pea. Vinelike, 4–6 ft. (1.2–1.8 m) long. Flowers fragrant, 3–5 (rarely 7), often 2 in. (5 cm) wide, in clusters; many colors now cultivated, perhaps originally only purple. Pod 2 in. (5 cm) long, hairy. Italy. About 50 cultivars, including compact, nonclimbing dwarfs, early flowering types, and some heat-resistant varieties. Hardy annual.

Lavatera
Mallow family
Malvaceae

La-va-tee′ra. Tree Mallow. A genus of 25 species of herbs mostly from the warmer regions of the Old World, a few grown in the flower garden.

Description
Stems hairy. Leaves alternate, somewhat maple-like, angled or lobed. Flowers rather showy, pink or purplish, below them a cluster of 3–9 bracts, united to form an involucre. Petals 5, notched or cut off at the tip, the base with a claw.

How to Grow
The species below do well in full sun and well-drained, enriched garden soil. They prefer cool weather.

arborea pp. *86, 137*
Tree Mallow. Tree or shrublike plant 4–10 ft. (1.2–3.0 m) high. Flowers 2 in. (5 cm) wide, pale to dark purplish red, veined at the base, in profuse, short, leafy racemes. Europe. Cultivar 'Variegata' has white-mottled leaves. Sow seeds in late summer. Or start indoors in late winter and transplant after last frost for first-season bloom. Plants will overwinter and bloom the following season, except where winters are severe or soil is poorly drained. Biennial grown as a hardy annual.

trimestris p. *87*
2–3 ft. (60–90 cm) high. Flowers usually solitary, to 4 in. (10 cm) wide, red, rose-pink, or white, very showy. Mediterranean region. Cultivar 'Splendens' has large rose-red or white flowers. Sow seeds in early spring. For heavy flowering, plant in dry, moderately rich soil. Hardy annual.

Layia
Daisy family
Compositae

Lay′i-a. A genus of mostly Californian herbs, comprising about 15 species, 2 grown for their showy flowerheads.

Description
Leaves alternate, generally without marginal teeth. Flowerheads solitary, stalks terminal. Ray flowers handsome, 8–20, yellow or white, and 3-toothed. Disk flowers tubular.

How to Grow
Where winters are severe, sow seeds in early spring for a good show of color before hot weather begins. Barely cover the seeds and firm them into prepared, well-drained soil. In Calif., sow seeds at the end of the summer dry season. The species below prefers cool weather and will bloom after frost.

platyglossa p. 229
Tidy-Tips. 1–2 ft. (30–60 cm) high in the wild, usually less in cultivation. Flowerheads showy, 2 in. (5 cm) wide, ray flowers usually yellow tipped with white. Calif. Hardy annual.

Limnanthes
False mermaid family
Limnanthaceae

Lim-nan'theez. A genus of 7 species of w. North American herbs, one of which is cultivated in the flower garden.

Description
Leaves alternate, dissected. Flowers solitary, sepals and petals 3–5 each, usually notched at tip.

How to Grow
In Calif. and the Deep South, sow seeds just before the fall rains; seedlings will bloom early the following summer. Where winters are severe, sow in very early spring in moist but well-drained soil. This species prefers cool weather.

Douglasii p. 201
Meadow Foam; Marsh Flower. 4–12 in. (10–30 cm) high, usually branching from the base. Flowers long-stalked, fragrant, nearly 1 in. (2.5 cm) wide, white, or yellowish toward the base. Oreg. and Calif. Hardy annual.

Limonium
Plumbago family
Plumbaginaceae

Ly-mo'ni-um. Sea Lavender; Sea Pink. About 150 species, several widely grown for cutting and for dried flowers.

Description
Leaves mostly basal, often tufted. Flowers small, numerous, in open, loose panicles or in branching spikes, prevailingly lavender, rose-pink, or bluish, but sometimes yellow or white. Calyx tubular, often membranous or colored. Corolla of 5 nearly separate and often clawed petals.

How to Grow
Start indoors in peat pots 8 weeks before last spring frost. Difficult to transplant unless plants are small. They prefer somewhat sandy soil and warm weather.

sinuatum p. 266
Statice. 12–30 in. (30–75 cm) high. Flowers blue, lavender, rose, red, salmon, yellow, or white, ⅜ in. (9 mm) wide, in panicles of 3- to 5-winged branches. Mediterranean to Asia Minor. Many hybrids available. Biennial grown as a tender annual.

Linaria
Snapdragon family
Scrophulariaceae

Ly-nay'ri-a. About 100 species from the north temperate zone, a few grown for ornament.

Description
Slender herbs with opposite or whorled leaves, the upper ones sometimes alternate. Flowers usually showy, in terminal spikes or racemes, corolla irregular, 2-lipped, with a long tube, and long-spurred. Stamens 4.

How to Grow
Sow seeds in very early spring. Seedlings are small and need careful weeding. Where winters are mild, plant seeds in well-drained, average soil in early fall. Will naturalize in poor soil if grasses don't compete aggressively. Prefers cool weather.

maroccana p. 110
Toadflax. To 18 in. (45 cm) high. Flowers
½ in. (13 mm) long, red- or violet-purple,
with yellow spotted lower lip. Morocco.
Cultivars in many colors. Hardy annual.

Linum
Flax family
Linaceae

Ly'num. Flax. Nearly 200 species of herbs,
grown for ornament, except for Common
Flax, which yields linseed oil and linen.

Description
Leaves generally alternate, stalkless, narrow,
without marginal teeth. Flowers in generally
terminal racemes or cymes, day-blooming
and rather fleeting. Sepals and petals 5 each,
separate. Stamens 5.

How to Grow
Quick to grow from seeds sown outdoors in
early spring or, where winters are mild, in
the fall. Plant in rows or clumps. The species
below prefer cool weather.

grandiflorum p. 83
Flowering Flax. 1–2 ft. (30–60 cm) high.
Flowers to 1 in. (2.5 cm) wide, red or pink.
N. Africa. Cultivar 'Caeruleum' has bluish-
purple flowers; 'Coccineum', scarlet flowers.
Many others are available. Hardy annual.

usitatissimum p. 136
Common Flax. 3–4 ft. (90–120 cm) high.
Flowers ½ in. (13 mm) wide, usually blue,
sometimes white. Europe, but often an
escape in North America. Hardy annual.

Lobelia
Lobelia family
Lobeliaceae

Lo-bee'li-a. Showy-flowered herbs comprising
about 375 species, popular for borders, wild
gardens, and edging.

Description
Leaves alternate and simple. Flowers in
terminal clusters, mostly spikes or racemes
that are sometimes leafy, nearly always
bracted. Corolla irregular, more or less

tubular below, but split to the base, 3 of the lobes forming a lip, the other 2 erect or turned backward. Stamens united by their anthers into a ring around the style.

How to Grow
To prevent damping-off, start seeds indoors in late winter in vermiculite, and water from the bottom. Transplant in clumps to 2 in. (5 cm) pots, and set out when seedlings are the size of a half dollar. Does best in cool or dry climates but will endure southern summers if given good drainage and afternoon shade. Grows quite slowly.

Erinus p. 129
Edging Lobelia. Erect or trailing, 3–8 in. (7.5–20.0 cm) high. Flowers ½–¾ in. (13–19 mm) long, typically blue on slender stalks. South Africa. Cultivars variously colored or with double flowers. Those with trailing stems are useful for hanging baskets. Hardy annual.

Lobularia
Mustard family
Cruciferae

Lob-you-lair′i-a. A small genus of about 5 species of Mediterranean herbs, related to *Alyssum*.

Description
Leaves alternate, with unbroken margin. Flowers white, with 4 petals and 4 sepals. Stamens 6.

How to Grow
The species below grows easily from seeds sown outdoors in early spring and again in late summer. Or start indoors 6–8 weeks before last spring frost. Only small seedlings transplant well. Self-sows readily. Not heat-resistant; prefers cool weather.

maritima pp. 116, 150
Sweet Alyssum; Snowdrift. To 1 ft. (30 cm) high, much-branched and spreading. Flowers pungent, numerous, tiny, white, lilac to pink, or purple, in umbels ¾ in. (19 mm) wide. Cultivars may be more compact, have larger or double flowers, or have variegated leaves. Good edging plant. S. Europe. Perennial treated as a hardy annual.

Lonas
Daisy family
Compositae

Lo'nas. Anthemis Tube. A single herb from
the Mediterranean region.

Description
Leaves alternate, coarsely toothed, divided
feather-fashion, with the segments linear.
Flowerheads small, tubular, without rays, in
dense corymbs.

How to Grow
Start seeds indoors 6–8 weeks before last
frost to prolong the flowering season. Or
sow outdoors when danger of frost is past.
Not heat-resistant, but will flower through
midsummer if planted in spring in
well-drained, average soil. Prefers cool
weather.

annua p. 212
African Daisy; Yellow Ageratum. To 1 ft.
(30 cm) high. Flowerheads yellow,
everlasting, ⅓ in. (8 mm) wide, in branched
clusters. Italy and nw. Africa. Also called
L. inodora. Half-hardy annual.

Lopezia
Evening primrose family
Onagraceae

Low-peez'ia. A genus of American herbs or
subshrubs, used chiefly as greenhouse plants.

Description
Leaves small, alternate, broadly lance-shaped,
the margin sawlike. Flowers small, produced
in clusters at ends of branches. Petals 5, the
upper 2 bent upward and having at the bend
a glossy piece of hard honeylike tissue that
deceives flies. The real nectaries are at the
base of the flower. Stamens 2, one fertile, the
other petal-like.

How to Grow
Sow seeds indoors in early spring; transplant
to the garden after danger of frost is past.
Prefers warm weather.

hirsuta p. 89
Mosquito Flower. 1–3 ft. (30–90 cm) high.
Flowers small, ½ in. (13 mm) long, white,

pink, or red. Mexico and El Salvador. Tender
annual.

Luffa
Cucumber family
Cucurbitaceae

Luf'fa. A small genus of tropical Old World
gourds, grown chiefly for their ornamental
fruits.

Description
Tendril-bearing, quick-growing, herbaceous
vines. Leaves alternate, 5- to 7-lobed. Flowers
yellowish or whitish, male flowers in
racemes, the female solitary. Petals 5. Fruit
with a dry or papery rind, the interior
fibrous. The dried, fibrous, cucumber- or
club-shaped skeletons of the fruit are sold in
tropical markets to be used as sponges.

How to Grow
Start seeds indoors in peat pots 4–6 weeks
before last frost. Transplant when soil is
warm. Run vines up trees or over buildings;
they grow too long for a trellis. On the
ground, the gourds will grow crooked and
clubby. These tropical plants prefer warm
weather.

acutangula p. 193
Angled Luffa; Sing-Kwa. Vines 10–15 ft.
(3.0–4.5 m) long. Leaves very rough, not as
large as in *L. aegyptica,* more angled than
lobed. Flowers yellow, showy, 3 in. (7.5 cm)
wide. Fruit club-shaped, 9–12 in. (22.5–
30.0 cm) long, ridged, the black seeds not
margined. Old World tropics. Tender
annual.

aegyptica p. 194
Sponge Gourd; Dishcloth Gourd. Vine
8–15 ft. (2.4–4.5 m) long. Leaves 5–12 in.
(12.5–30.0 cm) long, almost circular, with
3–7 lobes, the margins toothed. Flowers
yellow, showy, 3 in. (7.5 cm) wide. Fruit
cucumber-shaped, 12–18 in. (30–45 cm)
long, the black seeds margined. Also known
as *L. cylindrica.* Old World tropics. Tender
annual.

Lunaria
Mustard family
Cruciferae

Loo-nay'ri-a. Two Eurasian herbs cultivated for the satiny, parchmentlike divisions of their pods, used in dried bouquets.

Description
Leaves usually alternate, ovalish, and stalked. Flowers violet-purple or white, in a showy terminal raceme. Petals 4, long-clawed.

How to Grow
Easy to grow by sowing seeds outdoors in early spring. Where winters are mild, sow in fall. Rarely blooms the first season, but is quite winter-hardy and will live over to bloom in mid-spring. Plants die after blooming. Let a few plants set seeds for next year. The species below prefers cool weather.

annua *p. 88*
Honesty; Moonwort; Moneyplant; Satin Pod; Satinflower. 18–36 in. (45–90 cm) high. Flowers fragrant, purplish, to 1 in. (2.5 cm) long. S. Europe; naturalized in North America. Cultivar 'Alba' has white flowers; another has variegated leaves. Biennial grown as a hardy annual.

Lupinus
Pea family
Leguminosae

Loo-pine'us. Lupine. A genus of many species found in North America, South America, and around the Mediterranean; all annuals or perennials except for a tree.

Description
Herbaceous stems, with leaves compound and finger-shaped. Flowers pealike, produced in dense terminal racemes.

How to Grow
The lupines are not heat-resistant and need an early start to get a good show of color. In mild climates, sow seeds in a lightly shaded spot in fall. Where winters are severe, start seeds indoors in peat pots 8–10 weeks before last frost and transplant to garden after danger of frost is past. Seeds are often slow to sprout. Lupines prefer cool weather.

***subcarnosus** p. 142*
Bluebonnet. 8–10 in. (20–25 cm) high.
Flowers ½ in. (13 mm) long, blue, with a
white or yellow spot. Tex. Hardy annual.

***texensis** p. 141*
Texas Bluebonnet. To 12 in. (30 cm)
high. Differs from *L. subcarnosus* most
conspicuously in the darker-colored flowers,
¾ in. (19 mm) long. Tex. Hardy annual.

Lychnis
Pink family
Caryophyllaceae

Lick'nis. Catchfly; Campion. A genus of
about 35 herbs, mostly from the north
temperate zone and northward, some old
garden favorites.

Description
Erect plants, often with sticky hairs. Leaves
opposite, stipules absent. Calyx with 5 teeth.
Petals 5, with claw at base, limb rounded or
sometimes 2-cleft or fringed. Stamens 10.

How to Grow
Easy to grow in any ordinary, well-drained
soil in full sun. Sow in early spring or, for
more predictable performance, start indoors
and transplant when spring bulbs are
blooming. Protect seedlings from hard
freezes. Prefers warm weather.

***Coeli-rosa** p. 113*
Rose-of-Heaven. 12–20 in. (30–50 cm) high.
Flowers solitary, terminal, 1 in. (2.5 cm)
wide, rose-pink. Mediterranean region.
Sometimes sold as *Agrostemma* or as *Silene*.
There are cultivars with red- or purple-eyed
flowers or toothed petals, as well as dwarf
forms. Half-hardy annual.

Machaeranthera
Daisy family
Compositae

Ma-kee-ran'the-ra. A small genus of herbs
found in w. North America and closely
related to *Aster*.

Description
Leaves alternate, bristly. In the only

cultivated species (below), flowerheads rather showy.

How to Grow
This species needs well-drained soil with pH 6.0–7.0. It grows best in cool, dry climates, but will have 4–6 weeks of color in warm, humid climates. Start seeds indoors in early spring; break dormancy by mixing seeds with moist peat moss and refrigerating at 40° F (4.5° C) for 2–3 weeks. Transplant hardened-off seedlings after danger of hard frost is past. Or sow seeds outdoors in early spring or fall.

tanacetifolia p. 127
Tahoka Daisy. 1–2 ft. (30–60 cm) high. Flowerheads to 2 in. (5 cm) wide, lavender-blue, the rays slender and pointed. S. Dak. to Mexico and Calif. Half-hardy annual.

Malcolmia
Mustard family
Cruciferae

Mal-col'mi-a. A small genus of low, grayish herbs.

Description
Stems branching profusely, making a compact plant. Leaves simple, alternate, slightly cut. Flowers white, purple, or reddish, in loose clusters at end of branches, the petals 4, long and narrow.

How to Grow
Prepare soil in early spring as soon as it is dry enough to work. Sow seeds thinly, then barely cover with sand. Where winters are mild, sow in fall. Self-sows. Prefers cool weather and usually burns out by late summer.

maritima p. 112
Virginia Stock. 6–12 in. (15–30 cm) high. Flowers ¾ in. (19 mm) wide, purplish-pink to reddish to white. Grown for its sweet fragrance. Mediterranean region. Hardy annual.

Malope
Mallow family
Malvaceae

Ma-lo'pe. A genus of 3 smooth or hairy herbs found in the Mediterranean region.

Description
Leaves alternate, without marginal teeth, occasionally 3-parted. Flowers showy, white, violet, or pink, surrounded by 3 bracts.

How to Grow
Grown in Europe as a summer flower, but not sufficiently heat-resistant for prolonged color in U.S., except where summers are cool. Sow seeds 2–3 weeks before last frost. Plants grow bushy, so sow 3–5 seeds per hill with 2 ft. (60 cm) between hills. Cover with ¼ in. (6 mm) soil. Overly fertile soil will produce dense plants with few blossoms. Prefers cool weather.

trifida p. 89
2–3 ft. (60–90 cm) high. Flowers trumpet-shaped, 2–3 in. (5.0–7.5 cm) wide, rose or purple, growing singly on stalks from axils of leaves. Europe and n. Africa. Cultivar 'Grandiflora' has larger, deep rosy-red flowers, and is sometimes known as *M. grandiflora*. Hardy annual.

Malva
Mallow family
Malvaceae

Mal'va. Mallow. About 30 species of widely distributed herbs, several grown for ornament, but some rather weedy.

Description
Leaves alternate, usually angled, lobed, or dissected. Flowers mostly in the leaf axils, solitary or clustered, most with 2 or 3 involucre-like bracts beneath them. Calyx united, but 5-cleft. Petals 5, with a notch at the tip, mostly pink or white.

How to Grow
Easy to grow in any ordinary garden soil. Sow seeds where desired. These mallows tend to escape and become weeds. They are less satisfactory than those found in the closely related genus *Hibiscus*. Mallows prefer cool weather.

verticillata* var. *crispa *p. 165*
Curled Mallow. To 6 ft. (1.8 m) high.
Flowers white to purplish, with petals ¼ in.
(6 mm) wide, ½ in. (13 mm) long. Eurasia.
Hardy annual.

Martynia
Martynia family
Martyniaceae

Mar-tin′ee-a. A single species, related to
Proboscidea, occasionally grown by flower
arrangers for the seed pods.

Description
Leaves large, opposite, triangular, with long
petioles. Flowers large and bell-shaped in
loose racemes.

How to Grow
These sprawling plants are easy to grow in
full sun and enriched garden soil. Where
summers are short, start seeds indoors 6–8
weeks before last frost and transplant after
danger of frost is over. Where summers are
long, sow seeds in warm soil. Prefers warm
weather.

annua *p. 164*
To 6 ft. (1.8 m) high. Flowers bell-shaped,
white to reddish purple, spotted with yellow,
red, and purple, to 2 in. (5 cm) long. Fruit
to 1½ in. (4 cm) long. Tropical America.
Tender annual.

Matricaria
Daisy family
Compositae

Ma-tri-cay′ri-a. An Old World genus of
about 35 species, closely related to
Chrysanthemum, with which it is often
confused.

Description
Leaves finely cut, often strong-scented.
Flowers in heads, the disk flowers yellow, the
rays white or lacking.

How to Grow
Easy to grow from seeds sown in early spring
as soon as the ground can be worked. Plants
prefer cool weather.

recutita *p. 159*
German Camomile; Sweet False Camomile.
1–2½ ft. (30–75 cm) high. Flowerheads
1 in. (2.5 cm) wide, the disk flowers yellow,
with 10–20 white ray flowers. Europe and
n. Asia. Sometimes an escape in e. U.S.
Hardy annual.

Matthiola
Mustard family
Cruciferae

Mat-thy′o-la. A genus containing 50 species
of Old World annuals, perennials, or
subshrubs, only 2 species commonly in
cultivation.

Description
Leaves alternate, without marginal teeth, or
wavy or cut into segments. Flowers in
terminal racemes, with 4 long-clawed petals.

How to Grow
Easy to grow and quick to flower. Some of
the most cold-resistant annuals, but cannot
stand heat. Start seeds very early indoors so
that plants will be at early flower-bud stage
before transplanting. Or sow outdoors in
very early spring in full sun. Sow thickly and
do not thin plants; crowding will force them
to bloom early. Where winters are mild, sow
seeds in late summer for winter and spring
bloom. These plants prefer cool weather.

incana *p. 107*
Stock; Brompton Stock; Gillyflower. 1–2½ ft.
(30–75 cm) high. Flowers white, blue,
purple, reddish, pink, or yellowish, fragrant,
1 in. (2.5 cm) wide, usually double. S.
Europe. Cultivar 'Annua', Ten-Weeks Stock,
is early flowering and disease-resistant.
Biennial grown as a hardy annual.

longipetala *p. 92*
Evening Stock. Low-growing, much
branched, to 1½ ft. (45 cm) high. Flowers
¾ in. (19 mm) wide, scattered, purple to
white, very fragrant, opening in the evening.
Eurasia. Usually planted in clumps. Hardy
annual.

Mentzelia
Loasa family
Loasaceae

Ment-zee'li-a. About 60 species of American annual or perennial herbs, shrubs, or trees, usually with barbed, but not stinging, hairs.

Description
Leaves usually alternate, without marginal teeth, cut into lobes or cleft almost to the center. Flowers white, yellow, or red, often showy, borne singly, in terminal racemes, or in flat-topped cymes. Petals usually 5. Stamens numerous.

How to Grow
Best adapted to mild, dry climates where seeds sprout with fall rains and plants blossom at end of winter rainy season. Elsewhere, sow in full sun in very early spring. Plants do well in raised beds of well-drained, average soil. They do not transplant well and prefer cool weather.

Lindleyi p. 201
Blazing Star. 1–2 ft. (30–60 cm) high, single-stalked, or branched and straggling. Flowers 1½–2½ in. (4–6 cm) wide, bright yellow, very fragrant. Calif. Sometimes offered as *Bartonia aurea*. Hardy annual.

Mesembryanthemum
Carpetweed family
Aizoaceae

Me-sem-bri-an'thee-mum. Fig-marigold. Originally, the fig-marigolds made up a huge genus, but over the past 100 years, they have been divided into several separate genera. *Mesembryanthemum* contains the original species described by Linnaeus and 40–50 other species, the one below most widely grown.

Description
Leaves alternate or opposite, nearly cylindrical, some flecked with glistening specks. Flowers generally large and showy, often daisylike because of the great number of petals and stamens, mostly white, red, or yellow. Calyx tubular, with 4–5 rather leafy lobes.

How to Grow

Although best suited to dry soils and arid western climates, the species below will give 4–6 weeks of color in cool climates if grown in poor soil. Start early indoors in sandy potting soil to get good-sized plants for setting out in a sunny garden after the danger of frost is past. Prefers cool weather.

crystallinum pp. 101, 155

Ice Plant; Sea Fig; Sea Marigold. Prostrate, to 2 ft. (60 cm) long, fleshy, ovalish leaves. Flowers nearly stalkless, white or pale pink, ¾–1¼ in. (2–3 cm) wide. Grown for its glistening foliage. Naturalized along the Calif. coast. Tender annual.

Mimosa
Pea family
Leguminosae

My-mo′sa. An immense genus of 400–500 species of mostly tropical American herbs, shrubs, and trees, only 2 much cultivated in the U.S.

Description

Leaves alternate, twice-compound, the leaflets numerous, usually very small, arranged feather-fashion. Flowers small, more or less tubular, in dense, ball-like clusters. Stamens protruding.

How to Grow

Where summers are short, start seeds indoors very early in peat pots. Transplant to sunny, well-drained garden soil or large containers, 2 plants per container. Where frost-free period is 7–8 months, sow seeds outdoors 3 weeks before last frost. Thin so that plants are 12 in. (30 cm) apart. Prefers warm weather.

pudica p. 122

Sensitive Plant; Humble Plant. To 3 ft. (90 cm) high, stems more or less hairy and slightly spiny. Flowers rose-purple or lavender, small round heads ⅔ in. (17 mm) in diameter, in long-stalked clusters growing from leaf axils. Tropical America; naturalized in Fla. and along the Gulf Coast. Generally grown as a novelty, since the leaves fold up to the stems when touched or in cloudy weather. Tender perennial grown as a tender annual.

Mimulus
Snapdragon family
Scrophulariaceae

Mim'you-lus. A genus of about 150 declining or erect herbs or subshrubs found in North and South America, Asia, Australia, South Africa, and very numerous in w. North America. Sometimes called *Diplacus*.

Description
Plants smooth or hairy, often sticky or clammy. Leaves opposite, with or without marginal teeth. Flowers showy, 2-lipped, often spotted, giving the effect of a face, growing singly from the leaf axils or in terminal racemes.

How to Grow
Popular in Europe's cool gardens, but difficult to grow in most of U.S. except Calif. Good for large cold frames. Sow seeds indoors in midwinter or very early spring. Set out plants as soon as danger of frost is past. Light afternoon shade will prolong the bloom period. Water generously. Increase by cuttings and division. Can be brought indoors for winter bloom. These plants prefer cool weather.

guttatus p. 206
Monkey Flower. To 2 ft. (60 cm) high. Flowers yellow, generally with red or brown dots on the throat, 2-lipped, 1½ in. (4 cm) wide. Alaska to Mexico. Perennial grown as a half-hardy annual.

× *hybridus* p. 249
Monkey Flower. 12–14 in. (30–35 cm) high. Flowers 2 in. (5 cm) wide, red, or red and yellow. This species is probably derived from *M. luteus* and *M. guttatus,* as well as other species. Perennial grown as a tender annual.

Mirabilis
Four-O'Clock family
Nyctaginaceae

Mi-ra'bil-is. Sixty species of tropical American herbs, only the species below commonly in cultivation.

Description
Roots thickened or tuberous. Leaves

opposite, generally stalked. Flowers solitary, or a few from a calyxlike involucre, the true calyx corolla-like, tubular, and red, yellow, or white. Petals none. Stamens 5–6.

How to Grow
In the North, start seeds early indoors in peat pots and transplant after danger of frost is past. In mild climates, sow seeds in the garden during spring or fall. These warm-weather plants are perennials in the South and warm West, but will bloom reliably the first season. Plants quickly grow quite large, so space them 3 ft. (90 cm) apart in full sun.

Jalapa p. 82
Four-O'Clock; Marvel-of-Peru. 1½–3 ft. (45–90 cm) high. Flowers to 1 in. (2.5 cm) wide, red, pink, yellow, or white, sometimes striped, the tube 1–2 in. (2.5–5.0 cm) long, usually solitary in the involucre. Flowers open in the late afternoon. Many cultivars, some compact, dwarf, or variegated. Roots can be dug up in fall and stored over winter. Tender perennial grown as a tender annual.

Moluccella
Mint family
Labiatae

Mol-lew-sell′a. Two species of aromatic Old World annual herbs, both found in old-fashioned gardens, the one below widely cultivated for fresh and dried flowers.

Description
Leaves opposite, stalked, generously toothed. Flowers very small, in whorls in the leaf axils. Corolla tiny, irregular, white or pinkish, scarcely or not exceeding the bristly or prickly calyx.

How to Grow
Considered difficult to grow largely because seeds need light during germination. Where growing season is short, prepare soil as soon as it can be worked in spring. Sow seeds in moist soil, pressing them in with a board. Scatter a shallow covering of sand. Keep moist. In mild climates, sow seeds in previously flooded, deep furrows in late summer. Prefers cool weather.

laevis p. 197

Bells-of-Ireland; Molucca Balm; Shell-Flower.
2–3 ft. (60–90 cm) high. Leaves roundish or
heart-shaped, ¾–1½ in. (2–4 cm) long.
Flowers fragrant, green, 1–2 in. (2.5–5.0 cm)
wide, very numerous, the calyx with 5 small
prickles, but expanding in fruit and the
nutlets nestled in it. W. Asia. Can be forced
in the winter under medium heat. Half-hardy
annual.

Momordica
Cucumber family
Cucurbitaceae

Mo-more'di-ka. Over 40 species of
tropical Asian or African tendril-bearing,
high-climbing vines, 2 grown for their
decorative fruit.

Description
Leaves alternate, heavy, compound or deeply
divided. Male and female flowers separate,
sometimes on the same plant, both solitary
(in cultivated species), yellow or white, the
stalk bearing a prominent bract. Corolla
bell-shaped or more open, parted nearly to
the base. Fruit oblongish or globe-shaped,
splitting at maturity.

How to Grow
Where growing season is short, start seeds
indoors 6–8 weeks before last frost;
transplant near a sunny trellis when danger
of frost is past. Where summers are warm,
sow seeds ¼ in. (6 mm) deep in garden.
Run these quick-growing vines over
vegetable-garden fences or up supports. They
prefer warm weather.

Charantia p. 191

Balsam Pear. 8–10 ft. (2.4–3.0 m) long.
Leaves large, with 3–5 deep lobes. Flowers
yellow, the center darker, ¾ in. (19 mm)
wide, the bract on the flower-stalk without
teeth. Fruit oblongish or oval, 4–8 in.
(10–20 cm) long, warty, orange-yellow,
when split showing the bright scarlet arils of
its seeds. Old World tropics. The similar
looking Balsam Apple (*M. Balsamina*) is a
smaller vine with smaller egg-shaped fruit.
Both, tender perennials grown as tender
annuals.

Myosotis
Borage family
Boraginaceae

My-o-so'tis. Fifty species, mostly European, but a few throughout the north temperate zone.

Description
Usually branching, often weak or prostrate, generally hairy. Leaves alternate, without marginal teeth. Flowers small, in branched or unbranched, sometimes 1-sided, clusters. Calyx short, tubular, 5-toothed at the top. Corolla 5-lobed, the throat crested and often of a different color.

How to Grow
Where growing season is short, sow seeds outdoors in early spring. Where winters are mild, sow in the fall for spring color. Plants prefer light shade, especially where sunlight is intense. Self-sows readily at the edge of woodlands or around large shrubs. Crowding does not affect performance. Prefers cool weather.

sylvatica p. 145
Forget-Me-Not. 6–18 in. (15–45 cm) high. Flowers blue, but sometimes pink or white, to ⅓ in. (8 mm) wide, the eye differently colored, often yellow. Eurasia. Also sold as *M. alpestris*. Blooms spring to summer. Biennial grown as a hardy annual.

Nemesia
Snapdragon family
Scrophulariaceae

Ne-mee'she-a. African herbs or subshrubs, comprising 50 species.

Description
Stem square and grooved. Leaves simple, lance-shaped, not stalked, in alternating pairs, becoming smaller toward the top. Flowers in terminal clusters, yellow, brown, crimson, pink, blue, white, often 2-colored. Corolla short and tubular, the expanded limb wide, flat, and 2-lipped, the base of the lower lip forming a small spur, the upper being cut into 4 segments.

How to Grow
Difficult to grow outside of Calif. and the

Northwest, but worth the effort. Needs a long, cool growing season. Start seeds indoors in midwinter or very early spring. Set out in the garden after danger of frost is past. In the West, a fall crop can be grown; in protected areas, bloom will continue into winter.

strumosa pp. 106, 205
To 2 ft. (60 cm) high. Flowers to 1 in. (2.5 cm) wide, white, yellow, pink, orange, red, or purple, often deeply marked on the outside. South Africa. Many cultivars are available, including large-flowered and dwarf forms. Tender annual.

Nemophila
Waterleaf family
Hydrophyllaceae

Nem-off'i-la. A North American genus comprising 11 species of annual herbs, only a few of garden interest.

Description
Some species are climbing, others are dwarf or trailing plants. All are hairy. Leaves usually much cut, alternate or opposite. Flowers showy, growing at the tips of the branches in clusters. Corolla bell-shaped, blue, white, purple, or spotted. Calyx of 5 spreading sepals alternating with additional leafy growths.

How to Grow
These cool-weather wildflowers perform well in northern and high-altitude gardens. They provide good color before plants are killed by the heat or humidity. Where the climate is mild, sow seeds outdoors in the fall. Where winters are severe, wait until early spring. Grows quickly and easily, especially if given afternoon shade. Thin plants to 1 ft. (30 cm) apart.

maculata p. 131
Five Spot. Trailing, to 1 ft. (30 cm) long. Flowers bell-shaped, 1¾ in. (4.5 cm) wide, white, with a bluish to purple spot at the tip of each petal. W. and cen. Calif. Hardy annual.

Menziesii p. 130
Baby Blue-Eyes. Trailing, to 1 ft. (30 cm) long. Flowers bell-shaped, bright blue, to

1½ in. (4 cm) wide. There are white, and
blue and white forms. Good flower for
naturalizing. Calif. Hardy annual.

Nicandra
Potato family
Solanaceae

Ny-kan'dra. A single strong-growing species
from Peru that has escaped from cultivation
and become naturalized in tropical America
and U.S. Often grown in the garden for its
dried seed cases.

Description
Leaves alternate, ovalish, with toothed
margins. Flowers large, calyx 5-parted,
stamens 5. Fruit a 3- to 5-celled, many seeded
berry enclosed in an inflated calyx.

How to Grow
Sow seeds indoors, ⅛ in. (3.2 mm) deep in
light soil, in early spring. Set out hardened-
off seedlings 2–3 weeks before last frost.
Thin plants to 3–4 ft. (90–120 cm) apart.
Grow in full sun. Relegate large, rough-
looking plants to back of the garden. Prefers
warm weather.

Physalodes p. 136
Apple-of-Peru. Spreading, 4–8 ft. (1.2–2.4 m)
high. Flowers solitary, tubular, blue, or
violet and white, 1–2 in. (2.5–5.0 cm)
wide, on curving stalks. Occasionally offered
as Shoofly. Perennial grown as a half-hardy
annual.

Nicotiana
Potato family
Solanaceae

Ni-ko-she-a'na. Seventy herbaceous species,
occasionally shrubby or treelike, mostly
tropical, all American except for one found
in Australia. Prized for their long flowering
period.

Description
Whole plant more or less covered with
short, sticky hairs. Stems branching,
sometimes joined. Leaves large, soft,
alternate, simple, the juice having narcotic or
poisonous properties. Flowers in clusters at

ends of branches, sweet-scented, originally opening at night and remaining open on sunless days; white, greenish yellow, or purple. Calyx of 5 partly united green sepals. Corolla tubular or funnel-shaped. Stamens 5.

How to Grow
Easy to grow from seeds started indoors in early spring and transplanted to garden as soon as danger of frost is over. Lime and potash are beneficial. Water generously during hot, dry weather. Cut back fertilizer and water in late summer to rejuvenate plants. Sometimes grown as pot plants. They prefer warm weather.

alata pp. 92, 168, 169, 265
Flowering Tobacco. To 5 ft. (1.5 m) high, erect and slender. Flowers fragrant at night, the tube 2–4 in. (5–10 cm) long, and the limb 1 in. (2.5 cm) wide, in numerous colors including white, pink, mauve, red, maroon, purple, and even green. Brazil, Uruguay, Paraguay. Many cultivars are available, some with larger flowers, and some day-blooming dwarf kinds with showier but less fragrant blossoms. Also called *N. affinis*. Tender annual.

Tabacum p. 93
Tobacco. To 6 ft. (1.8 m) high. Flowers stalked, the corolla 2 in. (5 cm) long, the tube white, cream, rose, or purplish red, its lobes pointed. Grown commercially as smoking tobacco, but also a striking garden plant. Tropical America. Tender annual.

Nierembergia
Potato family
Solanaceae

Near-em-berg'i-a or near-em-ber'ji-a. Cupflower. Tropical American herbs or subshrubs comprising about 30 species, 4 grown for their attractive tubular flowers.

Description
Leaves alternate, somewhat scattered, without marginal teeth. Flowers white or pale blue, mostly near the ends of twigs. Calyx more or less bell-shaped, 5-parted. Corolla long-tubed, the 5-lobed limb abruptly expanded, throat yellow. Stamens 5, protruding, one shorter than the others.

How to Grow
Start seeds indoors in early spring. If
hardened off, seedlings are frost-hardy and
can be set out 2–3 weeks before last frost.
Needs moist, well-drained soil. Prefers warm
weather. These plants are good for hanging
baskets.

hippomanica var. *violacea* p. 135
Cupflower. 6–15 in. (15–38 cm) high.
Flowers numerous, 1 in. (2.5 cm) wide,
violet-blue with throat yellow. Argentina.
The hardiest of all cupflowers. Perennial
where winters are mild; elsewhere grown as a
half-hardy annual.

Nigella
Buttercup family
Ranunculaceae

Ny-jell′a. About 20 herbaceous annual
species, mostly natives of the Mediterranean
region.

Description
Leaves alternate, often of lacelike appearance
because of finely divided, threadlike
segments. Flowers blue or white, produced at
ends of branching stems, each flower
enclosed by much-branched, threadlike bracts
growing from base. Petals 5–8, notched.
Stamens indefinite in number. Pistils usually
5–10, separated at top, but united at base.

How to Grow
Easy to grow from seeds sown as soon as
ground can be worked in spring; seedlings
resent transplanting. Thin to 6–8 in. (15–
20 cm) apart. Where winters are mild, sow
seeds in fall in average, well-drained soil.
Prefers cool weather.

damascena p. 124
Love-in-a-Mist; Devil-in-the-Bush. 12–18 in.
(30–45 cm) high. Flowers light blue, white,
pink, rose, mauve, or purple, 1½ in. (4 cm)
wide, set in the midst of threadlike bracts.
S. Europe. New ultra dwarf types are good
edging plants; standard tall type can be
grown for dried seed pods. Hardy annual.

Ocimum
Mint family
Labiatae

Os'si-mum. Aromatic herbs (rarely shrubs) comprising 150 species, the one below cultivated for its fragrant, edible foliage.

Description
Leaves opposite, mostly toothed. Flowers small, irregular, crowded in whorls grouped in branching racemes. Corolla very small, usually not exceeding the toothed calyx, the lobes or teeth recurved in fruit.

How to Grow
Sprouts quickly and easily from seeds sown indoors in warm soil about 8 weeks before last frost. Set outdoors when danger of frost is past. Sow seeds in warm soil in full sun. To rejuvenate plants, cut back to half the stem length, feed generously, and water. Where seasons are warm and long, sow again in midsummer. Prefers warm weather.

Basilicum p. 185
Basil; Sweet Basil. 1–2 ft. (30–60 cm) high. Leaves ovalish, 3–5 in. (7.5–12.5 cm) long. Flowers small, white or purplish. Tropical Old World. Several ornamental cultivars, including 'Dark Opal', with purple leaves; 'Spicy Globe', with very fine leaves; and 'Citriodorum', with lemon-scented leaves. Tender annual.

Oenothera
Evening primrose family
Onagraceae

Ee-no-thee'ra or ee-noth'er-ra. The evening primroses and their day-blooming relatives, the sundrops. Eighty species of American herbs. Formerly included in *Hartmannia*.

Description
Leaves alternate, simple, with smooth edge. Flowers showy, prevailingly yellow, but also white or rose-color in some species, generally 1 or 2 in the leaf axils. Calyx tubular, usually 4-sided, its 4 lobes often bent backward and usually soon falling. Petals 4, mostly very broad.

How to Grow
To grow these perennials and biennials for

first-year bloom, sow seeds outdoors in early spring. Or start seeds indoors 8–12 weeks before last frost. Where winters are mild, sowing outdoors in fall works well. Plant seeds or transplants in patches. All prefer warm weather.

biennis p. 217
Evening Primrose. 3–6 ft. (0.9–1.8 m) high. Flowers night-blooming, yellow turning gold, 1–2 in. (2.5–5.0 cm) wide. North America and naturalized in Europe. The var. *grandiflora,* chiefly from the South, has larger flowers and is best for the garden. Biennial grown as a hardy annual.

deltoides p. 161
Desert Evening Primrose. 2–10 in. (5–25 cm) high. Flowers night-blooming, 3 in. (7.5 cm) wide, white turning pink. Sw. deserts of U.S. Half-hardy annual.

erythrosepala p. 216
Evening Primrose. 2–8 ft. (0.6–2.4 m) high. Flowers night-blooming, yellow turning orange or red, 3½ in. (9 cm) wide. Established in northern areas. Also sold as *O. Lamarckiana.* Hardy biennial grown as a hardy annual.

laciniata p. 219
Evening Primrose. 6–24 in. (15–60 cm) high. Flowers night-blooming, yellow turning red, 2½ in. (6 cm) wide. Me. and S. Dak. to Tex. Perennial grown as a hardy annual.

missourensis p. 203
Missouri Evening Primrose. Spreading branches to 15 in. (38 cm) long. Flowers night-blooming, yellow turning red, to 7 in. (17.5 cm) long and 5 in. (12.5 cm) wide. Cen. U.S. A garden favorite. Perennial grown as a hardy annual.

primiveris p. 203
Evening Primrose. 6–9 in. (15.0–22.5 cm) high. Flowers night-blooming, yellow turning orange, 2–3 in. (5.0–7.5 cm) wide. Sw. deserts of U.S. Hardy annual.

speciosa p. 87
Showy Evening Primrose. 1–2 ft. (30–60 cm) high. Flowers day-blooming, white turning pink, 3 in. (7.5 cm) wide. Cen. U.S. Sometimes sold as *Hartmannia.* Can become a weed. Perennial grown as a hardy annual.

Omphalodes
Borage family
Boraginaceae

Om-fa-lo'dez. Low herbs, comprising about 25 species, closely allied to *Cynoglossum,* which they resemble. Europe and Asia.

Description
Stems smooth or slightly hairy. Leaves basal, long-stalked, lance- or heart-shaped, the stem leaves smaller, fewer, and alternate. Flowers blue, sometimes pinkish, arranged in loose 1-sided racemes. Calyx joined halfway down. Corolla united to form a short tube, usually white with veinlike markings radiating from the center, giving it a starlike appearance. Stamens 5, not protruding.

How to Grow
Sow in moist garden soil (neutral or slightly alkaline) in partial shade. Seeds sown in spring will flower that season; those sown in fall in mild climates will flower in early spring. Prefers cool weather.

linifolia p. 150
Navelwort. To 1 ft. (30 cm) high. Flowers white, ½ in. (13 mm) wide, the corolla tube twice as long as the calyx. Spain and Portugal. Hardy annual.

Origanum
Mint family
Labiatae

Or-rig'a-num. A genus of herbs or dwarf shrubs. Mediterranean region to cen. Asia.

Description
Leaves opposite and simple. Flowers few to many, arranged in spikelets, inflorescences with enlarged, overlapping bracts.

How to Grow
Easy to grow from seeds started indoors 6–8 weeks before last spring frost. Transplant to the garden after danger of frost is past. Prefers warm weather.

Majorana p. 196
Sweet Marjoram; Annual Marjoram. To 2 ft. (60 cm) high. Leaves opposite, stalked, elliptical, ½ in. (13 mm) long, without marginal teeth. Flowers small, purple or

white. Europe. Leaves are eaten as an herb.
Tender perennial grown as a tender annual.

Orthocarpus
Snapdragon family
Scrophulariaceae

Or-tho-kar′pus. A genus of 25 species of
New World herbs, generally called owl's
clover in Calif., where some species originate.
Related to *Castilleja*.

Description
Leaves alternate with smooth or cut edges.
Flowers in spikes, often with colored bracts.

How to Grow
Easy to grow from seeds sown outdoors in
early spring. Prefers warm weather.

purpurascens p. 94
Owl's Clover; Escobita. To 12 in. (30 cm)
high. Flowers irregular, 2-lipped, 1 in.
(2.5 cm) long, rose-purple or crimson, the
lower lip white with yellow or purple
streaks. Bracts tipped with red. Calif. Hardy
annual.

Osteospermum
Daisy family
Compositae

Os-tee-o-sperm′um. Seventy species of South
African herbs and shrubs, allied to *Calendula*.

Description
Leaves alternate, occasionally opposite, entire,
sometimes with toothed edges. Flowers
solitary on terminal stems or in loose
panicles.

How to Grow
Cultivars are best suited to the West,
Southwest, and North. In dry, mild climates,
sow in late summer for fall and winter
bloom. In the humid South, sow in mid-
spring on raised beds. In the North, start
seeds indoors 6–8 weeks before last frost.
After danger of frost is past, set plants out
1 ft. (30 cm) apart in full sun. The species
below prefer warm weather.

'Buttermilk' *p. 154*

12–18 in. (30–45 cm) high. Flowers 2–3 in. (5.0–7.5 cm) wide, white with dark center, heads solitary or loosely clustered. Probably derived from *O. Ecklonis*. South Africa. Half-hardy annual.

hyoseroides p. 243

To 2 ft. (60 cm) high. Flowers to 2 in. (5 cm) wide, disk flowers yellow tipped with violet, ray flowers yellow-orange, in loose corymbs. South Africa. Half-hardy annual.

Oxypetalum
Milkweed family
Asclepiadaceae

Ox-y-pèt'a-lum. About 125 species of Central or South American herbs.

Description
Leaves opposite. Flowers with 5-part corolla, in open cymes.

How to Grow
Easy to grow from seeds started indoors 6–8 weeks before last spring frost. Transplant to garden after danger of frost is past. Prefers cool weather.

caeruleum p. 146

Southern Star. Twining stem, to 3 ft. (90 cm) long. Flowers pale blue darkening with age, ⅛ in. (3.2 mm) long, starlike, solitary to a few. Brazil, Uruguay. Tender perennial grown as a tender annual.

Panicum
Grass family
Gramineae

Pan'i-kum. Panic Grass. A large genus of over 500 species of grasses found in all parts of the world, but mostly in the tropics.

Description
Creeping or erect, varying considerably in height and leaf size. Leaves usually flat. Flowers usually in light feathery clusters, in which the upper flowers are fertile and the lower ones rarely so.

How to Grow
In early spring work up the soil and lay down a 2–3 ft. (60–90 cm) square of clear plastic. Secure the edges with soil. Cut a 6-in. (15-cm) cross in center, and plant seeds where they can grow through the slits. Cover plastic with dried grass clippings to shade out weeds. Prefers warm weather.

miliaceum pp. *175, 178*
Millet; Broomcorn Millet. 3–4 ft. (90–120 cm) high. Spikelets ¼ in. (6 mm) long, green, drooping, in 1-ft. (30-cm) panicles, the stalks slender and crowded. Cultivated from earliest times for fodder and grain. East Indies. 'Violaceum' has purple spikelets. Hardy annual.

Papaver
Poppy family
Papaveraceae

Pap-a'ver. The true poppies comprise a genus of about 50 species of herbs found mostly in the temperate regions of Europe and Asia and a few in w. North America.

Description
Leaves basal, generally many, usually deeply segmented and hairy. Flowers solitary, on a long slender stalk, nodding when in bud, but straightening as the flower opens. Calyx of 2 sepals, which fall when the petals open. Corolla of 5 petals, vividly colored red, violet, yellow, or white, sometimes blotched at the base. Stamens numerous. If cut or broken, plant exudes a milky substance.

How to Grow
Because poppies do not transplant well, sow seeds where plants are to remain or start indoors in peat pots. Where winters are mild, sow outdoors in fall or very early spring. Elsewhere, start seeds indoors in midwinter and plant out when seedlings are a good size. They prefer cool weather.

nudicaule p. *252*
Iceland Poppy. To 12 in. (30 cm) high. Flowers fragrant, 1–3 in. (2.5–7.5 cm) wide, yellow, orange, reddish, or white, petals 4 or 8. Many cultivars, some with double blossoms. Arctic regions south to Colorado, Eurasia. One of the more difficult poppies to grow but a favorite for winter and early

spring color in Calif., warm Southwest, and
Deep South. Perennial grown as a half-hardy
annual.

Rhoeas p. 255
Corn Poppy; Flanders Poppy. To 3 ft.
(90 cm) high. Stems branching and wiry.
Flowers red, deep purple, scarlet, or
occasionally white, 2 in. (5 cm) wide, petals
4. Europe and Asia, naturalized in North
America. The Shirley Poppy came from this
species and has become a great garden
favorite. Hardy annual.

somniferum p. 254
Opium Poppy. 3–4 ft. (90–120 cm) high.
Flowers often double, white, pink, red, or
purple, 3–4 in. (7.5–10.0 cm) wide, petals
sometimes fringed. Greece and the Orient.
The juice of the unripe pod yields opium,
the production of which is illegal in the U.S.
Hardy annual.

Pelargonium
Geranium family
Geraniaceae

Pee-lar-go′ni-um. Garden Geranium; Stork's-
Bill Geranium. A large genus of 250 species
of South African herbs and shrubs, their
habits being very diverse.

Description
Stems strong-growing or trailing, herbaceous
or woody. Leaves alternate, stalked, simple,
entire and roundish, or much cut and often
fernlike, some deeply marked on the upper
side, a few fragrant. Flowers showy, irregular,
ranging from pure white to pink, crimson,
and bright scarlet, in umbel-like clusters
growing on leafless stalks from leaf axils.
Calyx of 5 sepals joined at the base. Petals 5.
Stamens 10.

How to Grow
Start seeds indoors in late winter or early
spring. Bottom heat of 70–75° F (21–24° C)
helps seeds sprout in 14–21 days. Start early
so that plants will have flower buds when
planted outdoors after frost. Although these
are warm-weather plants, midsummer heat
and humidity, especially in Deep South, can
cause them to burn out and die. Direct
seeding will not work.

× *domesticum* p. 108
Martha Washington Geranium; Summer Azalea. To 18 in. (45 cm) high. Flowers 1½–3 in. (4.0–7.5 cm) wide, white, pink, or red, 2 upper petals usually blotched darker. Needs cool nights. Tender perennial grown as a tender annual.

× *hortorum* p. 257
Zonal Geranium; Fish Geranium. 1–3 ft. (30–90 cm) high. Umbels many-flowered and flat-topped. Flowers 2–2½ in. (5–6 cm) wide, red, salmon-pink, white, coral, peach, and bicolored, some with double blossoms. Faint fishlike odor. This group of hybrids based on *P. zonale* and *P. inquinans*. Tender perennial grown as a tender annual.

peltatum p. 260
Ivy Geranium; Hanging Geranium. Stems trailing to 3 ft. (90 cm) long. 5- to 7-flowered. Flowers 2–2½ in. (5–6 cm) wide, white to deep rose, upper petals having dark markings. Many cultivars and hybrid derivatives are available. Tender perennial grown as a tender annual.

Pennisetum
Grass family
Gramineae

Pen-i-see'tum. A genus of 80 species of chiefly tropical grasses, some ornamental.

Description
Leaf blades flat and narrow, sometimes colored. Flowers in a spikelike panicle, the spikelets having beneath them bristles, sometimes plumed, often longer than the spikelets.

How to Grow
In early spring work up the soil and lay down a 2–3 ft. (60–90 cm) square of clear plastic. Secure the edges with soil. Cut a 6-in. (15-cm) cross in center, and plant seeds where they can grow through the slits. Cover plastic with dried grass clippings to shade out weeds. These grasses prefer warm weather.

setaceum pp. 172, 177
Fountain Grass. 3–4 ft. (90–120 cm) high. Leaf blades many, green or variously colored. Spikes to 14 in. (35 cm) long, curved or

nodding, the bristles ¾ in. (19 mm) long.
Ethiopia. Cultivars, with the spikes and
foliage pink, rose-purple, coppery, or reddish.
The leading ornamental species. Also called
P. Ruppelii. Perennial grown as a half-hardy
annual.

villosum *p. 173*
Feathertop. To 2 ft. (60 cm) high. Leaf
blades many. Spikes to 4 in. (10 cm) long,
off-white, feathery, with many bristles, to
2 in. (5 cm) long. Africa. Also called
P. longistylum. Perennial grown as a
half-hardy annual.

Penstemon
Snapdragon family
Scrophulariaceae

Pen-stee'mon. Beardtongue. A large genus of
250 species of herbs, rarely shrubs, chiefly
from the w. U.S. Many of the species are
important bee plants in the West.

Description
Leaves opposite or whorled, and showy.
Flowers 2-lipped, tubular, mostly in terminal
racemes or panicles. Calyx 5-parted. Corolla
with the lower lip 3-lobed, the upper lip
2-lobed. Stamens 5, with 4 fertile, the fifth
sterile and often bearded.

How to Grow
Start seeds indoors in very early spring. Seeds
need light for germination and sprout slowly
and unevenly. Transplant outdoors after last
frost. Well-drained, enriched soil, with a pH
6.5–7.0, produces the best results. Grow in
full sun in cool climates, but give afternoon
shade where summers are long and hot.
Plants prefer cool weather.

gloxinioides *p. 256*
Penstemon. 2–3 ft. (60–90 cm) high.
Flowers 2 in. (5 cm) wide, bell-shaped with
flared lip, colors ranging from white to
crimson and blue. Mexico. This hybrid
derives from *P. Hartwegii* and *P. Cobaea.*
Much grown on the West Coast. Half-hardy
annual.

Perilla
Mint family
Labiatae

Per-rill′a. A small genus of tender herbaceous annuals, natives of e. Asia.

Description
Leaves green or dark reddish brown, in opposite pairs, inversely heart-shaped. Flowers small, in pairs, borne in the axils or bracts in terminal racemes.

How to Grow
Sow seeds indoors in late winter or early spring. Transplant outdoors after last frost. Or sow outdoors after danger of frost is over. Self-sows in warm areas. Frequently escapes and becomes a weed. Prefers warm weather.

frutescens pp. 184, 185
Beefsteak Plant. To 3 ft. (90 cm) high. Leaves green on both sides, occasionally marked reddish brown, slightly wrinkled, the margins slightly toothed, 3–6 in. (7.5– 15.0 cm) long. Flowers small, 3–8 in a raceme, the corolla white, sometimes tinged red. India and Japan. Cultivar 'Atropurpurea' has dark purple leaves. Cultivar 'Crispa' has deeply cut, wrinkled leaves of dark reddish purple with bronze sheen. Tender annual.

Petunia
Potato family
Solanaceae

Pe-too′ni-a. An important group of garden flowers, comprising about 30 species of herbs, nearly all from Argentina.

Description
Leaves soft, without marginal teeth, alternate below but the upper ones opposite. Flowers variously colored, the corolla funnel-shaped. Stamens 5, 4 in pairs, the odd one smaller, rudimentary, and sterile.

How to Grow
Sow seeds indoors 8–10 weeks before last spring frost. Seeds are tiny and need not be covered. Transplant outdoors after danger of frost is past. During hot weather, water frequently. Shear back after blooming, feed and water to rejuvenate plants. Remove

self-sown seedlings, since they tend to have washed-out colors. Prefers warm weather.

× *hybrida* pp. 82, 247
Common Garden Petunia. 8–18 in. (20–45 cm) high. Flowers 2–4 in. (5–10 cm) wide, sometimes fringed, double, or wavy, ranging from white to pink, red, purple, blue, or yellow, often striped, barred, or otherwise marked. Grandiflora types have large, fancy blossoms. Multiflora kinds have smaller, simpler flowers, but are more disease resistant. These hybrids derive from *P. axillaris* and *P. violacea*. Half-hardy annual.

Phacelia
Waterleaf family
Hydrophyllaceae

Fa-see′li-a. About 175 species of American herbaceous plants, found mostly in the northwestern states.

Description
Leaves simple or compound, alternate, fleshy, sometimes hairy, veins prominent on underside. Flowers blue, purple, or white, arranged in rolled 1-sided racemes, the raceme unrolling as the flowers open. Individual flowers on short stalks. Calyx of 5 narrow sepals, widening toward the apex, but joined at the base. Corolla bell-shaped, the petals 5, sometimes with sterile anther lobes between the petals. Stamens 5, conspicuous.

How to Grow
Where winters are mild, sow outdoors in late summer or fall. Where winters are severe, wait until early spring. Prefers cool weather and well-drained average to dry soil, such as sandy or gravelly banks with pH 6.5–7.0. Best when planted in masses.

campanularia p. 131
California Bluebell. To 8 in. (20 cm) high. Flowers to 1 in. (2.5 cm) wide, bell-shaped, deep blue, with 5 white anther lobes between petals. Deserts of s. Calif. Hardy annual.

Phalaris
Grass family
Gramineae

Fal'ar-ris. About 15 species of ornamental and seed-yielding grasses in the north temperate zone, cultivated for the variegated foliage, the species below a source of birdseed.

Description
Leaf blades flat and narrow. Flower cluster terminal, usually a narrow spike or panicle, its spikelets flattened but not bristled.

How to Grow
In early spring work up the soil and lay down a 2–3 ft. (60–90 cm) square of clear plastic. Secure the edges with soil. Cut 6-in. (15-cm) crosses, and plant seeds where they can grow through the slits. Cover plastic with dried grass clippings to shade out weeds. Prefers warm weather.

canariensis p. 176
Canary Grass. 18–24 in. (45–60 cm) high. Spikelets broad, more or less egg-shaped, ⅝ in. (16 mm) long, pale with green stripes. Europe, but naturalized in the U.S. Hardy annual.

Phaseolus
Pea family
Leguminosae

Fa-see'o-lus. Twenty species of mostly tropical herbs, including important beans grown for food or forage. The species below grown for ornament.

Description
Chiefly twining plants with compound leaves, mostly with 3 leaflets. Flowers pealike, but the keel coiled, variously colored. Fruit a somewhat flattened or cylindrical pod, edible itself or grown for its highly nutritious seeds.

How to Grow
Sow seeds a week or so before last spring frost. Plant 2 or 3 seeds 1 in. (2.5 cm) deep, then thin to the best seedling. Provide tall, strong supports early so vines will not be injured in the wind. Prefers warm weather.

coccineus p. 262
Scarlet Runner; Flowering Bean; Painted
Lady. A tall-growing vine, 6–8 ft. (1.8–
2.4 m) long. Flowers scarlet, showy, 1 in.
(2.5 cm) long. Tropical America. Young
pods are delicious. Also sold as *P. multiflora.*
The variety *albus,* called the White Dutch
Runner or Dutch Case-Knife Bean, has
white flowers and edible seeds; there is also a
dwarf, bushy form. Perennial grown as a
half-hardy annual.

Phlox
Phlox family
Polemoniaceae

Flocks. About 60 species of usually hardy
herbs found mostly in North America.

Description
Leaves lance-shaped, opposite and in pairs, or
alternate. Flowers showy, in loose or closely
packed terminal clusters, ranging from white
to red, pale lilac, or purple, the corolla
tube usually having an eyelike marking at
the opening. Calyx of 5 sepals united
halfway down. Corolla of 5 united petals
forming a short, narrow tube. Stamens 5,
usually enclosed in the corolla tube.

How to Grow
Easy to grow and long-flowering. Sow
outdoors in very early spring or, in mild
climates, late summer through fall. Where
growing season is short, start seeds indoors
8–10 weeks before last frost and set out
seedlings 2–3 weeks before danger of frost is
past. Harden off before transplanting. Prefers
well-drained soil, pH 6.5–7.0, and full sun.
Heat-resistant in dry seasons. Does best with
cool weather, but will bloom in spring in
warm-weather areas.

Drummondii p. 246
Annual Phlox; Drummond Phlox; Texan
Pride. To 18 in. (45 cm) high. Flowers
ranging from white and yellow to lavender,
blue, pink, and red, 1–1½ in. (2.5–4.0 cm)
wide, in umbel-like clusters. Tex. Cultivars
include 'Twinkle', which has fancy star-
shaped, often 2-colored blossoms. Hardy
annual.

Pimpinella
Carrot family
Umbelliferae

Pim-pi-nell′a. Numerous species of perennial or annual herbs from the north temperate zone, only the one below grown in gardens.

Description
Leaves twice- or thrice-compound, the ultimate segments mostly toothed. Flowers small, in a compound umbel.

How to Grow
In the North, start seeds indoors in peat pots about 8 weeks before last spring frost and set out in the garden when the soil is warm. Seeds germinate slowly. In mild areas, sow outdoors after frost. Prefers cool weather.

Anisum p. 213
Anise. To 2 ft. (60 cm) high. Flowers yellowish white in loose cluster, to 2 in. (5 cm) wide. S. Europe and Egypt. Hardy annual.

Platystemon
Poppy family
Papaveraceae

Plat-i-stee′mon. A single, attractive species from Calif.

Description
Leaves entire. Flowers with 3 sepals and 6 petals.

How to Grow
When weather becomes warm, sow seeds where plants are to remain. Likes plenty of water but not soggy soil. Prefers cool weather.

californicus p. 200
Creamcups. 6–12 in. (15–30 cm) high. Flowers solitary, 1 in. (2.5 cm) wide, long-stalked, cream-colored or light yellow. Stamens numerous, some of them flattened and petal-like. Hardy annual.

Polygonum
Knotweed family
Polygonaceae

Pol-lig'o-num. Smartweed; Knotweed. Erect,
trailing, or climbing herbs, comprising about
150 worldwide species of very diverse habits.

Description
Stems angled, swollen at the joints where
leaf base clasps the stem, sometimes spotted
or streaked brown. Leaves alternate and
simple. Flowers small, in terminal spikes or
loose racemes. Calyx of 5 sepals generally
colored pink or white. Corolla absent.
Stamens 3–9.

How to Grow
Seeds sprout in warm soil. Start indoors in
early spring and transplant after danger of
frost is past. Needs sunny locations. Will
persist for years through volunteer seedlings.
The species below prefer warm weather.

capitatum p. 117
Knotweed. Trailing to 10 in. (25 cm) long,
and to 6 in. (15 cm) high. Flowers tiny,
pink, with 5 sepals, in dense heads to ¾ in.
(19 mm) wide. Himalayas. Perennial treated
as a half-hardy annual.

orientale p. 94
Kiss-Me-Over-the-Garden-Gate; Prince's-
Feather. To 6 ft. (1.8 m) high. Flowers tiny,
pink or rose, clustered on dense branching
spikes to 3½ in. (9 cm) long. Asia and
Australia, naturalized in North America.
Perennial grown as a hardy annual.

Polypogon
Grass family
Gramineae

Pol-li-po'gon. About 10 species of grasses
with soft silky inflorescences.

Description
Leaf blades flat and narrow. Flowers in
spikelike panicles.

How to Grow
In early spring work up the soil and lay
down a 2–3 ft. (60–90 cm) square of clear
plastic. Secure the edges with soil. Cut
6-in. (15-cm) crosses, and plant seeds

where they can grow through the slits.
Cover plastic with dried grass clippings to
shade out weeds. Prefers warm weather.

monspeliensis p. 175
Rabbit-Foot Grass. To 30 in. (75 cm) high,
usually to 24 in. (60 cm) high in the
garden. Leaf blades flat, 6 in. (15 cm) long.
Spikelets green or pale yellow, to 6 in.
(15 cm) long and covered with fine bristles.
Admired for its furry flower and seed heads.
Europe. Hardy annual.

Portulaca
Purslane family
Portulacaceae

Por-tew-lak′a. Purslane. Low-growing, mostly
trailing herbs, comprising about 100 species
from tropical and temperate regions.

Description
Stems soft and fleshy, often reddish. Leaves
alternate, small, thick, entire, often spoon-
shaped, 1–2 in. (2.5–5.0 cm) long. Flowers
usually terminal, usually opening only in
full sunlight, sometimes inconspicuous,
sometimes showy. Calyx of 5 sepals. Corolla
of 5 petals, in varying colors. Stamens
numerous.

How to Grow
Seeds are very fine and tend to wash away or
be buried if sown directly in the garden.
Start seeds indoors 6–8 weeks before last
frost and set out when soil is warm. Plants
need full sun and sandy, well-drained soil.
They prefer warm weather.

grandiflora p. 253
Rose Moss; Garden Portulaca; Sun Moss;
Wax Pink. Trailing to 10 in. (25 cm) long,
much branched. Flowers terminal, showy,
1 in. (2.5 cm) wide, ranging from white,
pink, and yellow to red and purple. Suitable
for dry banks or rock gardens. Brazil. Tender
annual.

oleracea p. 208
Purslane; Pussley. Trailing to 18 in. (45 cm)
long. Flowers small, ⅜ in. (9 mm) wide,
yellow. India. The cultivar 'Giganthes' has
1-in. (2.5-cm) flowers; 'Wildfire Mixed'
comes in several colors. Hardy annual.

pilosa p. 85

Trailing to 12 in. (30 cm) long. Flowers rose-red, ½ in. (13 mm) wide, with 5 petals and many stamens. N.C. to Fla. 'Hortualis' has reddish-purple flowers, ¾ in. (19 mm) wide. Tender annual.

Primula
Primrose family
Primulaceae

Prim'you-la. Primrose. A large genus of over 400 species of low-growing, herbaceous plants of the northern hemisphere, found mostly in alpine and cool localities.

Description
Stems short or none. Leaves crowded, stalked, long and narrow, or roundish or tufted, the midrib generally prominent on underside. Flowers on leafless stalks, sometimes with leafy bracts, solitary, or in loose umbels, in whorled tiers, or in rounded heads. Flowers yellow, white, red, blue, pink, or purple. Calyx of 5 sepals, joined halfway, usually slightly inflated, generally pale green. Corolla of 5 lobes, tubular at the base. Stamens 5, not protruding.

How to Grow
After refrigerating them for 3 weeks, sow fresh seeds indoors in fall for spring flowers. Transplant seedlings to progressively larger pots. Plant out after spring frost. Seedlings can also winter in protected cold frames. In low elevations of Calif., direct seed in fall. All species prefer cool weather.

malacoides p. 114

Fairy Primrose. 4–18 in. (10–45 cm) high. Flowers lilac or pink, to ½ in. (13 mm) wide, in several whorls on each stalk. China. 'Alba' has white flowers, 'Rosea' bright rose-colored flowers. In low elevations of Calif., will bloom in winter and early spring. In northern and coastal gardens, blooms in summer. Perennial grown as a half-hardy annual.

obconica p. 115

German Primrose. To 12 in. (30 cm) high. Flowers lilac, pink, red, and white, 1 in. (2.5 cm) wide, in many-flowered umbels. China. Many good cultivars. Same blooming times as *P. malacoides*. Leaves can cause mild skin irritation. Perennial grown as a half-hardy annual.

× *polyantha* p. 247

Polyanthus. To 12 in. (30 cm) high. Flowers 1½–2 in. (4–5 cm) wide, purple, blue, rose, yellow, white, or scarlet, in profuse clusters. Blooms in spring. Hybrids derived from *P. elatior, P. veris,* and *P. vulgaris.* The easiest primrose to grow. Perennial treated as a hardy annual.

Proboscidea
Martynia family
Martyniaceae

Pro-bos-sid′i-a. Nine species of curiously fruited, clammy or sticky American herbs. Grown for ornament or edible seed pods.

Description
Leaves large, with long stems. Flowers in a loose raceme, the corolla 5-lobed, stamens 4. Sepals fused in a tubelike structure.

How to Grow
Where summers are short, start seeds indoors 6–8 weeks before last frost. Transplant to garden when danger of frost is past. Where summers are long, sow seeds in warm soil. Does best with enriched garden soil. Prefers warm weather.

louisianica p. 165

Unicorn-Plant; Devil's-Claw; Proboscis-Flower. Sprawling, to 3 ft. (90 cm) long. Flowers bell- or funnel-shaped, the limb slightly 2-lipped, creamy white to purple or pinkish, in few-flowered clusters in axils, having a musky odor. Corolla 1–2 in. (2.5–5.0 cm) long. Stamens 4, joined by the anthers. In the South, young pods are used like pickling cucumbers. Se. U.S. Tender annual.

Pueraria
Pea family
Leguminosae

Poo-er-ray′ri-a. A genus of Asiatic and East Indian rapid-growing vines, related to *Canavalia.*

Description
Leaves compound, with 3 leaflets. Flowers
blue or purple, pea-shaped, borne in racemes
in leaf axils.

How to Grow
Sow seeds outdoors when danger of frost is
past. Plant near a trellis or other support.
Prefers warm weather.

lobata p. 96
Kudzu Vine. A somewhat woody, hairy-
stemmed vine, to 60 ft. (18 m) long.
Flowers purple to pinkish, ½ in. (13 mm)
wide, fragrant, in dense upright racemes
nearly 12 in. (30 cm) long. China and Japan.
Sometimes called *P. hirsuta.* A quick grower
useful for making dense shade over arbors.
Widely grown in the South as a forage
crop. May become a weedy pest. Perennial
grown as a half-hardy annual.

Reseda
Mignonette family
Resedaceae

Re-zee′da. A genus of 50–60 species of erect
or reclining herbs, sometimes woody at the
base, from the Mediterranean region. A few
species are cultivated.

Description
Leaves alternate or clustered, simple or
divided pinnately in some species. Flowers
small, in long spikes, and composed of 4–7
petals.

How to Grow
Plant outdoors in early spring and again in
late summer to prolong period of bloom.
They need enriched soil and sun to partial
shade. Thin seedlings since plants are
difficult to transplant. The species below
prefer cool weather.

alba p. 167
White Mignonette. To 3 ft. (90 cm) high.
Flowers ½ in. (13 mm) wide, in clusters,
greenish white, with 5–6 sepals and petals.
Mediterranean region. Hardy annual.

lutea p. 214
Wild Mignonette. To 30 in. (75 cm) high.
Flowers ¼ in. (6 mm) wide, greenish
yellow, in clusters, usually with 6 sepals

and petals. Mediterranean region. Biennial grown as a hardy annual.

odorata p. 215
Common Mignonette. To 1 ft. (30 cm) high. Flowers ⅓ in. (8 mm) wide, yellowish, in terminal clusters or spikes, petals 4–7. Mediterranean region and the Red Sea. Grown for its sweet fragrance. Hardy annual.

Ricinus
Spurge family
Euphorbiaceae

Ris'i-nus. A single species of gigantic herbs or trees, probably originally native to Africa, but now widespread throughout the tropics and subtropics. Beans are a source of castor oil and poison. Grown in the garden for its leaves.

Description
Leaves alternate, simple, with long stems. Flowers in panicles, male below, female above.

How to Grow
Where summers are short, start seeds indoors 6–8 weeks before last spring frost. Where summers are long, sow outdoors in warm soil. Do not peel or nick seeds because their juice can cause severe allergic problems. Seeds are highly poisonous and should not be planted in households with children. Plant prefers warm weather.

communis pp. 266, 267
Castor Bean; Castor-Oil Plant. 4–15 ft. (1.2–4.5 m) high, though in the tropical areas it grows to 30 ft. (9 m) high. Leaves often 3 ft. (90 cm) wide. Flowers in dense terminal clusters often 1–2 ft. (30–60 cm) long, the individual flowers ½ in. (13 mm) wide, reddish brown, without petals. Tropical Africa. Many cultivars, including one with much larger green leaves, another with red stems and bluish-gray leaves, and several others with red, variegated, or white-veined leaves. Tender annual.

Rudbeckia
Daisy family
Compositae

Rood-beck′i-a. Coneflower. North American hardy herbs, comprising about 25 species.

Description
Leaves usually alternate, simple or compound, in some species much cut and lance-shaped, veins prominent, margins deeply toothed toward the tip. Flowers in terminal or axillary heads, generally yellow, in most species the disk flowers being brown or black.

How to Grow
Easy to grow. Sow outdoors in warm soil. Where growing season is short, start seeds indoors 8–10 weeks before last spring frost. Seedlings transplant easily. Plants grow rather large and should be set 18 in. (45 cm) apart. They prefer warm weather.

hirta p. 223
Black-eyed Susan. 1–3 ft. (30–90 cm) high, covered with short stiff hairs. Flowers daisylike, 2–3 in. (5.0–7.5 cm) wide, ray flowers yellow, disk flowers purplish brown. Originally restricted to the Midwest, now naturalized from s. Canada to n. Mexico. Many desirable cultivars have been created by hybridizing *R. hirta* and by breeding for tetraploid forms such as the 'Gloriosa Daisy' below. In the process, a rough-looking wildflower has become a mainstay in summer gardens. Very resistant to heat and drought. Short-lived perennial grown as a half-hardy annual.

hirta 'Gloriosa Daisy' pp. 222, 241
2–3 ft. (60–90 cm) high. Flowers to 6 in. (15 cm) wide, from yellow and gold to mahogany, red, or bicolored. Some with double or semidouble blossoms. Short-lived perennial grown as a half-hardy annual.

Sabatia
Gentian family
Gentianaceae

Sab-bay′she-a. American Centaury; Sea Pink; Rose Pink. A genus of 17 species of mostly weak herbs found in e. North America and occasionally cultivated.

Description
Erect, branching herbs with opposite, stalkless leaves, usually ovate but linear in some species. Flowers in clusters at ends of branches.

How to Grow
These plants like damp soil and partial shade. Sow seeds in early spring. They prefer cool weather.

angularis p. 153
Rose Pink. To 3 ft. (90 cm) high. Flowers 1½ in. (4 cm) across, pink, sometimes so pale as to appear whitish, with 5 petals and yellow center. E. North America. Hardy annual.

Salpiglossis
Potato family
Solanaceae

Sal-pi-gloss´is. Chilean herbs comprising about 5 species, mostly covered with short, sticky hairs.

Description
Leaves alternate, broadly lance-shaped, margins wavy or slightly cut. Flowers in loose terminal clusters growing from the axils of small leafy bracts. Individual flowers large, showy, velvety, colors varying, generally veined with gold. Calyx of 5 sepals, joined three-quarters of their length. Corolla funnel-shaped, widely open at the throat, the 5 lobes notched. Stamens 5.

How to Grow
Start seeds indoors in early spring. Don't cover seeds; simply press into soil. Water from bottom. Transplant seedlings to the garden 2 weeks before last frost. The larger seedlings are when transplanted outdoors, the longer the bloom before hot weather or humidity kills plants. Will bloom through summer only in very cool gardens. They prefer cool weather.

sinuata p. 248
Painted-Tongue. To 3 ft. (90 cm) high, branching. Flowers showy, 2 in. (5 cm) wide, funnel-shaped, with wide, open throat, in gold, red, pink, blue, or many other colors and patterns, including herringbone markings. Chile. Tender annual.

Salvia
Mint family
Labiatae

Sal'vi-a. Sage. About 750 species of herbs, subshrubs, or shrubs distributed throughout the tropical and temperate world. The leaves of some species are used as a seasoning.

Description
Stems usually square. Leaves in pairs, opposite, simple, ovalish or lance-shaped, sometimes hairy, the margins toothed or deeply cut into segments, smaller toward the top. Flowers in whorls, the clusters 2- to many-flowered, growing from the axils of small, leafy bracts and arranged in terminal spikes or racemes. Colors varying. Calyx 5-lobed, joined about halfway down. Corolla 2-lipped, 3 lobes in the lower lip and 2 in the upper lip. Stamens 4, in pairs.

How to Grow
All species benefit from being started indoors, but they grow fairly reliably if sown outdoors in warm soil where summers are hot. Start seeds indoors 10 weeks before last frost. Give 75° F (24° C) bottom heat. When danger of frost is past, set out in open, sunny position. Give plenty of water in dry weather. In the South, Southwest, and low elevations of Calif., plants need light to moderate shade. Will not perform well where humidity is quite low. All prefer warm weather.

argentea *p. 183*
Silver Sage. 2–4 ft. (60–120 cm) high. Basal leaves broadly ovalish, to 6 in. (15 cm) long, cut into lobes or irregularly toothed, covered with white woolly hairs. Flowers 4–8 in interrupted whorls. Individual flowers to ½ in. (13 mm) long, showy, upper lip longer than lower lip, whitish yellow or purplish. Mediterranean region. Perennial grown as a half-hardy annual.

farinacea *p. 142*
Mealy-Cup Sage. To 3 ft. (90 cm) high, covered with whitish, short hairs, and mealy. Flowers ½ in. (13 mm) long, in many-whorled racemes, violet-blue. Flower-stalks sometimes bluish. Tex. Good for cutting. Perennial grown as half-hardy annual.

patens p. 140
Gentian Sage. To 3 ft. (90 cm) high and covered with short sticky hairs. Flowers blue, 2–3 in. (5.0–7.5 cm) long, in pairs, in widely spaced racemes. Mts. of Mexico. Cultivar 'Alba' has white flowers. Perennial grown as a half-hardy annual.

Sclarea p. 95
Clary; Clear-Eye. To 3 ft. (90 cm) high. Bracts white at base, rose at tip. Flowers bluish white, 1 in. (2.5 cm) long, in loose, whorled racemes. S. Europe. Perennial or biennial grown as a half-hardy annual.

splendens p. 264
Scarlet Sage. To 3 ft. (90 cm) high. Bracts colored. Flowers typically scarlet, also white or rose-colored, 1½ in. (4 cm) long, in whorled racemes. Brazil. Widely used for summer bedding. Tender annual.

viridis p. 141
To 18 in. (45 cm) high. Flowers white, rose, reddish purple or deep purple, ½ in. (13 mm) long, in unbranched, elongated spikes. S. Europe. Also called *S. Horminum.* Half-hardy annual.

Sanvitalia
Daisy family
Compositae

San-vi-tal′i-a. North American tender herbaceous annuals comprising about 7 species.

Description
Leaves simple, opposite, ovalish. Flowers in small terminal heads. Ray flowers yellow or white, the disk flowers brown or purplish black.

How to Grow
Easy to grow. Prefers warm weather and light, open soil in full sun. Sow in early spring indoors or in a cold frame, or direct seed when warm weather arrives. Resistant to heat and humidity.

procumbens p. 221
Creeping Zinnia. Trailing to 6 in. (15 cm) long. Flowerheads numerous, to 1 in. (2.5 cm) wide. Ray flowers yellow, disk flowers purple. Mexico. New golden forms. Good

for hanging baskets and ground covers.
Tender annual.

Satureja
Mint family
Labiatae

Sat-you-ree′a. Savory. About 30 species of
aromatic herbs or small shrubs, distributed
through the temperate regions of the world.
The species below is used as an herb.
Sometimes spelled *Satureia*.

Description
Stems usually square. Leaves opposite,
ovalish or lance-shaped, the margins
sometimes toothed. Flowers pink, white, or
purplish, in whorls, in axillary or terminal
racemes. Calyx 5-lobed, usually tubular.
Corolla a narrow tube opening into 2 lips,
upper lip 2-lobed and flat, lower lip 3-lobed
and widely flaring. Stamens 4, in pairs.

How to Grow
Grown chiefly for its flavorful leaves;
sometimes for its flowers. Easy to grow in
average to dry soil. Sow seeds outdoors in
early spring. This species prefers warm
weather.

hortensis p. 151
Summer Savory. To 18 in. (45 cm) high.
Flowers pink, lavender, or white, ½ in.
(13 mm) long, in loose whorls, in spikes.
Europe, naturalized in the U.S. Hardy
annual.

Saxifraga
Saxifrage family
Saxifragaceae

Sacks-iff′ra-ga. Saxifrage; Rockfoil. About
300 species of herbs found chiefly in the
temperate regions of Europe and America.
Very diverse, but usually low-growing, or
creeping, the rootstocks spreading by offsets
or runners.

Description
Leaves thick and fleshy or soft and mosslike,
roundish or spoon-shaped to ovalish,
sometimes arranged in a rosette. Margins
generally toothed, often encrusted as with

lime, hence silvery. Flowers pink, white, purple, or yellow, in clusters. Calyx of 5 sepals, spreading. Corolla of 5 or more petals. Stamens 10 or more.

How to Grow
Sow in garden in early spring. For best results, plant in positions shaded from midday sun in average, well-drained soil supplemented with lime. Prefers cool weather.

Cymbalaria p. 200
Low, spreading, to 2 in. (5 cm) high. Flowers star-shaped, yellow, ¼ in. (6 mm) wide. Caucasus Mts. of Asia. Self-sows. Half-hardy annual.

Scabiosa
Teasel family
Dipsacaceae

Skay′bi-o′sa. Scabious; Pincushion. About 80 species of herbs found mostly in the temperate regions.

Description
Leaves simple, opposite, ovalish or lance-shaped, often lobed or deeply cut. Flowering stalk long. Flowers in terminal heads, surrounded by 2 rows of small leafy bracts, blue, purple, brownish black, reddish brown, pink, cream, or white. Calyx represented by bristles. Corolla tubular, sometimes 2-lipped, with lower lip greatly extended. Stamens 4.

How to Grow
Easy to grow and long-flowering in average garden soil. Sow indoors or in a cold frame in early spring. Transplant outdoors, 1 ft. (30 cm) apart, in sunny spot after danger of frost is past. A quick second crop can be grown in the South by sowing seeds in late summer. The species below prefer warm weather.

atropurpurea p. 119
Sweet Scabious; Mourning Bride. 2–3 ft. (60–90 cm) high, branching. Flowers double, dark purple, pink, or white, the heads to 2 in. (5 cm) across. Europe. One of the best cut flowers. There are many cultivars. Half-hardy annual.

stellata p. 118
To 18 in. (45 cm) high. Flowers blue or
rose-violet, in heads to 1¼ in. (3 cm) wide.
Whole plant finely-hairy. Good dried flower.
W. Mediterranean region. Half-hardy annual.

Schizanthus
Potato family
Solanaceae

Sky-zan'thus. Fringe Flower; Butterfly
Flower; Poor Man's Orchid. Chilean brittle
annuals, comprising about 10 species.

Description
Leaves alternate, broadly lance-shaped, usually
cut into many fernlike, light green segments.
Flowers showy, in terminal, loose, many-
flowered clusters, of many colors. Corolla
margins of contrasting colors or shades,
with streaks and spots of another color or
shade at the base. Calyx 5-lobed, joined at
the base. Corolla a short tube opening
widely into 2 lips, the upper 2-lobed, the
lower 3-lobed. Stamens 2, prominent.

How to Grow
Grown from seed as a winter or spring
annual in protected gardens in Calif. In
northern and cool coastal gardens grow in a
cold frame to flower-bud stage, then set out
in garden as soon as danger of frost is past.
Will not do well elsewhere. The species
below prefer cool weather.

pinnatus p. 105
Butterfly Flower. To 4 ft. (120 cm) high;
usually less. Flowers 1½ in. (4 cm) wide,
lower lip lilac or purplish, upper lip usually
paler, lower part of upper lip marked yellow,
and spotted or marked purple toward the
base. Cultivars are available in white, red, or
rose. Stamens prominent. Chile. Tender
annual.

× *wisetonensis* p. 104
Butterfly Flower. 1–2 ft. (30–60 cm) high.
Flowers white, blue, pink, yellow, red,
magenta, or combined colors, upper lip
streaked yellow. Hybrid derived from
S. *pinnatus* and S. *retusus* 'Grahamii'. Tender
annual.

Senecio
Daisy family
Compositae

Sen-ee′si-o. Groundsel; Ragwort. Over 2000
species of herbs, shrubs, or small trees, and a
few climbers, found throughout the world.

Description
Leaves alternate or basal. This large and
diverse genus is difficult to define, the chief
difference being in the rings of bracts that
surround the head. These do not overlap
each other, and the lower bracts are scale-
like, giving a calyxlike appearance to the
upper ring of bracts. Flowerheads generally
yellow, but sometimes purple, red, blue, or
white; solitary or in clusters. Heads often
showy, composed of ray and disk flowers,
but sometimes lacking ray flowers.

How to Grow
Of the 3 species below, *S. Cineraria,* a warm-
weather annual, and *S. elegans,* a cool-
weather annual, can be grown from seeds
started early indoors. Do not cover seeds,
because they need strong light and heat of
65–70° F (18.5–21.0° C) to germinate. Set
out in the garden 2–3 weeks before last
frost. These species need full sun and well-
drained soil. *Senecio × hybridus* is difficult to
grow, and is successful outdoors only in
coastal areas of Calif. Buy plants at the early
bloom stage and set out in the garden.
Plants in full bloom will not adjust. They
prefer cool weather.

Cineraria *p. 181*
Dusty Miller. To 2½ ft. (75 cm) high,
covered with long, white, matted hairs.
Leaves alternate, thick, cut into narrow,
rounded lobes. Flowers yellow or cream, in
small terminal clusters. Mediterranean region.
Many varieties available, some nearly white.
Grown for its foliage. Perennial grown as a
half-hardy annual.

elegans *p. 104*
Purple Ragwort. To 2 ft. (60 cm) high,
covered with sticky hairs. Flowerheads to
1 in. (2.5 cm) wide, the rays rosy purple or
white, the center yellow; heads in loose
branching clusters. South Africa. Also sold as
Jacobaea elegans. Many cultivars are available.
Perennial grown as a half-hardy annual.

× *hybridus* pp. 128, 245
Cineraria. 1–3 ft. (30–90 cm) high.
Flowerheads 2 in. (5 cm) wide, white to
reddish pink, blue, or purple, never yellow,
some with contrasting rings. Borne in
broadly branching clusters. Very variable.
This hybrid derives from *S. cruentus* and
S. Heritieri. Tender perennial grown as tender
annual.

Setaria
Grass family
Gramineae

See-tair′i-a. Chiefly agricultural, warm-
country grasses, comprising about 125
species, the one below chiefly a forage or
fodder grass.

Description
Leaf blades flat and narrow. Flowers in a
large, spikelike panicle, the spikelets having
beneath them bristles that persist after the
spikelet has fallen. Fruit an edible grain in
S. italica.

How to Grow
In early spring work up the soil and lay
down a 2–3 ft. (60–90 cm) square of clear
plastic. Secure the edges with soil. Cut a
6-in. (15-cm) cross in center, and plant seeds
where they can grow through the slits.
Cover plastic with dried grass clippings to
shade out weeds. Prefers warm weather.

italica p. 176
Foxtail Millet. 3–5 ft. (0.9–1.5 m) high. Leaf
blades rough, the basal sheath fringed with
hairs. Spikes to 12 in. (30 cm) long, the
bristles green, purplish, or brown. Eurasia.
Many cultivars are available, some with very
large spikes. Drooping plumes are attractive
cut. Hardy annual.

Silene
Pink family
Caryophyllaceae

Sy-lee′ne. Catchfly; Campion. About 500
species of herbs distributed throughout the
world. The species below useful for rock
gardens or borders.

Description
Erect, tufted or spreading plants, the stems or calyx sometimes sticky. Leaves opposite, simple, without teeth. Flowers solitary or in loose-branching clusters, white, pink, or red. Calyx tubular, its 5 lobes teethlike. Corolla of 5 separate petals. Stamens 10.

How to Grow
Easy to grow. Sow seeds in the fall or spring where plants will remain. They prefer warm weather.

Armeria p. 112
Sweet William Catchfly; None-So-Pretty. To 18 in. (45 cm) high. Flowers light or deep pink, to ½ in. (13 mm) across, in terminal clusters. S. Europe, naturalized in U.S. Hardy annual.

Silybum
Daisy family
Compositae

Sil-ly'bum. Annual or biennial herbs, comprising only 2 species, natives of the Mediterranean region. The species below grown as an ornamental plant for its silvery leaves. Also grown as a vegetable, since its roots, leaves, and flowerheads are edible.

Description
Leaves alternate, with white spots and veins on the upper side, the margins lobed and spiny. Flowerheads purplish, solitary and nodding. Many bracts surround the head, forming a globe-shaped receptacle.

How to Grow
Easy to grow from seeds. Sow outdoors in ordinary garden soil. Will bloom the first year if sown early. Can become a troublesome weed. Prefers cool weather.

Marianum p. 98
Holy Thistle; Lady's-Thistle; Milk Thistle. To 4 ft. (120 cm) high. Flowerheads rose to purplish red, to 2½ in. (6 cm) across. Bracts surrounding heads curved and spiny. Mediterranean region, naturalized in Calif. Hardy annual, sometimes biennial.

Solanum
Potato family
Solanaceae

So-lay'num. Nightshade. A huge genus of
herbs, shrubs, vines, and sometimes trees,
comprising about 1700 species of nearly
worldwide distribution, but overwhelmingly
tropical. The genus includes the Potato and
Eggplant, as well as ornamental plants for
the greenhouse or outdoor culture in the
South; some are pernicious weeds.

Description
Leaves alternate, the juice of the wilted
leaves deadly in some species, suspect in
most others. Flowers often borne in the leaf
axils or near them, often solitary or in
few-flowered clusters. Calyx united. Corolla
regular, shallowly bell- or wheel-shaped, the
5 stamens usually inserted on its throat.
Fruit edible in some species, deadly
poisonous in others.

How to Grow
Start seeds indoors 8–10 weeks before the
last spring frost. If given heat of 75° F
(24° C), seeds will sprout in 10–14 days. Set
out in the garden when the soil and weather
are warm. In cool climates, a black-plastic
mulch is recommended. The species below
prefers warm weather.

Melongena 'Golden Eggplant' *p. 190*
Ornamental Eggplant. To 2 ft. (60 cm)
high, with angled or lobed leaves. Flowers
violet-purple, nearly 2 in. (5 cm) wide,
usually nodding. Fruit 3–5 in. (7.5–
12.5 cm) wide, white turning golden yellow.
Africa, Asia. Several other cultivars available.
Tender annual.

Tagetes
Daisy family
Compositae

Tay-gee'teez. Marigold. A group of about
30 species of annual herbs, all native from
N. Mex. to Argentina, not from Africa or
France as implied by the common names
African Marigold and French Marigold. The
name "marigold" is commonly applied to
several different kinds of plants in addition
to *Tagetes*. The best known are the Pot
Marigold (*Calendula*), the Cape Marigold

(*Dimorphotheca*), and the Sea Marigold (*Mesembryanthemum*).

Description
Leaves strong-scented, mostly opposite and usually finely dissected. Flowerheads showy, solitary, or clustered. Below each head is a series of involucral bracts, united into a cuplike base.

How to Grow
Most of the species below are easy to grow from seeds sown outdoors 2–3 weeks before the last frost. Allow room to expand. They do well with enriched soil and full sun, except in the South and Southwest, where afternoon shade will prolong bloom. Triploid hybrids of *T. erecta* and *T. patula* have a low germination rate. Start seeds indoors at 65–70° F (18.5–21.0° C), 6–8 weeks before the last spring frost. Set out when the soil is warm. All kinds prefer warm weather.

erecta *pp. 231, 234*
African Marigold; Aztec Marigold; American Marigold. 18–36 in. (45–90 cm) high, branched and bushy. Flowerheads 2–6 in. (5–15 cm) wide, yellow or orange, the rays with a long claw, or even quilled in some forms. The stalk of the head is swollen just below the cluster. Mexico. Numerous cultivars, with large double flowers. There are also many new triploid hybrid forms derived from *T. erecta* and *T. patula*. Bred for early flowers that last up to frost, these hybrids also include white and mahogany-red blooms. Half-hardy annual.

patula *pp. 234, 235, 237*
French Marigold. To 18 in. (45 cm) high, much-branched. Flowerheads 2–3 in. (5.0–7.5 cm) wide, the numerous rays yellow with red markings. Mexico and Guatemala. There are many cultivars, ranging from pure yellow to nearly pure red, most with double or crested blossoms. Dwarf varieties are useful for edging. Half-hardy annual.

tenuifolia *p. 204*
Dwarf Marigold; Signet Marigold. To 12 in. (30 cm) high. Flowers yellow or orange, 1 in. (2.5 cm) wide. Mexico and Central America. Many cultivars are available, the most commonly grown belonging to the 'Pumila' group of dwarf forms. Half-hardy annual.

Thelesperma
Daisy family
Compositae

Thell-e-sper'ma. Coreopsis-like herbs
comprising about 12 species of w. North
America and s. South America.

Description
Leaves alternate and opposite, much divided
into threadlike segments. Flowerheads
solitary on long stems. The species below
differing only in technical characters from
Coreopsis.

How to Grow
Sow seeds outdoors in an open, sunny place
after the danger of frost is past. Plants prefer
warm weather.

Burridgeanum p. 227
12–18 in. (30–45 cm) high. Flowerheads
1½ in. (4 cm) wide, the ray flowers reddish
brown or orange, the margins yellow. Tex.
Also called *Coreopsis atrosanguinea* and
Cosmidium Burridgeanum. Hardy annual.

Thunbergia
Acanthus family
Acanthaceae

Thune-ber'ji-a. Mostly Asiatic or African
tender woody or herbaceous vines or shrubs
comprising about 100 species, the species
below grown for ornament. Sometimes called
clock vine.

Description
Leaves opposite, often arrow-shaped at the
base. Flowers showy, solitary in the leaf axils,
variously colored, and below them 2 or more
leafy bracts. Corolla funnel- or bell-shaped,
sometimes curved, the limb regular or nearly
so, not 2-lipped.

How to Grow
In mild-winter areas, sow seeds in the garden
in early spring. Elsewhere, start indoors 6–8
weeks before the last frost. Seeds germinate
slowly. Set out hardened-off seedlings when
soil is warm. Provide a support. These fairly
rampant vines will cover trellises or porches
in a short time. They prefer warm weather.

alata p. 221
Black-eyed Susan Vine. Twining vine to 6 ft. (1.8 m) long. Flowers long-stalked, 1½ in. (4 cm) long and 1–2 in. (2.5–5.0 cm) wide, white or orange-yellow, with purple throat. Tropical Africa. Many cultivars are available. Perennial but will bloom from seed in the first year if the growing season is long. Treated as a tender annual.

Tithonia
Daisy family
Compositae

Ti-tho′ni-a. Ten species of tall sunflowerlike shrubs or woody perennial herbs native in Mexico and Central America and naturalized elsewhere in the tropics. One species grown as an annual in the North.

Description
Leaves alternate or sometimes opposite on lower stem, broadly ovalish, deeply lobed, or coarsely round-toothed. Flowerheads usually solitary on long, hollow stems, the disk flowers bisexual, fertile, yellow, the ray flowers neutral, golden to orange.

How to Grow
Start seeds indoors 6–8 weeks before last spring frost. Plant outdoors when danger of frost is past. Prefers warm weather.

rotundifolia p. 237
Mexican Sunflower. 4–6 ft. (1.2–1.8 m) high, shrubby or woody. Flowerheads nearly 3 in. (7.5 cm) wide, the ray and disk flowers orange or yellow. Mexico and Central America. One of the most heat-resistant flowers. Tender annual.

Tolpis
Daisy family
Compositae

Toll′pis. A genus of about 20 species of small annual and perennial herbs, chiefly from the Mediterranean region, and allied to *Crepis*.

Description
Stems with a milky juice. Leaves basal, lance-shaped, remotely toothed. Flowerheads

composed only of ray flowers, not particularly showy. Beneath the head is a series of threadlike bracts, some of which are also on the upper part of the flowering stalk.

How to Grow
Sow seeds outdoors in spring after the danger of frost is past. Prefers warm weather.

barbata p. 228
Yellow Hawkweed. 8–12 in. (20–30 cm) high. Flowerheads with outer flowers yellow, the inner flowers red-brown with yellow tips, to 1¼ in. (3 cm) wide. Blooms from midsummer to frost. S. Europe. Tender annual.

Torenia
Snapdragon family
Scrophulariaceae

Tor-ren′i-a. African and Asiatic perennial or annual herbs comprising over 40 species and related to *Mimulus.*

Description
Stems much-branched, prostrate or erect, 4-angled. Leaves opposite, ovalish, toothed, and stalked. Flowers in stout, stalked clusters in leaf axils, or few-flowered terminal racemes. Corolla 2-lipped, the upper lip faintly 2-lobed, the lower lip 3-lobed, the central lobe blotched yellow at base.

How to Grow
Start seeds indoors 8–10 weeks before last spring frost. Transplant after danger of frost is past. Colors will be richer if plants receive light afternoon shade. Often planted beneath dripline of live oak trees in the Deep South. Prefers warm weather.

Fournieri p. 133
Wishbone Flower. 10–12 in. (25–30 cm) high, upright. Flowers 1 in. (2.5 cm) long, 2-toned purplish blue, white with purplish-blue spots, or pink and white, all with yellow throats. Vietnam. Many cultivars are available, including compact or large-flowered types. A useful flower for borders, edges, and rock gardens, or for hanging baskets. Tender annual.

Trachelium
Bellflower family
Campanulaceae

Tra-kee′li-um. Widely grown perennial herbs
comprising about half a dozen species from
the Mediterranean region. Closely related to
Campanula.

Description
Leaves alternate, ovalish, unequally toothed.
Flowers in dense terminal cyme. Corolla
tubular, its limb with 5 narrow lobes.

How to Grow
In the Deep South, sow seeds outdoors in
the early spring. Elsewhere, start seeds
indoors 8–10 weeks before the last spring
frost. Plant in the garden when danger of
frost is past. For first-year bloom, plants must
be started early. Prefers warm weather.

caeruleum p. 147
Throatwort. 1–4 ft. (30–120 cm) high.
Flowers blue or, rarely, white, 3–5 in.
(7.5–12.5 cm) wide. S. Europe. Hardy only
in the Deep South; in the North, it should
be treated as a tender annual.

Trachymene
Carrot family
Umbelliferae

Tra-kee-mee′ne. Chiefly Australian annual or
perennial herbs comprising over 12 species.
Often offered as *Didiscus.* The species below,
a very popular garden and greenhouse
annual, is grown for its beautiful flowers,
which strongly suggest a pale blue or
lavender edition of the common Wild Carrot
or Queen Anne's-Lace.

Description
Erect, weak-stemmed plants. Leaves twice- or
thrice-compound, the ultimate segments
narrow and cut into 3 narrow lobes. Flowers
minute but numerous and borne in a flat
umbel.

How to Grow
Start seeds early indoors and plant outdoors
when danger of frost is past. Or sow directly
where wanted in early spring as soon as
ground can be worked. Blooms better in

well-drained soil and when somewhat crowded. Prefers cool weather.

coerulea p. 122
Blue Laceflower. 18–30 in. (45–75 cm) high. Flowers tiny in flat umbels, 2–3 in. (5.0– 7.5 cm) wide, light blue to lavender. Hardy annual.

Triticum
Grass family
Gramineae

Trit′i-kum. Wheat. About 30 species of annual or biennial grasses, allied to *Secale* (Rye) and *Agropyron,* which includes Quackgrass. The species below cultivated since antiquity. W. Asia. Next to Rice, the most important cereal grass in the world.

Description
Leaf blades flat and narrow. Flowers in relatively stout spikelike panicle, the spikelets crowded, awned in some varieties, but without awn in others. Fruit, the Wheat grain, grooved.

How to Grow
In warm climates, plant in fall; elsewhere, in early spring. Work up the soil and lay down a 2–3 ft. (60–90 cm) square of clear plastic. Secure the edges with soil. Cut a 6-in. (15-cm) cross in center, and plant seeds where they can grow through the slits. Cover plastic with dried grass clippings to shade out weeds. Prefers warm weather.

aestivum p. 174
Wheat. To 4 ft. (1.5 m) high. Leaf blades flat, to 4 in. (10 cm) long. W. Asia. Includes both common winter and spring wheats. There are many other varieties for special agricultural purposes. Hardy annual.

Tropaeolum
Nasturtium family
Tropaeolaceae

Tro-pee′o-lum. Nasturtium. The common garden nasturtiums comprise a genus with about 50 species of annual or perennial soft-stemmed herbs, most of which are climbing, natives of the cooler parts of South America.

Description
Leaves alternate, more or less round, light green, with strongly marked veins radiating from the center from which the stalk arises. Leafstalk fleshy and sensitive, curling round any object with which it comes in contact, enabling the tall kinds to climb as much as 10 ft. (3 m). Flowers are showy and solitary, growing from the axils of the leaves, pale yellow, orange, scarlet, crimson, or dark red. Sepals 5, joined at the base, 3 prolonged into a spur at the back of the flower. Petals usually 5, broad, suddenly narrowing at the base into a kind of stalk where they join the sepals. Stamens 8, curving toward the back of the flower.

How to Grow
Easy to grow from seeds or cuttings. Sow seeds in garden 2 weeks before last frost. Or sow indoors in peat pots early and transplant when danger of frost is past. Soil should not be too rich or plants will produce lots of foliage and few flowers. Cuttings made from young shoots in fall make excellent indoor plants. Susceptible to aphids and mealybugs. Requires relatively cool temperatures; does not do well in the se. U.S. during summer.

majus p. 249
Nasturtium; Indian Cress. Climbing 8–12 ft. (2.4–3.5 m) high. Flowers 2½ in. (6 cm) wide, yellow or orange, sometimes striped and spotted with red, also scarlet or mahogany. South America. Newer, compact varieties hold blossoms well above foliage. Excellent coverings for trellises, posts, and rocks. Tender annual.

peregrinum p. 209
Canary-Bird Flower. Climbing to 8 ft. (2.4 m) high. Flowers pale yellow, 1 in. (2.5 cm) wide. A particularly dainty type used in English cottage gardens. Peru. Tender annual.

Ursinia
Daisy family
Compositae

Ur-sin'i-a. Annual or perennial herbs or subshrubs comprising about 40 species,

natives of South Africa. Showy garden
plants, but only the tender annuals are
cultivated.

Description
Leaves alternate, usually deeply cut into
narrow lobes, the margins toothed. Flowers
in solitary heads, daisylike. Ray flowers
orange or yellow, sometimes purplish brown
at base, the disk flowers dark bluish purple
or brown. Sometimes spelled *Ursinea.*

How to Grow
Because the plants prefer a long cool
growing season, start seeds indoors 6–8
weeks before last frost. Set out after danger
of frost is past. Will tolerate a considerable
period of drought.

anthemoides p. 226
Growing to 18 in. (45 cm) high.
Flowerheads daisylike, 2½ in. (6 cm) wide,
the ray flowers yellow or orange with reddish
purple at the base, the disk flowers purple.
South Africa. Also known as *U. pulchra* and
Sphenogyne speciosa. Half-hardy annual.

Venidium
Daisy family
Compositae

Ve-nid'i-um. South African annual or
perennial herbs comprising about 25 species.

Description
Leaves alternate, deeply cut, stalked, grayish
green, of cobwebby appearance when young.
Flowers in solitary heads, daisylike. Ray
flowers yellow or orange, sometimes with
purple band at the base. Disk flowers
purplish black.

How to Grow
Sow seeds indoors in early spring. Shift
seedlings to progressively larger pots to
produce good-size plants with flower buds by
last frost. In Calif., plant after spring rains.
Needs well-drained soil. To reduce incidence
of stem rot, plant in raised beds topped with
1 in. (2.5 cm) of sand. The species below
prefers cool weather.

fastuosum p. 225
Cape Daisy. 2–3 ft. (60–90 cm) high.
Flowerheads 4–6 in. (10–15 cm) across, the

ray flowers yellow-orange with purplish band
at base, the disk flowers purplish black. Will
withstand to 5° F (−15° C) of frost in
Calif., but often does not do well in the East,
especially if watered too freely. Excellent
as cut flowers, continuing to open in
morning and close at night. Tender annual.

Verbena
Verbena family
Verbenaceae

Ver-bee′na. Vervain. Tender or hardy annual
or perennial herbs, comprising about 200
species, natives of America, with the
exception of a few species found in Eurasia.

Description
Leaves generally opposite, usually lobed or
toothed. Flowers in various shades of white,
lilac, red, and purple, small, sometimes
stalked, in terminal spikes or terminal
roundish clusters. Calyx tubular, 5-toothed.
Corolla tubular, its lobes 5, the tube long
and narrow. Stamens 4, in pairs.

How to Grow
Verbena seed is notoriously hard to
germinate—only 40 percent can be expected
to grow. At 70–75° F (21–24° C)
germination occurs in 14–21 days. Sowing
seeds early indoors usually gives more
predictable results than direct-seeding. Sow
seeds indoors in light sandy soil or use a
cold frame. Transplant outdoors when
danger of frost is past. Set plants out in full
sun except in the Deep South and desert
areas, where light shade will be needed to
reduce drought stress and insect damage.
Susceptible to leafminers. Verbenas prefer
warm weather.

× *hybrida pp. 106, 107, 246, 259*
Garden Verbena. To 12 in. (30 cm) high.
Flowers fragrant, pink, red, purple, yellow, or
white, in compact terminal clusters, 2–3 in.
(5.0–7.5 cm) wide. Many cultivars are
available, including upright, trailing, or
dwarf kinds. This hybrid derives from
V. peruviana and probably some other
subspecies. Tender annual.

peruviana p. 258
Creeping 12–24 in. (30–60 cm) long, rooting
at the nodes. Flowers bright red in clusters,

1–2 in. (2.5–5.0 cm) wide. S. Brazil to
Argentina. Tender annual.

Viola
Violet family
Violaceae

Vy-o′la. Violet. Hardy perennial, and a few
annual herbs, comprising about 500 species
distributed throughout temperate regions.

Description
Low-growing plants. Leaves basal or growing
on the stems. Basal leaves simple, heart-
shaped or ovalish, sometimes cut into
fingerlike lobes, slightly wrinkled, stalked.
Stem leaves alternate, simple, ovalish, usually
stalked, the margins with rounded teeth.
Two leafy appendages at base of the stem
leaves are usually cut into 3 lobes. Flowers
stalked, solitary, sometimes nodding, violet,
blue, reddish purple, lilac, yellow, or white.
Calyx of 5 sepals. Corolla of 5 petals, 4
arranged in pairs, each pair differing, the
lower petal spurred. Stamens 5, with an
orange, shield-shaped appendage at the top
of each anther. Some species have 2 kinds of
flowers: nonfertile, showy spring flowers and
fertile, summer flowers, which never open
and are self-fertilizing. Most bloom in the
spring.

How to Grow
Start seeds indoors 10–12 weeks before last
spring frost for bloom in late spring. Or
start in late summer and protect in a cold
frame for flowering the following spring. To
prolong spring bloom in warm climates,
provide afternoon shade. All species prefer
cool weather.

cornuta pp. 161, 207
Horned Violet; Bedding Pansy; Tufted
Pansy. To 8 in. (20 cm) high. Flowers
1½ in. (4 cm) wide, solitary, in a wide range
of colors, from purple to red, orange, or
white. Spain and the Pyrenees. Many cultivars
are available. Perennial treated as a hardy
annual.

Rafinesquii p. 160
Field Pansy. 3–8 in. (7.5–20.0 cm) high.
Flowers bluish white to creamy, ½ in.
(13 mm) wide. E. U.S. west to Colo. and
Ariz. Hardy annual.

tricolor *p. 132*

Johnny-Jump-Up; Pansy; Heartsease. To
12 in. (30 cm) high or more. Flowers
tricolored, purple, white, and yellow, solitary,
¾ in.(19 mm) long. They differ from the
other violas in that the corolla is flattish and
roundish and the petals overlap. A favorite
for planting over tulip and daffodil beds.
Europe, naturalized in North America.
Perennial grown as a hardy annual.

× *Wittrockiana* *pp. 132, 206, 207, 248*

Pansy; Viola; Heartsease. To 9 in. (22.5 cm)
high. Flowers flat, 2–5 in. (5.0–12.5 cm)
wide, solid colors and those with "facelike"
markings, ranging from purple, blue,
maroon, and red to yellow, orange, and
white, some with 3 colors. Numerous
cultivars available, including winter-
blooming kinds. This hybrid derives from
V. tricolor, V. lutea, V. altaica, and possibly
other species. Perennial grown as a hardy
annual.

Xanthisma
Daisy family
Compositae

Zan-this′ma. Sleepy Daisy. A single species,
native in Tex. The flowerheads close at night.

Description
Wandlike stems with narrow, alternate
leaves. Flowerheads long-stalked, mostly
solitary, with 18–20 ray flowers.

How to Grow
Start seeds early indoors and transplant
hardened-off seedlings outdoors after danger
of frost is past. (Seedlings are not frost-
hardy.) This species does well in a well-
drained or even dry location, and with a soil
pH of 6.5–7.0. Blooms the first year; in mild
climates, will live over winter and bloom
the following spring. Prefers cool weather.

texana *p. 222*

Sleepy Daisy; Star-of-Texas. 2–4 ft. (60–
120 cm) high. Flowers yellow, 2½ in.
(6 cm) wide. Native to dry, open prairies,
and well-suited to open places with poor
soil. Hardy annual.

Xeranthemum
Daisy family
Compositae

Zer-ran'the-mum. Everlasting. A small group
of Mediterranean annual herbs, related to
Carlina. The species below is one of the
oldest and perhaps the best known of the
everlastings.

Description
Leaves alternate, entire. Flowerheads solitary,
long-stalked, composed entirely of disk
flowers surrounded by small, papery or chaffy
bracts, colored like the heads.

How to Grow
Where the growing season is long, sow seeds
in garden when danger of frost is past.
Where summers are short, sow seeds early
indoors. Do not thin. After frost danger is
past, dig holes in the garden and fill with
water. Carefully set a clump of plants in each
hole at the same depth as it grew in the pot.
Water again to settle soil. Prefers cool
weather.

annuum *p. 98*
Everlasting; Immortelle. 2–3 ft. (60–90 cm)
high. Flowerheads single or double, 1½ in.
(4 cm) wide, composed of white, purple, or
pink disk flowers and papery petal-like
bracts. S. Europe. Several varieties available.
Excellent dried flower. Hardy annual.

Zinnia
Daisy family
Compositae

Zin'ee-a. Annual or perennial herbs or
subshrubs comprising about 15 species,
chiefly found in Mexico, but also in Tex.,
Colo., and Chile.

Description
Rather stiff erect stems with short bristly
hairs. Leaves opposite, ovalish or lance-
shaped, usually stem-clasping. Flowers in
solitary, flattish or cone-shaped, showy heads,
each flower growing in the axil of a scale-
like bract, the tip of which is often colored.
Ray flowers of every shade except blue, the
underside often greenish, arranged in one to
many rows. Disk flowers yellow or purplish
brown.

How to Grow

Where growing season is short, start seeds indoors at least 6 weeks before plants will be set out. Do not let soil dry out, and maintain temperature at 65–70° F (18.5–21.0° C). When danger of frost is past, set out in garden. Where growing season is long, sow outdoors in early spring, or earlier in the South. Sow groups of 3–4 seeds 12 in. (30 cm) apart. Thin when 3 in. (7.5 cm) high. Best results come from enriched soil. Keep moist until established. To prevent mildew disease, do not wet leaves. Water freely in hot, dry weather. In very hot climates, provide afternoon shade. All zinnias prefer warm weather. They make excellent cut flowers. Strip off leaves, because foliage deteriorates quickly and will smell rank.

angustifolia p. 229

Zinnia. 12–16 in. (30.0–40.5 cm) high. Flowerheads to 1½ in. (4 cm) wide, the disk black-purple, the rays orange with a yellow stripe. Mexico. New dwarf cultivars are excellent for edging or ground covers. Tolerates dry soil. Also sold as *Z. linearis.* Tender annual.

elegans pp. 235, 242

Common Zinnia; Youth-and-Old-Age. To 3 ft. (90 cm) high. Flowerheads to 4 in. (10 cm) wide, the rays purple or reddish lilac, the disk yellow or orange. Mexico. Cultivars are available in every color except blue, including green and bicolors. Most have double flowers, some with giant blossoms, to 6 in. (15 cm) wide, or quilled petals. "Come-and-come-again" kinds are long-flowering. Disk flowers often absent in cultivars. Tender annual.

Haageana pp. 238, 241

Mexican Zinnia. To 2 ft. (60 cm) high. Flowerheads to 2½ in. (6 cm) wide, the rays orange, the disk yellow, red, or orange. Mexico. Tolerates dry soil. Tender annual.

Appendices

Garden Design

Planning your flower garden can be as much fun as planting or gathering flowers: It lets you visualize scenarios for the seasons to come. Time spent planning will pay off richly when you see your flowers bloom in just the right sequence, colors, and location. If you are a beginner, the following steps will tell you what to do and how to avoid common pitfalls. If you are an experienced gardener, you may discover alternatives to your present landscaping.

Assessing Your Time and Energy

A small, well-tended garden is often more gratifying than large beds that tax your time and strength. While vigorous, healthy retirees usually have the time to create impressive, spacious gardens, people with demanding jobs or small children have fewer available hours. If you spend little time commuting or if your children are no longer underfoot, you may want to consider large flower beds. But it is a different matter if you work on weekends, commute, or aren't up to the physical demands of weeding or digging soil. Then, small flower beds or containers of flowers are much more sensible.

Mapping Your Land

The first step in designing an outdoor garden is to draw a map showing your house and the surrounding land. To establish the shape of your lot, measure the distances between the corners of your property and roughly estimate the corner angles. Measure the space occupied by the house, walks, drives, and outbuildings. Then, draw a plot plan on a sheet of graph paper, showing all of these elements. Use a circle to indicate the spread of a tree or shrub. Be sure to include all construction and existing gardens. Make a few photocopies for future use.

On your working copy, mark key features such as high knolls, poorly drained spots where water stands for long periods, bad views that need screening, channels followed by rain runoff, shady spots, and wind tunnels created by buildings or fences. Next, draw a compass arrow on your map to indicate due north. If possible, show the directions of the morning and afternoon sun.

Choosing a Site

The simplest and easiest-to-care-for flower beds are those set against fences and buildings or those bordering property lines. Islands of flowers placed in the lawn may be attractive, but they will need extra care when mowing and edging.

In most parts of the country, annuals do best in full sun; in the South and warm West, summer annuals appreciate afternoon shade. Avoid sites where the invasive roots of trees or hedges could compete with flowers. Keep away from drainage channels, and if the site is poorly drained, plan to build raised beds. Don't let soil influence your choice of a site. Almost any soil can be improved sufficiently to grow vigorous plants.

Be aware of the effect of reflected heat. Drives, walks, and masonry walls reflect and radiate heat. This can work to the advantage of many annuals in the North, but in warm climates, it can weaken plants already suffering from heat and drought. All flower beds should be within easy reach of a faucet so that they can be watered during dry spells and so that transplants can be kept moist until they are established.

Determining the Size and Shape of Flower Beds

Each bed should be at least three feet by six feet, except, of course, for narrow strips of earth between construction features. In this relatively small 18-square-foot garden, you need to plant only three different kinds of annuals; more would make it look too busy. Larger beds require a greater variety. For beds deeper than three feet from front to back, you will need a path for access. Flowers will soon hide the path, and it will allow you to weed and harvest without stepping on plants. Never walk on the cultivated soil around flower plants or you will compact the soil, injure roots, and restrict growth.

Rectangular beds adapt easily to simple designs. As you progress in gardening skills, you can embellish your garden with curving beds and peninsulas. Such oddities as round beds or diamond and squash shapes cut out of the lawn were popular in Victorian days but are seldom seen now.

Giving Each Bed a Special Function

The Pennsylvania Dutch have a quaint way of explaining why they grow flowers: "Just for pretty." True, all flower beds are beautiful, but they can also serve special purposes—to hide the knees of tall, leggy perennials or lanky shrubs; to screen homely vistas or to soften the stark lines of buildings, walls, and walks; to provide flowers for cutting, fragrance, or drying; to lead your eye deeper into the garden or to serve as a focal point of bright color at the back of the garden; to enliven the green hues of vegetable and herb gardens; and, most important, to give your home a cheerful face. What a lift the sight of your beautiful flower garden will bring as you approach your home!

Integrating several flower beds into an overall garden design is an art unto itself. No two people would draw the same design for a garden, nor would they choose the same flowers. You have great latitude of choice in designing your garden—so much, in fact, that you will soon come to appreciate garden design as a true art form.

Selecting the Right Spot

Assume that you are designing the garden for yourself and your family. You can simplify the planning of flower beds for your home garden by, at first, considering the front, side, and back yards as

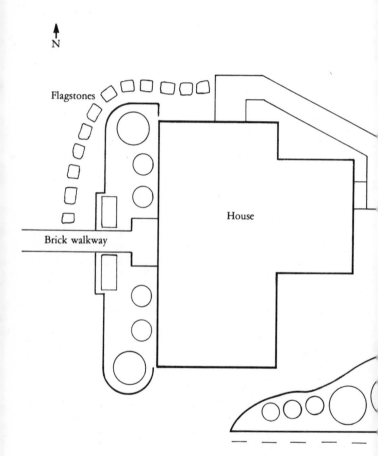

N

Flagstones

Brick walkway

House

To make a base map, draw an outline of your property on a piece of graph paper, then draw in the house, any outbuildings, driveways, fences, trees and bushes, and any preexisting flower beds.

Indicate the northern point of a compass with an arrow. Make several copies of your base map and store the original in a safe place.

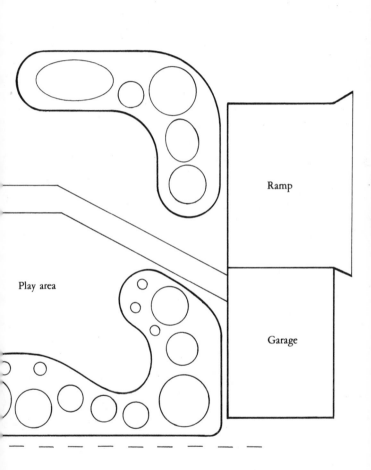

Ramp

Garage

Play area

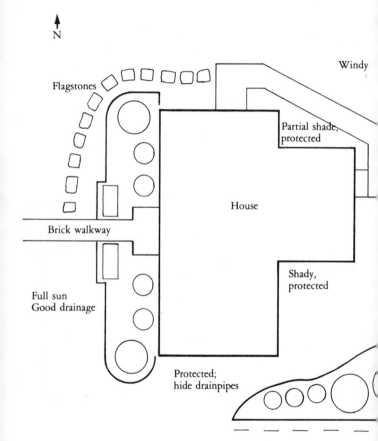

N

Flagstones

Windy

Partial shade,
protected

House

Brick walkway

Shady,
protected

Full sun
Good drainage

Protected;
hide drainpipes

On a clean copy of your base map, indicate which areas receive strong sun, which are cast in shade, and which have partial sun. Indicate, too, windy spots, protected spots, views that you want to hide, areas that are poorly drained, and those that are elevated. Use this information to select suitable plants for your garden.

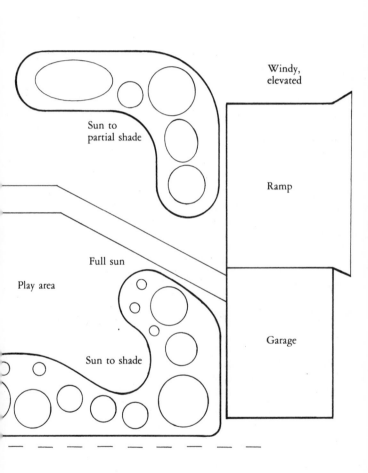

Windy, elevated

Sun to partial shade

Ramp

Full sun

Play area

Sun to shade

Garage

Garden Design

separate elements. Later on, you can try to unify the three sections into a single grand design, but bear in mind that your efforts may be lost on visitors.

Walk through the house and look out the windows so that you will know the spots most frequently viewed from inside. Next, go outside and put stakes in the ground, outlining areas in full or partial view of "popular" windows. Consider the front yard slightly differently: Since most homeowners spend little time looking out of their front windows, mark spots that are well displayed as you approach the house.

Returning to the back yard, stand or sit in your favorite spots for relaxing. If possible, place flower beds where they can be enjoyed from your outdoor overlooks as well as from the house. This exercise will help you determine which way to orient the flower beds.

Refining the Overall Garden Plan

In earlier times, gardens were arranged with a view toward leading visitors on grand tours of the entire garden. Walkways led from vista to vista, and garden features and decorations were cunningly placed. Such complex garden plans are still possible, either by hiring a landscape architect or building the essential features bit by bit yourself and changing whatever fails to suit you.

A few well-situated flower beds are perhaps equally effective. Without attempting to integrate the beds in an overall garden plan, each bed would have its own design in a size and shape appropriate to the setting, and would complement existing trees, shrubs, perennials, and construction features.

Creating the Right Illusion

Although spacious gardens may feature streams, terraces, ponds, swimming pools, bogs, large trees, and meandering walks, unless these are near the house, they are not appropriate for annuals. Annual flowers are resolutely domestic: They look best close to the house and appear alien in a wild setting.

At the other extreme, gardens in most of today's residential areas are usually small, located on flat or gently rolling land, devoid of trees, and lacking in privacy. It is a greater challenge to design a landscape for these small yards than for larger country homes or even mobile homes in rural settings. The challenge in small-lot design is to draw attention away from intrusive features and to create the illusion of privacy, serenity, and intimacy in a crowded environment.

Certain manmade attractions, such as pools, fountains, stonework, patios, and decks, can look good on small lots. Annuals can help blend these features into the landscape. The brighter flowers should be placed beyond the construction feature and lighter colors positioned in the foreground.

Selecting Garden Flowers

At least six considerations should enter your selection of garden flowers:

1. Adaptability to your climate
2. Preference for sun or shade
3. Compatibility of colors and your personal color preferences
4. Height and spread of each variety
5. Time span of blooming
6. Extra benefits: fragrance, attracting birds, suitability for cutting and drying, and use for screening or other landscape needs.

Climate

Most annuals will thrive in every state in the United States if you plant them at the right time. However, the cool-weather varieties will give only a brief display of color if you live where hot summers quickly follow winter's end. Conversely, the varieties that love heat do not get going until the soil is warm, and bloom quite late in northern or highland gardens. Coastal climates present special problems with fog, salt spray, and winds. Very windy areas, such as the Texas Panhandle, are best suited to low-growing flowers.

Preference for Sun or Shade

Seed catalogues and packets will tell you whether a variety prefers sun or shade. This information is of limited value if you do not understand the sources of shade and its degrees—light, moderate, or deep.

Shade can be cast by buildings or other constructions, hills, trees, and taller plants. The shade from walls, fences, and buildings is easier to deal with than that from other plants, because trees and shrubs have strong roots that extend well beyond the foliage canopy. Annuals have a hard time competing for plant nutrients and water when planted too close to these robbers.

Light shade is usually perceived as mottled shade cast by an open canopy of foliage or by trees trimmed high to remove the lower branches. Moderate shade is solid shade during morning or afternoon, with at least half a day of full sun. Such shade will often cause flowers to bloom later and somewhat sparsely, and to grow taller than in full sun. Deep shade means shade from sunup to sundown, with little sunlight filtering through.

Virtually no annuals will thrive in deep shade, but you can slip in a quick show of color before the deciduous trees leaf-out in late spring. Flowers listed as shade-tolerant will grow well in moderate shade, but most annuals grow best in full sun. In the hot, dry West and Southwest, however, they may prefer moderate afternoon shade or light shade.

Garden Design

Colors
It is amazing how attractive disparate flower colors—even clashing hues—can look together. But if you feel pain when you see vivid pink and orange blossoms growing side by side, you might wish to follow these suggestions for combining colors:

Compatible Hues
Group pastels and warm hues in separate beds. The blue, pink, lavender, and violet shades look good together. Certain light yellows will work well with the pastels. Orange, red, strong yellows, and mahogany also combine well. Monochromatic shades can look very attractive together. Try planting different shades of pink, yellow, or blue, each in separate groups.

Accent Colors
Use very dark colors like purple, deep red, deep magenta, and brown sparingly. These deep hues "drop out" of the landscape as the sun fades and can also overpower a color scheme if overused. Between strong colors, plant white and light blue flowers or annuals with silvery foliage.

Color Clichés
Patriotism notwithstanding, try to resist planting red, white, and blue next to each other. The three colors just don't blend. Similarly, in the North, planting red salvia and white petunias in front of shrubs has become a landscaping cliché that is also to be avoided.

Mixed Colors
Flower-seed packets of mixed colors are always cheaper to buy than the separate colors. Save them for large beds or box the mixed colors in between complementary separate colors. Avoid using more than one kind of flower for mixed colors in a single bed; the resulting bed would look more haphazard than planned.

Height and Spread of Plants
Seed packets and catalogues are generally accurate in their statements about the height of flowers at maturity. But bear in mind that high temperatures and humidity, or shade, can make plants grow taller than you expected. If you buy bedding plants (seedlings usually sold in six-packs, peat pots, or larger four-to-six-inch pots), their tags seldom give the height of varieties; you will need to check the heights in seed catalogues. While finding maximum height is relatively easy, few descriptions list the spread of plants, and this can be a trap for beginners. Some annual flowers are genetically tiny; others can spread to four feet across. Failure to leave sufficient space or leaving too much room between plants can lead to funny-looking flower beds. Never guess on plant heights; look up this information and plan the beds accordingly. Stair-stepped flower beds with

low-edging flowers in the front, medium-height bedding flowers in the middle, and tall flowers in the back are ideal. But how odd it looks to have tall plants blocking lower-growing kinds! You can cluster groups of taller flowers here and there and surround them with a carpet of lower-growing annuals rather than planting each kind in soldier-straight rows.

Time Span of Blooming

Combining flowers that will bloom at the same time can be a challenge to beginning gardeners. Yet with a little experience, you will know instinctively which types of flowers bloom in the winter or spring, such as pansies, stock, or calendula, and which ones start to blossom when the days grow hot, such as marigolds or zinnias. It is more difficult to learn the few flowers that can stand up to the extremes of heat and humidity in southern areas and in low-elevation western gardens. If you live in these regions, consult your local Cooperative Extension Service for heat-resistant varieties. It looks strange to see an annual flower bed mostly green with just a few patches of color. Synchronized blooms work better. The easiest approach is to keep the spring-blooming and summer-blooming annuals in separate beds.

Growing Annuals in Containers

Annuals are a natural for containers. In all except mild climates, perennials and woody plants grown in containers often die in winter because their root balls freeze solid and the soil is dry. Grow annuals and avoid this problem.

Container gardening is an ancient art now enjoying a revival. The easy availability of large, decorative containers, excellent potting soils, long-feeding fertilizers, and labor-saving watering devices are hastening this trend. Containers appeal to apartment- and condominium-dwellers who only have balcony or courtyard space. They also provide excellent accents for patios and entranceways, and portable color spots for a combination flower, vegetable, or herb garden. Beneath aggressive surface-rooted trees, containers are literally the only way to grow flowers.

Small containers should be avoided because they dry out quickly and the wind will easily blow them over. Avoid dark-colored containers, too, because they absorb more heat, and if the sides are exposed to afternoon sun, they may become too hot for good root growth.

Trailing annuals are much in demand for window boxes, large planters, stone retaining walls, and hanging baskets. Here the selection among bedding plants is somewhat limited; you may have to grow choice trailing varieties from seeds.

Cut Flowers

Beautiful flower arrangements can be created by anyone who has a feeling for line, mass, balance, and color, and it doesn't require absolute commitment. Find a good amateur, however, and you will usually uncover a shrewd observer who has read elementary texts on flower arranging and has gone to the trouble of accumulating the tools and accessories that help build arrangements with grace, stability, and holding power.

Pleasing Your Senses
Flower arranging is like a hybrid between painting and sculpture. The successful arranger visualizes not only the size and shape of an arrangement but also its line or flow, texture, and apparent weight. You can satisfy all of these considerations in an arrangement and still keep it simple and pleasing.

Make your first arrangements just for yourself. When you feel sufficiently confident to ask for comments on your work, be prepared for a chastening experience. Praise will be mixed with criticism, for most advanced arrangers "go by the book" and their rules often reward conformity more than spontaneity.

The gardener with a thriving, diverse flower garden has a distinct edge on those who must rely on florists for raw materials. While elegant arrangements can be constructed from annuals alone, variety can be added by combining annuals with perennials, branches from shrubs or fruit trees, foliage from woody plants, seeds and flowerheads from meadow weeds, driftwood, moss, and other found materials.

Starting a Cutting Garden
The catalogues of seed specialists are good places to begin planning a cutting garden. You might prefer the simple approach of planting a packet of flower seeds containing assorted kinds for cutting. These packets are full of surprises—the flowers contained in them are seldom identified on the package. For a more planned approach, follow these guidelines:

1. Decide how much area you can devote to a cutting garden and if you can grow flowers for cutting in other places in the yard as well.
2. Set a reasonable limit on the number of plants your space will accommodate.
3. Plant successive crops for extended bloom.
4. Include the three basic flower shapes—spire-shaped flowers, round flowers, and lacy, delicate blossoms.
5. Select compatible colors.
6. Don't overlook ornamental herbs and plants grown principally for foliage.

Garden Size
In a postage-stamp-sized garden it is difficult to grow enough flowers

for complete and rich arrangements. It is interesting to watch how larger gardens are transformed in the hands of budding flower arrangers. Ordinary shrubs and single-purpose landscaping flowers soon give way to cutting flowers. Excess lawn areas are gradually turned into flower beds. Containers start to sprout flowers and hanging baskets become filled with trailing fronds.

Number of Plants
As a rule of thumb, provide at least three to four plants of each kind so that you'll have plenty of flowers to cut. For example, a three- by six-foot bed can hold only three or four kinds of plants, a skimpy choice. To broaden the selection of plant material, try to find room for at least six to eight kinds.

Successive Blooms
As soon as spring flowers have burned out, replace them with those that bloom in the summer. In vegetable gardening, this is called succession cropping. The technique and its advantages are comparable for both flowers and vegetables.

Flower Shapes
Try to include different flower shapes: spire-shaped flowers, round flowers, and flowers that act as filler. Spire shapes come from the flowers that form tall heads, the more slender the better. You need these flowers for height and line in arrangements. Round flowers are the most common; they add mass to arrangements. Filler flowers have tiny, airy blossoms that decorate the spaces between larger blossoms without adding apparent weight.

Unusual Complements
Herbs such as bee balm and lavender contain some of the finest flowers for fresh and dried arrangements. These are usually medicinal or scenting herbs rather than culinary kinds and are perennial rather than annual. Use them to complement annual flowers. Include, also, some of the plants that have silvery foliage such as dusty miller and wormwood.

How to Cut Flowers
The best time to cut flowers is in the coolest part of the day, either in the morning after the dew has dried or just before sundown. Avoid cutting flowers during midday heat. Cut the stems diagonally with a sharp knife. Do not use a scissors because this crushes stems. Never rip off stems; you could damage the entire plant.
To prevent wilting, place flowers in water as quickly as possible. (Some gardeners like to carry a bucket of water with them to the garden.) Keep the flowers in the water out of sunlight until the leaves look crisp. Some kinds of flowers need special attention before they are put in water: Flowers with milky juice, such as poppies,

must have the stem tips seared with a flame to stop bleeding. To revive wilted flowers, stand them in warm water.

Before starting your arrangement, strip off any foliage that would be under water. Bacteria will cause the leaves to quickly deteriorate. Numerous additives are available to prolong flower life. The most consistently successful are the professional compounds that contain soluble silver as a preservative.

To keep your flowers looking fresh, change the water every day or so and recut the stems. If you are planning an arrangement for a party a few days off, cut the flower buds before they are fully open, then refrigerate them in water until you need them. The flowers will look fresh when you take them out of the refrigerator, although they will not last as long as fresh-picked ones.

How to Dry Flowers

It is quite easy to dry annuals for dried-flower arrangements. Certain kinds with papery petals can be simply dried by hanging them head down in a cool, dark, dry place. These flowers are called everlastings. Strawflowers and statice are some of the most popular everlastings.

Many other annuals can also be transformed into dried flowers if treated with special drying agents, such as silica gel. Cover the flowers completely with the drying agent. You can use either a large bowl or a tray. Depending on the flower variety, drying takes four to six days. All moisture must be removed. To prevent faded colors, keep the blossoms away from all light during the drying process.

Consider the Setting

A flower arrangement should fit effortlessly into a room and not appear as an afterthought. It should be in keeping with a room's architecture, color, and furnishings.

Every arrangement should be prepared for a specific setting, and the setting should determine the choice of flowers, the container, and the design. Contemporary homes call for stronger, bolder designs than colonial homes. Arrangements that blend easily with traditional furnishings may look too fussy in a modern room.

Principles of Design

Great arrangements do not have to be large masses of bold foliage or flowers. A single flower in a bud vase, or a few field flowers in a jar on the kitchen table can be charming and effective. In general, the height of an arrangement should be in proportion to the size of the container and the space in which it is placed. A good rule of thumb is to make the arrangement two and a half times the height of the container. This of course depends upon the width and the type of flower container. If you're using a bud vase, the arrangement may be lower; if it's a low ceramic bowl, a higher arrangement is in order.

Every arrangement is made up of lines, masses, and spaces. Lines can be manipulated within a single dimension or used to produce a feeling of depth. Mass is dependent not only on the size of the flowers but also on their color and, to a lesser extent, their texture. The spaces between flowers can either be closed with filler flowers or left open, whichever treatment most effectively accentuates the line and mass you are trying to achieve.

Most arrangements fall into four basic categories: vertical, horizontal, circular, or triangular. Vertical arrangements convey strength and force. They can relieve the bareness of a plain wall or reinforce the dignity of a partitioning column.

Horizontal compositions suggest quiet and repose. They look good on low tables or when viewed from above, as do circular patterns. Low-profile designs lend themselves to table centerpieces, particularly if the occasion is informal or the table is small.

Triangular designs are the most popular because they are flexible and can be adapted to almost any setting where height isn't a problem. When visualizing a triangular arrangement, you should consider the shape of the triangle as well as its size. The symmetrical triangle is the most formal shape and can be used on a mantel, on a table in a formal entryway, or on an occasional table in a large living room. Although construction is challenging, a symmetrical triangle can be used for centerpieces on formal dining tables. The plant material must be arranged openly so that it does not interfere with conversation across the table. Formal triangular arrangements can be made large for tea tables, where height and mass do not interfere with conversation, or in church displays.

Asymmetrical triangles are suitable for corner tables or at one end of a buffet table. For variation, place two matching asymmetrical designs in a mirror-image position to create a more formal atmosphere. Place them at the ends of a mantel or on a long table.

Texture

Manipulation of texture is an important principle of flower arranging. Slick materials reflect light and, therefore, add brilliance. Rough, prickly materials suggest informality or strength.

Color

Use color discreetly. Designers often base their color patterns on the 12-step color wheel: red, red-orange, orange, yellow-orange, yellow, yellow-green, green, blue-green, blue, blue-violet, violet, and red-violet.

One-color Arrangements

A design can consist of only one hue. This monochromatic arrangement may comprise both light and dark values of the chosen color; such a simple pattern is satisfying through its quiet charm. The effect can be enlivened by the use of flowers that differ in form,

Cut Flowers

When you arrange flowers, the vase you use is almost as important as the flowers you select. Low, rounded vases are a good choice for large, rounded arrangements.

Simple crockery containers produce a casual effect, ideal for daisylike flowers. In contrast, both crystal and silver vases are perfect for elegant, sophisticated arrangements.

Cut Flowers

size, and texture, yet are of the same color. Variety of this sort vivifies the pattern.

Harmonious Combinations

A design of closely related hues of different colors is called an analogous harmony. Any combination, such as red-orange, orange, and yellow-orange, or green, blue-green, and blue, has a unity of color that is very attractive. If the hues are not skillfully blended, the arrangement may seem spotty; but spottiness can be avoided by placing the colors so that the transitions from hue to hue pass easily through the composition.

Dramatic Effects

The most dramatic color pattern is the complementary harmony, or the combining of opposites; that is, of hues that stand opposite each other on the color wheel, like blue and orange. Because there is no unity in blue and orange, an arrangement built entirely of these hues is almost too noticeable for the average room. The violence of the complementary harmony can be softened by modifications of the scheme.

A good color pattern combines near-complementary colors. It also uses two hues; but the second hue, instead of being the direct complement of the first, is the hue adjacent to the complement. If, then, blue is the first hue, the second hue will be red-orange or yellow-orange instead of orange. Another modification, the split-complementary, uses with the first hue the two hues bordering the complement; that is, with blue, both red-orange and yellow-orange. These two modifying harmonies are more successful than the pure complement because the blends suggest the presence of an additional color.

The last color harmony is the triad, which uses a hue from each of the three main segments of the color wheel; for example, orange, green, and violet. Because of its variety; the triad design is vivid and animated.

Containers

Select a container for its appropriateness to the flowers it is to hold and the setting it is to occupy. Like plant material, it is judged by its form, color, and texture. Good containers are so simple that they do not attract attention to themselves, and they are in harmony with their contents. Large, heavy plant material belongs in a container whose size, form, and texture suggest strength; small, dainty arrangements require delicate vases.

Holders

The pin-type of holder is probably the most helpful for the home because it will work with most vases. It is always good with low bowls. It can be used in a deep vase, such as an urn, by placing layers of cloth within the container and then setting the holder on top of the cloth far enough below the rim so that the mechanics do not show. In a transparent container or bowl that is so low that the holder shows, pebbles, rocks, or interesting shapes of wood can be piled about the holder to conceal the needles. Pin-type holders must be handled with care, however, to avoid puncturing fingers.

Holders for Glass Vases

For glass containers in which the stems are to show, it is often possible to build a lattice of several twigs wedged together, then set at the edge of the water. Contrivances of wire mesh are sometimes placed at the top of the container, but if these are rigid enough to hold the stems immovable, there is danger that they may scratch the glass. Arrangements that are not too heavy can be made, then held firmly while the stems are wrapped first with wire, then with narrow strips of plumber's lead. A short end of the lead must be left to bend over the edge of the vase at one side to keep it secure.

Plastic or Metal Holders

In recent years the formed plastic material called Oasis has begun to replace holders for use in opaque containers. Oasis stores water so that you can transport arrangements without fear of spills. Be sure this material is soaking wet and heavy before you use it.

Non-rusting metal holders can be obtained in several sizes, shapes, and styles to fit vases and stem diameters. The pin-type and wire-mesh holders are both popular. Galvanized hardware cloth or chicken wire can also be molded into shapes that will fit tightly in containers.

Garden Diary

Garden records can be quickly jotted on a calendar tacked to the toolshed wall, entered in a loose-leaf notebook, or written in a diary. Even if your entries are sporadic, once you start you will find much to record. Your journal will soon grow in usefulness, both as a keepsake and as a source of gardening information.

The rewards of keeping a garden diary outweigh the little work that goes into daily or weekly jottings-down. Without some record, just sit down and try to recall last year's date for the final spring frost or the date when you sowed zinnia seeds.

Finding Solutions

Unconscious rumination and occasional verbalization between you and your plants come naturally when you garden. Your mind may find a solution to a problem without your being aware of any question. You may have read an entire seed catalogue without a single inspiration for new flowers. Yet later, while working in the garden, you suddenly think, "Why not plant cleome here next spring; it would be just right for this spot!" If you fail to write down your idea, you might find yourself in front of a seed rack next year without a clue as to the flower you wanted: "Now what was I thinking about? Celosia?"

How can you determine whether there is still time to grow a crop of dwarf marigolds before the fall frost? You know they will take the first light frost, but on what date will a hard freeze end Indian summer? If you had taken the time to jot down last year's date for the first hard frost, you would know the answer to your quandary. Notes keep you from repeating mistakes or unproductive practices. Did you sow seeds that failed to sprout in dry soil last summer? Be sure to make a note for next year to try seeding them in a moistened furrow and then to cover the seeds with burlap.

What Kind of Diary?

Although garden journals can consist solely of facts—weather, flower varieties planted, bloom duration, or future planting schemes—it would be a mistake to include only hard facts, empirical notes, and dry statistical observations. Leave room for the juice-of-life notations that make keeping a journal fun: "Tell family before planting 'Diablo' cosmos again. They pulled it up; thought it was ragweed." Or, "Would like to plant ornamental peppers in patio containers, but how can I keep grandkids from eating them. Hot, hot!" Even plaintive notations make for lively reading later: "How can George grow such beautiful calendulas? They make mine look sick. Ask and hear him gloat, or inquire through third party?"

A Personal Record

Garden diaries are very personal records, extensions of the writer's unique thought processes, problem-solving techniques, creative mechanisms, vanities, fantasies, and strengths. A collection of diaries

*To help you maintain
your garden
throughout the year,
this calendar outlines
basic garden duties for
each season. Copy the
relevant parts into your
garden diary.*

Calendar

Winter

Turn compost after the first hard frost to evict field mice.

Cover compost to prevent leaching of nutrients.

Clean off spent flowers after birds have gleaned the seeds.

Top-dress garden with chicken manure or sterilized, packaged, mud-free steer manure.

Trim off low-hanging branches to give flowers more sun.

Clean, sharpen, and oil garden tools. Paint or wipe handles with linseed or tung oil.

Install or inspect fluorescent lights to be used later for starting seeds. Replace tubes every third year.

Plan next year's flower garden. Order seeds, containers, and seed-starting media.

Early Spring

Have soil tested every other year for nutrient levels.

Start seeds of slow-growing flowers indoors.

Dig or till soil as soon as the soil has dried enough to break into fine particles when worked.

Add lime or fertilizers as directed by soil tests.

Incorporate compost or purchased organic matter into the soil. Don't overdo it; too much compost will encourage foliage and inhibit flowering.

Cover flower beds temporarily with clear plastic to trap the heat of the sun.

Direct-seed frost-hardy flowers outdoors.

Start a new compost heap.

Set out bedding plants of frost-hardy species.

Mid-spring through Late Spring

Start seeds of fast-growing flowers indoors.

Direct-seed or transplant cool-weather tender flowers in the garden.

On bulb beds sow seeds of low-growing annual flowers that will hide the yellowing foliage after the bulbs bloom.

Garden Diary

Calendar

Early Summer

Transplant frost-tender seedlings to the garden after hardening off.

Spray or dust if insects or plant diseases become serious. Use biological controls as your first line of defense.

Direct-seed fast-growing, warm-weather plants.

Cultivate the soil while weed seedlings are small.

Midsummer through Late Summer

Feed plants water-soluble fertilizers if foliage color fades or performance is poor.

Water flowers in containers frequently and move them to shaded areas to reduce stress of sun and wind.

Visit seed company and botanical garden flower trials to gather ideas for next year.

Replace spent plants with quick-growing, heat-resistant kinds.

Turn the compost heap. Soak it occasionally.

Early Fall

Start flowers in cold frame to prolong fall color. Paint and caulk the frame before planting.

Send for seed catalogues.

In the Deep South and warm West, plant seeds or seedlings of frost-hardy species for winter and spring bloom.

Take cuttings of easily rooted plants to grow as houseplants: coleus, impatiens, begonias.

Spray or dip cuttings to remove insects before taking cuttings inside.

Use a rooting hormone to improve rooting.

Fall

Have soil tested if you failed to do so in the spring. The fall is a good time to add lime if tests indicate it is needed.

Enlarge flower gardens; it is easier now than during the spring rush.

Throw clear plastic over flower beds at night to protect them from snap freezes. Drape the plastic over stakes to prevent it from breaking stems.

over the years would provide a better measure of the man or woman than interviews, recollections by friends or family, or notes deliberately set down for reading by others.

Getting Started
It would be presumptuous to suggest that anyone keep a journal by filling in forms designed by someone else. That would be like painting by numbers. Yet forms do provide a good starting point and can be modified to suit your personality and penchant for writing.

To help you design a garden diary for yourself or a friend, the suggestions outlined below show the kinds of information you may wish to include. Many gardeners like to keep garden records in a loose-leaf binder. But there are numerous other ways to organize garden diaries. You will have to determine your own needs.

Weather Record
Draw a generalized calendar that can be xeroxed. For each month, write in the days. As often as possible, mark the daily high and low temperatures and the humidity level. Write down rainfall, frosts, freezes, freak snowfalls, high winds, or any unusual weather. This record will help you to improve your planting schedule next year.

Flower Record
Note the new varieties you plant each year and describe their performance so that you can decide whether to plant them again. Make a chart with seven column headings: variety name, source and cost, seeds or plants, date sown or planted, date of first bloom, duration of bloom, and comments.

Soil Improvement Record
Keep a log of all tests and test results. Make a chart with four columns: flower-bed size, location, amendments, and fertilizers. Soil amendments include lime, gypsum, manure, peat moss, compost, or seaweed. Enter the name of the product and the amount used per 100 square feet; also note whether it was top-dressed or incorporated into the soil, as well as the date of application and cost. For fertilizers, note the brand and analysis, the amount applied per 100 square feet, whether it was top-dressed, incorporated, or liquid-fed, the date of application, and the cost.

Pest and Disease Problems
To help you learn the most effective control measures, record all pest and disease problems and your method of control. Make a chart with six columns: flower variety, damage and date, insect, disease, rodent or other pest, and control. Describe the insect, disease, or pest fully. Under the control column, note the type—biological, spray, dust, or dilution—and rate its effectiveness.

Pests & Diseases

Because plant pests and diseases are a fact of life for a gardener, it is helpful to become familiar with common pests and diseases in your area and to learn how to control them.

Symptoms of Plant Problems
Because the same general symptoms are associated with many diseases and pests, experience is needed to determine their causes.

Diseases
Both fungi and bacteria are responsible for a variety of diseases ranging from leafspots and wilts to root rot, but bacterial diseases usually make the affected plant tissues appear wetter than fungi do. Diseases caused by viruses and mycoplasma, often transmitted by aphids and leafhoppers, display such symptoms as mottled yellow or deformed leaves and stunted growth. Aster yellows, one such mycoplasma disease, affects marigolds, asters, and some other annuals.

Insect Pests
Numerous insects attack plants. Sap-sucking insects—including aphids, leafhoppers, and scale insects—suck plant juices. The affected plant becomes yellow, stunted, and misshapen. Aphids and scale insects produce honeydew, a sticky substance that attracts ants and sooty mold fungus growth. Other pests with rasping-sucking mouthparts, such as thrips and spider mites, scrape plant tissue and then suck the juices that well up in the injured areas.
Leaf-chewers, namely beetles and caterpillars, consume plant leaves, whole or in part. Leafminers make tunnels within the leaves, creating brown trails and causing leaf tissue to dry. In contrast, borers tunnel into shoots and stems, and their young larvae consume plant tissue, weakening the plant. Some insects, such as various grubs and maggots, feed on roots, weakening or killing the plant.

Nematodes
Microscopic roundworms called nematodes are other pests that attack roots and cause stunting and poor plant growth. Some nematodes produce galls on roots and others produce them on leaves.

Environmental Stresses
Some types of plant illness result from environment-related stress, such as severe wind, drought, flooding, or extreme cold. Other problems are caused by salt toxicity, rodents, birds, nutritional deficiencies or excesses, pesticides, or damage from lawnmowers. Many of these injuries are avoidable if you take proper precautions.

Controlling Plant Problems
Always buy healthy disease- and insect-free plants, and select resistant

varieties when available. Check leaves and stems for dead areas or off-color and stunted tissue.

Routine Preventives
By cultivating the soil routinely you will expose insects and disease-causing organisms to the sun and thus lessen their chances of surviving in your garden. In the fall be sure to destroy infested or diseased plants, remove dead leaves and flowers, and clean up plant debris. Do not add diseased or infested material to the compost pile. Spray plants with water from time to time to dislodge insect pests and remove suffocating dust. Pick off the larger insects by hand. To discourage fungal leafspots and blights, always water plants in the morning and allow the leaves to dry off before nightfall. For the same reason, provide adequate air circulation around leaves and stems by spacing plants properly.
Weeds provide a home for insects and diseases, so pull them up or use herbicides. But do not apply herbicides, including "weed-and-feed" lawn preparations, too close to flower beds. Herbicide injury may cause elongated, straplike, or downward-cupping leaves. Spray weed-killers when there is little air movement, but not on a very hot, dry day.

Insecticides and Fungicides
To protect plant tissue from injury due to insects and diseases, a number of insecticides and fungicides are available. However, few products control diseases due to bacteria, viruses, and mycoplasma. Pesticides are usually either "protectant" or "systemic" in nature. Protectants protect uninfected foliage from insects or disease organisms, while systemics move through the plant and provide some therapeutic or eradicant action as well as protection. Botanical insecticides such as pyrethrum and rotenone have a shorter residual effect on pests, but are considered less toxic and generally safer for the user and the environment than inorganic chemical insecticides. Biological control through the use of organisms like *Bacillus thuringiensis* (a bacterium toxic to moth and butterfly larvae) is effective and safe.
Recommended pesticides may vary to some extent from region to region. Consult your local Cooperative Extension Service or plant professional regarding the appropriate material to use. Always check the pesticide label to be sure that it is registered for use on the pest and plant with which you are dealing. Follow the label concerning safety precautions, dosage, and frequency of application.

Recognizing Pests and Diseases
Learning to recognize the insects and diseases that plague garden plants is a first step toward controlling them. The chart on the following pages describes the most common pests and diseases that attack annuals, the damage they cause, and control measures to take.

Aphids

Cutworms

Grasshoppers

Leaf-feeding Beetles

Leaf-feeding Caterpillars

Description	Damage	Controls
Tiny green, brown, or reddish, pear-shaped, soft-bodied insects in clusters on buds, shoots, and undersides of leaves.	Suck plant juices, causing stunted or deformed blooms and leaves. Some transmit plant viruses. Secretions attract ants.	Spray with malathion or rotenone late in the day in order not to kill bees. Encourage natural predators such as ladybugs.
Smooth, brown or green, wormlike moth larvae.	Feed near soil line, cutting off stems of transplants.	Place cardboard collars around stems of transplants, extending 2 inches above and below soil line.
Elongated, yellow, green, or brown insects with long hind legs and hard outer covering.	Feed on and consume aerial plant parts.	Handpick. Spray with hot pepper and soap solution or carbaryl (Sevin). Protect plants with fine netting.
Hard-shelled, oval to oblong insects on leaves, stems, and flowers.	Chew plant parts leaving holes. Larvae of some feed on roots.	Handpick and destroy. Spray with Sevin or rotenone.
Soft-bodied, wormlike crawling insects with several pairs of legs. May be smooth, hairy, or spiny. Adults are moths or butterflies.	Consume part or all of leaves. Flowers and shoots may also be eaten.	Handpick and destroy. Spray with *Bacillus thuringiensis,* pyrethrum, or malathion.

Pests and Diseases

Garden Pests

Leafhoppers

Leafminers

Mealybugs

Plant Bugs

Slugs and Snails

Description	Damage	Controls
Small, greenish, wedge-shaped, soft-bodied insects on undersides of leaves. Quickly hop when disturbed.	Suck plant juices, causing discolored leaves and plants. Some transmit plant virus and mycoplasma diseases.	Spray with malathion or dust plants with diatomaceous earth.
Small pale larvae of flies or beetles. Feed between leaf surfaces.	Leaves show yellow, then brown, oval or meandering papery blotches. Leaves may drop.	Remove badly infested leaves. Spray with malathion before mines appear.
White, waxy, oval soft-bodied insects on leaves, leaf axils, and shoots. Produce sticky honeydew.	Suck plant juices, causing off-color and stunted plants.	Clean foliage frequently. Pick off with alcohol swab. Spray with malathion or pyrethrum. Encourage natural predators and parasites.
Oblong, flattened, greenish-yellow insects, ¼–⅓ inch long. Some with black stripes. Wings held flat over abdomen.	Suck plant juices, causing spots on leaves. Some deform roots and shoots.	Spray with malathion or rotenone.
Gray, slimy, soft-bodied mollusks with or without a hard outer shell. Leave slime trails on leaves; found in damp places.	Feed at night, rasping holes in leaves.	Trap slugs using stale beer in pie pans. Eliminate trash and hiding places around garden. Use bait containing metaldehyde. Pick off.

Pests and Diseases

Garden Pests

Spider Mites

Spittlebugs

Stalk Borers

Thrips

Whiteflies

Description	Damage	Controls
Tiny golden, red, or brown arachnids on undersides of leaves. Profuse fine webs seen with heavy infestations.	Scrape leaves and suck plant juices. Leaves become pale and dry. Plant may be stunted.	Spray leaves with water or a diluted soap solution. Use a miticide on undersides of leaves.
Brown, green, or gray, ¼ inch long, robust sucking insects. Young covered with frothy spittle mass.	Suck plant juices. Can stunt and weaken plants, but often causes little but cosmetic harm.	If damage occurs, spray with malathion.
Cream and brown or purple, striped caterpillars found on or inside stems of herbaceous plants.	Burrow inside stems, plant wilts and dies.	Remove infested plants. Slit stems and kill borers. Clean up weeds in area.
Very small, slender, brown, yellow, or black insects with narrow fringed wings. Rasping-sucking mouthparts.	Scrape and suck plant tissue. Cause browning, white flecking, and gumminess. Sometimes deform flowers, buds, and leaves.	Remove infested flowers and buds. Spray with malathion, or dust with sulfur or diatomaceous earth.
Tiny flies with white, powdery wings. Fly up in great numbers when disturbed. Secrete honeydew.	Suck plant juices. Plants look yellow, sickly, and stunted.	Spray with insecticidal soap, resmethrin, or malathion.

Pests and Diseases

Garden Diseases

Damping-off and Wirestem

Leafspots

Powdery Mildew

Viruses

Wilts

Description	Damage	Controls
Soil-borne fungal diseases that attack seeds and seedlings.	Rotting of seeds and seedlings, resulting in poor stands. Stems may become black, dry, and hard.	Start seed in sterile perlite or vermiculite, or treat seed before planting with thiram or captan. Don't overwater.
Spots on leaves or flowers caused by fungi encouraged by humid or wet weather.	Tan, brown, or black spots on leaves or flowers. If serious, leaves may drop from plant.	Increase air circulation around plant. Remove badly diseased leaves and flowers. Spray with zineb or benomyl if serious.
White, powdery fungal disease on aerial plant parts.	Reddish spots and powdery fungal growth. Leaves may be distorted and drop. Stems, buds, and flowers are also affected.	Remove badly infected leaves. Increase air circulation. Spray with Karathane, benomyl, or sulfur.
Various diseases, including mosaics, that cause off-color, stunted plants. May be transmitted by aphids.	Crinkled, mottled, deformed leaves, stunted plants, poor growth.	Remove and destroy infected plants. Control the insect vector (aphids) if present. Buy only healthy plants.
Soil-borne fungal diseases that cause wilting, stunting, and eventual death of plants.	Leaves turn yellow and entire plant may wilt and die. Roots may rot.	Remove infected plants. Practice crop rotation. Use resistant varieties.

Seed Sources

Abundant Life Seed Foundation
P.O. Box 772, Port Townsend, WA 98368

Applewood Seed Company
5380 Vivian Street, Arvada, CO 80002

W. Atlee Burpee Company
Warminster, PA 18974

D. V. Burrell Seed Growers Company
P.O. Box 150, 405 N. Main, Rocky Ford, CO 81067

Chiltern Seeds
Bortree Stile, Ulverston, Cumbria LA12 7PB, England

Clyde Robin Seed Company
P.O. Box 2366, Castro Valley, CA 94546

The Country Garden
Route 2, Box 455A, Crivitz, WI 54114

Far North Gardens and International Grower's Exchange
P.O. Box 52248, Livonia, MI 48152

Gurney Seed & Nursery Company
Yankton, SD 57079

Harris Seeds
3670 Buffalo Road, Rochester, NY 14624

J. L. Hudson, Seedsman
Box 1058, Redwood City, CA 94064

Jackson & Perkins
83-A Rose Lane, Medford, OR 97501

Johnny's Selected Seeds
Albion, ME 04910

J. W. Jung Seed Company
Randolph, WI 53956

Earl May Seed & Nursery Company
Shenandoah, IA 51603

Nichol's Herbs and Rare Seeds
1190 N. Pacific Highway, Albany, OR 97321

Over much of the country, annual seeds and plants are widely available in retail stores from late winter through early summer. In mild-winter areas, plants and seeds are sold almost year-round. Experienced gardeners often prefer the wider choices offered by mail-order seed and plant specialists. The mail-order houses listed below are good sources.

Park Seed Company
Highway 254 N., Greenwood, SC 29647

Plants of the Southwest
1812 Second Street, Sante Fe, NM 87501

Stokes Seeds Inc.
Box 548, Buffalo, NY 14240

Thompson & Morgan
P.O. Box 1308, Jackson, NJ 08527

Otis S. Twilley Seed Company, Inc.
P.O. Box 65, Trevose, PA 19047

Glossary

Acid soil
Soil with a pH value of 6 or lower.

Alkaline soil
Soil with a pH value of more than 7.

Alternate
Arranged singly along a twig or shoot, and not in whorls or opposite pairs.

Annual
A plant whose entire life span, from sprouting to flowering and producing seeds, is encompassed in a single growing season.

Anther
The terminal part of a stamen, containing pollen.

Awn
A bristlelike projection on a spikelet of a grass.

Axil
The angle formed by a leafstalk and the stem from which it grows.

Axis
The central stalk of a compound leaf or flower cluster.

Basal leaf
A leaf at the base of a stem.

Biennial
A plant whose life span extends to two growing seasons, sprouting in the first growing season and then flowering, producing seed, and dying in the second.

Bisexual flower
A flower with both stamens and pistils present.

Blade
The broad, flat part of a leaf.

Bract
A modified and often scale-like leaf, usually located at the base of a flower, a fruit, or a cluster of flowers or fruits.

Bud
A young and undeveloped leaf, flower, or shoot.

Bulb
A short underground stem, the swollen portion consisting mostly of fleshy, food-storing scale leaves.

Calyx
Collectively, the sepals of a flower.

Capsule
A dry fruit containing more than one cell, splitting along more than one groove.

Clasping
Surrounding or partly surrounding the stem, as in the base of the leaves of certain plants.

Claw
The narrowed basal portion of a petal in certain plants.

Cleft leaf
A leaf divided at least halfway to the midrib.

Clone
A group of plants all originating by vegetative propagation from a single plant, and therefore genetically identical to it and to one another.

Compound leaf
A leaf made up of two or more leaflets.

Corm
A solid underground stem, resembling a bulb but lacking scales; often with a membranous coat.

Corolla
Collectively, the petals of a flower.

Corona
A crownlike structure on some corollas, as in daffodils and the Milkweed family.

Corymb
A flattened flower cluster in which the individual stalks grow from the axis at different points, rather than at the same point as in an umbel, and blooming from the edges toward the center.

Creeper
Technically, a trailing shoot that takes root at the nodes; used in the captions to denote vines and trailing, prostrate plants.

Creeping
Prostrate or trailing over the ground or over other plants.

Crest
A ridge or appendage on petals, flower clusters, or leaves.

Cross-pollination
The transfer of pollen from one plant to another.

Crown
Part of a plant between the roots and the stem, usually at soil level.

Cultivar
A manmade plant variety, produced and maintained by vegetative propagation rather than from seed.

Cutting
A piece of plant without roots; set in a rooting medium, it develops roots, and is then potted as a new plant.

Cyme
A branching flower cluster that blooms from the center toward the edges, and in which the tip of the axis always bears a flower.

Dead-heading
Removing blooms that are spent.

Disbudding
The pinching off of selected buds to benefit those left to grow.

Disk flower
The small tubular flowers in the central part of a floral head, as in most members of the Daisy family. Also called a disk floret.

Dissected leaf
A deeply cut leaf, the clefts not reaching the midrib; same as a divided leaf.

Division
Propagation by division of crowns or tubers into segments that can be induced to send out roots.

Double-flowered
Having more than the usual number of petals, usually arranged in extra rows.

Everlasting
A plant whose flowers can be prepared for dried arrangements.

Fall
One of the sepals of an iris flower, usually drooping.

Filament
The thread-like lower portion of a stamen, bearing the anther.

Floret
One of many very small flowers in a dense flower cluster, especially in the flowerheads of the daisy family.

Flowerhead
A short, tight cluster of flowers, such as those found in the daisy family.

Genus
A group of closely related species; plural, genera.

Germinate
To sprout.

Glaucous
Covered with a waxy bloom or fine pale powder that rubs off easily.

Herbaceous perennial
An herb that dies back each fall, but sends out new shoots and flowers for several successive years.

Horticulture
The cultivation of plants for ornament or food.

Humus
Partly or wholly decomposed vegetable matter; an important constituent of garden soil.

Hybrid
A plant resulting from a cross between two parent plants belonging to different species, subspecies, or genera.

Inflorescence
A flower cluster.

Invasive
Aggressively spreading away from cultivation.

Irregular flower
A flower with petals that are not uniform in shape but usually grouped to form upper and lower "lips."

Lanceolate
Shaped like a lance; several times longer than wide, pointed at the tip and broadest near the base.

Lateral bud
A bud borne in the axil of a leaf or branch; not terminal.

Layering
A method of propagation in which a stem is induced to send out roots by surrounding it with soil.

Leaf axil
The angle between the petiole of a leaf and the stem to which it is attached.

Leaflet
One of the subdivisions of a compound leaf.

Leaf margin
The edge of a leaf.

Loam
A humus-rich soil containing up to 25 percent clay, up to 50 percent silt, and less than 50 percent sand.

Lobe
A segment of a cleft leaf or petal.

Lobed leaf
A leaf whose margin is shallowly divided.

Margin
The edge of a leaf.

Midrib
The primary rib or mid-vein of a leaf or leaflet.

Mulch
A protective covering spread over the soil around the base of plants to retard evaporation, control temperature, or enrich the soil.

Naturalized
Established as a part of the flora in an area other than the place of origin.

Neutral soil
Soil that is neither acid nor alkaline, having a pH value of 7.

Node
The place on the stem where leaves or branches are attached.

Offset
A short, lateral shoot arising near the base of a plant, readily producing new roots, and useful in propagation.

Opposite
Arranged along a twig or shoot in pairs, with one on each side, and not alternate or in whorls.

Ovary
The swollen base of a pistil, within which seeds develop.

Palmate
Having veins or leaflets arranged like the fingers on a hand, arising from a single point.

Panicle
An open flower cluster, blooming from bottom to top, and never terminating in a flower.

Peat moss
Partly decomposed moss, rich in nutrients and with a high water retention, used as a component of garden soil.

Pedicel
The stalk of an individual flower.

Perennial
A plant whose life span extends over several growing seasons and that produces seeds in several growing seasons, rather than only one.

Petal
One of a series of flower parts lying within the sepals and next to the stamens and pistils, often large and brightly colored.

Petiole
The stalk of a leaf.

pH
A symbol for the hydrogen ion content of the soil, and thus a means of expressing the acidity or alkalinity of the soil.

Pinnate
With leaflets arranged in two rows along an axis; pinnately compound.

Pistil
The female reproductive organ of a flower, consisting of an ovary, style, and stigma.

Pollen
Minute grains containing the male germ cells and released by the stamens.

Propagate
To produce new plants, either by vegetative means involving the rooting of pieces of a plant, or by sowing seeds.

Prostrate
Lying on the ground; creeping.

Raceme
A long flower cluster on which individual flowers each bloom on small stalks from a common, larger, central stalk.

Radial flower
A flower with the symmetry of a wheel; often called regular.

Ray flower
A flower at the edge of a flowerhead of the Daisy family, usually bearing a conspicuous, straplike ray.

Regular flower
With petals and sepals arranged around the center, like the spokes of a wheel; always radially symmetrical.

Rhizome
A horizontal underground stem, distinguished from a root by the presence of nodes, and often enlarged by food storage.

Rootstock
The swollen, more or less elongate stem of a perennial herb.

Rosette
A crowded cluster of leaves; usually basal, circular, and at ground level.

Runner
A prostrate shoot, rooting at its nodes.

Seed
A fertilized, ripened ovule, almost always covered with a protective coating and contained in a fruit.

Sepal
One of the outermost series of flower parts, arranged in a ring outside the petals, and usually green and leaflike.

Sessile
Without a petiole.

Sheathing base
A tubular covering around the base of a stem or around the lower part of an internode above the node; found in grasses.

Simple leaf
A leaf with an undivided blade; not compound or composed of leaflets.

Solitary
Borne singly or alone; not in clusters.

Spadix
A dense spike of tiny flowers, usually enclosed in a spathe.

Spathe
A bract or pair of bracts, often large, enclosing the flowers.

Species
A population of plants or animals whose members are at least potentially able to breed with each other, but which is reproductively isolated from other populations.

Spike
An elongated flower cluster; individual flowers lack stalks.

Spur
A tubular elongation in the petals or sepals of certain flowers, usually containing nectar.

Stamen
The male reproductive organ of a flower, consisting of a filament and a pollen-containing anther.

Standard
The upper petal or banner of a pea flower. An iris petal, usually erect.

Stipule
A small appendage, often leaflike, on either side of the base of some petioles.

Style
The elongated part of a pistil between the stigma and the ovary.

Subshrub
A partly woody plant.

Subspecies
A naturally occurring geographical variant of a species.

Succulent
A plant with thick, fleshy leaves or stems that contain abundant water-storage tissue. Cacti and stonecrops are examples.

Tap root
The main, central root of a plant.

Terminal
Borne at the tip of a stem or shoot, rather than in the axil.

Throat
The opening between the bases of the corolla lobes of a flower, leading into the corolla tube.

Toothed
Having the margin shallowly divided into small, toothlike segments.

Tuber
A swollen, mostly underground stem that bears buds and serves as a storage site for food.

Tufted
Growing in dense clumps, cushions, or tufts.

Two-lipped
Having two lips, as in certain irregular flowers.

Umbel
A flower cluster in which the individual flower stalks grow from the same point, like the ribs of an umbrella.

Unisexual flower
A flower bearing only stamens or pistils and not both.

Variegated
Marked, striped, or blotched with some color other than green.

Variety
A population of plants that differ consistently from the typical form of the species, either occurring naturally or produced in cultivation.

Vegetative propagation
Propagation by means other than seed.

Volunteer seedling
A plant that sprouts from seeds formed the previous year.

Whorl
A group of three or more leaves or shoots, all emerging from a stem at a single node.

Wing
A thin, flat extension found at the margins of a seed or leafstalk or along the stem; the lateral petal of a pea flower.

Credits

Gillian Beckett
Contributor Gillian Beckett is a well-known English horticultural photographer.
84A, 84B, 90A, 93B, 98B, 104A, 125A, 126A, 130B, 140A, 143A, 193A, 196B, 200B, 209B, 215A, 215B, 216B, 220A, 243B, 254A

Sonja Bullaty and Angelo Lomeo
A celebrated husband-and-wife team, Sonja Bullaty and Angelo Lomeo have contributed to many leading publications, including the Time-Life gardening series.
131A, 187A, 208A

Al Bussewitz PHOTO/NATS
Former sanctuary director at the Massachusetts Audubon Society, Al Bussewitz is a photographer for the Arnold Arboretum, Boston.
110A

Thomas E. Eltzroth
Coauthor of *How to Grow a Thriving Vegetable Garden* and a dedicated home gardener, Thomas E. Eltzroth is also a professor of horticulture.
102A, 105B, 108A, 109A, 114A, 115A, 116A, 118A, 118B, 119B, 130A, 141B, 144B, 181A, 190A, 204B, 206B, 207B, 208B, 221A, 221B, 225B, 234B, 237A, 238A, 238B, 241A, 241B, 242B, 247A, 247B, 248A, 249A, 250A, 252B, 262B, 263B, 266A, 267A, 269B

Entheos
A highly respected photographic agency, Entheos specializes in nature and horticultural photography.
96A, 97A

Derek Fell
A widely published garden writer, Derek Fell has also photographed thousands of plants. His publications include *Annuals,* an HPBook.
92B, 93A, 96B, 100B, 103B, 126B, 135B, 136A, 152B, 157A, 166B, 193B, 194A, 196A, 219B, 222A, 269A

Charles Marden Fitch
Photographer Charles Marden Fitch is a media specialist and horticulturist. Most of his plant and flower pictures are taken in his own garden.
Cover

Judy Glattstein
An instructor at the New York Botanical and Brooklyn Botanic Gardens, Judy Glattstein is also a freelance writer and photographer.
81B, 102B, 131B, 154A, 169A, 170, 181B, 186A, 190B, 220B, 224B, 251A, 265A

Pamela J. Harper

A well-known horticultural writer and lecturer, Pamela Harper has also taken more than 80,000 photographs of plants and gardens.
78, 80B, 86A, 87B, 88A, 89A, 90B, 91B, 94A, 95A, 97B, 99B, 101A, 103A, 104B, 105A, 106A, 106B, 107A, 111A, 112A, 112B, 113A, 115B, 119A, 120, 122A, 123A, 123B, 124A, 124B, 125B, 127B, 128B, 129A, 129B, 134A, 135A, 138A, 139A, 139B, 141A, 143B, 144A, 145A, 145B, 146A, 146B, 148, 150A, 150B, 151A, 153A, 157B, 158B, 161B, 162B, 163A, 164B, 166A, 168A, 169B, 172B, 173A, 173B, 174A, 175A, 177B, 179B, 180B, 182A, 183A, 184A, 184B, 185A, 187B, 189A, 191A, 194B, 195A, 195B, 198, 203A, 205B, 210B, 211B, 212A, 212B, 214B, 217A, 218A, 223B, 224A, 226A, 227A, 228A, 229A, 231B, 234A, 240A, 243A, 244A, 245A, 245B, 246A, 246B, 248B, 249B, 253A, 253B, 254B, 255A, 256A, 257A, 259B, 260B, 261B, 262A, 263A, 264A, 264B, 265B, 270A, 270B

Walter H. Hodge

A leading botanist, Walter Hodge has photographed plants and animals throughout the world. He is the author of *The Audubon Society Book of Wildflowers*.
81A, 83A, 85A, 94B, 100A, 116B, 117B, 122B, 128A, 132A, 142A 155A, 156A, 159A, 159B, 161A, 162A, 164A, 174A, 176A, 178A, 186B, 191B, 192A, 192B, 197B, 207A, 210A, 213B, 214A, 230A, 235A, 244B, 251B, 257B, 258B, 261A

Peter Loewer

Editor of the flower descriptions in this guide, Peter Loewer has written and illustrated many books on garden flowers.
82B, 137A, 165A, 197A, 201B, 211A, 227B, 229B, 271B

John MacGregor

A biologist, John MacGregor works for the Kentucky Department of Fish and Wildlife Resources. He is also a freelance wildlife photographer.
160B

Gary Mottau

A respeᵗed horticultural photographer, Gary Mottau is a frequent contributor to *Horticulture* magazine.
101B, 239B, 240B

Sarah Pletts

Artist Sarah Pletts has had drawings published in numerous books and magazines. She also designs for the theater.
Title page drawing

Credits

Dolores R. Santoliquido
Artist Dolores Santoliquido has illustrated numerous books,
including the Audubon Society field guide series and the Audubon
Society nature series.
20, 80–119, 122–147, 150–169, 172–197, 200–231, 234–271

Joy Spurr
A nature photographer for over 30 years, Joy Spurr manages a
photographic agency in Seattle, Washington, that features natural
history subjects. Her photographs have been published in numerous
books and magazines.
83B, 85B, 91A, 98A, 133B, 137B, 151B, 152A, 167B, 200A, 202A, 202B,
206A, 223A, 250B, 259A, 266B, 271A

Alan D. Singer
Painter, illustrator, and writer, Alan Singer is best known for his
1982 U.S. Postal Stamp Collection "Birds and Flowers of the Fifty
States," which he illustrated with his father Arthur.
18–19, 39, 43, 47, 424–427, 436–437

Mary Jane Spring
A nature studies artist, Mary Jane Spring has been a scientific
illustrator at the University of Connecticut for the last ten years. She
also does watercolors, taxonomic plates, and landscapes in oil.
21, 446, 448, 450, 452

Steven M. Still
A prolific photographer, Steven M. Still teaches horticulture
at Ohio State University in Columbus.
80A, 82A, 86B, 89B, 92A, 95B, 107B, 108B, 109B, 110B, 111B, 113B,
114B, 117A, 132B, 133A, 134B, 138B, 140B, 142B, 153B, 154B, 155B,
156B, 158A, 163B, 167A, 172A, 175B, 176B, 177A, 178B, 179A, 180A,
182B, 183B, 185B, 188A, 188B, 189B, 201A, 204A, 205A, 209A, 213A,
216A, 217B, 222B, 225A, 226B, 228B, 230B, 232, 235B, 236A, 236B,
237B, 239A, 242A, 252A, 255B, 256B, 258A, 260A, 267B, 268A, 268B

David M. Stone PHOTO/NATS
A successful freelancer since 1979, David M. Stone's nature and life
science photographs have been published in several garden books,
textbooks, and nature magazines.
87A, 88B, 147A, 147B, 160A, 165B, 203B, 219A, 231A

Thomas K. Todsen
An assistant professor at New Mexico State University, Thomas
Todsen teaches biology, and specializes in plant taxonomy. He has
been an avid photographer for more than 30 years.
99A, 127A, 136B, 168B, 218B

Index

Numbers in boldface refer to pages on which color plates appear.

Chanticleer Staff

Publisher: Paul Steiner
Editor-in-Chief: Gudrun Buettner
Executive Editor: Susan Costello
Managing Editor: Jane Opper
Series Editor: Mary Beth Brewer
Assistant Editors: David Allen,
Leslie Ann Marchal
Production: Helga Lose, Gina Stead
Art Director: Carol Nehring
Art Associate: Ayn Svoboda
Picture Library: Edward Douglas
Natural History Editor: John Farrand, Jr.
Drawings: Sarah Pletts, Dolores R.
Santoliquido, Alan D. Singer, and
Mary Jane Spring
Frost Date Map: Paul Singer

Design: Massimo Vignelli